DRIVEN WEST, TAKEN EAST

DRIVEN WEST, TAKEN EAST

A World War II Memoir of the Eastern Front

VILNIS BANKOVIČS

Translated from the Latvian
by Maris Roze

To order additional copies of this book, contact:
Xlibris
1-888-795-4274
www.Xlibris.com
Orders@Xlibris.com
703713

CONTENTS

TRANSLATOR'S NOTE

Vilnis Bankovičs's WWII memoir provides an eyewitness-participant account of the war in Russia and Eastern Europe that has remained largely unreported in English and American histories focused on Western Europe and the Pacific. As such, Bankovičs's account is authentic history, told in spare, straightforward prose, detailing the rush of events in the war's latter half and several varieties of captivity in the years afterward. The translation aims to render the author's unadorned but compelling account into contemporary, idiomatic English. Footnotes and in-text translations of German and Russian phrases are provided. A foreword outlines the military and political situation in Latvia and the Baltic states on the eve of the war, as well as during it, and highlights the narrow and unpalatable range of choices available to young Latvian men and to a nation caught up in two successive occupations.

Pronunciation: Latvian Names and Place Names

Latvian vowels and consonants are pronounced as they are in Continental Europe, rather than in Britain or the United States. The vowels *a, e, i,* and *u,* for example, are pronounced *ah, eh, ee,* and *oo,* rather than *ei, ee, eye,* and *you.* The consonant *c* is pronounced *ts* and not *k.* The letter *j* is pronounced like the *y* in *you,* not like the *j* in *judge.*

The names of persons and places in this translation retain the diacritical marks used in the original Latvian. These marks change the pronunciation of the letters (and the words) they are assigned to. The most common marks are the horizontal stripe above a vowel that makes that vowel sound long. Thus, the *a* in *labi* (good) is pronounced *ah*, as in *ago*; the ā in *māte* (mother) is pronounced like the *a* in *car*. Similarly, the long vowels ē, ī, ō, ū stretch these letters out: *egle* (spruce) starts with an *eh* sound, as in *bed*; *ērglis* (eagle) starts with a lengthened *ee* sound that has no exact English equivalent. The *i* in *mitrs* (moist) is pronounced as in *little*, while the ī in *mīkla* (riddle) is lengthened to an *ee* sound, as in *meet*.

Other common diacritical marks are the little checkmarks above certain consonants that produce a softening and thickening of the sound. The *s* in *sargi* (guards), pronounced like the *s* in *swan*, becomes the *sh* of *show* when the letter is š as in *šaurs* (narrow). There are also č and ž, which produce *ch* and *zh* sounds, as in *check* and *azure*. You can also soften *n*, *k*, *l*, and *g* by using short accent marks below or above the letters to produce ņ, ķ, ļ, and ģ, as in *ņemi* (take), *ķeri* (catch), *baļķis* (log), and *vāģis* (wagon).

Another key aspect of Latvian pronunciation is that the stress in a word is almost always on the first syllable. Thus, the author's last name, which includes the *ch* sound of the letter č, is pronounced *Ban'-ko- vichs* and not *Ban-ko'-vichs*.

Symbol	Pronunciation as in Common English (and Other) Words
ā	father, harpoon, car
ē	long **eh** sound, with no exact English equivalents
ī	meet, feet, seal
ō	(approx.) work
ū	future, music, duplex
š	short, ashen, champagne
č	chaplain, change, bachelor
ž	leisure, azure, genre
ņ	(Sp.) baño (bath), mañana (tomorrow)
g	gain, wing, glass
j	young, yard, yellow—as in the common men's name **J**ānis
dz	ku**dz**u
dž	jar, judge, badge—as in the author's friend **Dž**onis

FOREWORD

Reconstructing Humanity on the East European Killing Grounds of War and Peace

"Don't shoot at anyone," Vilnis Bankovičs's mother told him when he left for the war. "If you have to shoot, then shoot in the air, but never aim at a person. Your enemy is also some mother's son. Do this, and God will protect you."

If all mothers seeing their sons off pleaded like this, there would be fewer wars. Unfortunately, those who make the wars have different goals. Human compassion is the first thing left behind when men go to war. Mothers don't matter, except as mourners when their sons don't return.

If wars were ever human, World War II in Eastern Europe was probably the most inhuman war of them all. It spared nobody and nothing. It was almost a miracle that anybody and anything were left when the worst was over. Even when it was, it was not over.

World War II was not really a war in the classical sense, as even World War I had been. In Eastern Europe, it assumed the form of a quasi-religious war of annihilation between two totalitarian ideologies that were both hell-bent on nothing less than world domination, each in its own way. Countries and peoples that happened to be between the two were trampled and became what historian Timothy Snyder describes as the *bloodlands*.[1] Disregard of international law and basic human rights became the norm; killing was deliberate and ubiquitous,

---

[1]   Timothy Snyder, *Bloodlands: Europe Between Hitler and Stalin* (New York: Basic Books, 2010).

not only as the consequence of military operations but also as deliberate policy. Millions upon millions perished. From the Baltic Sea down to the Black Sea stretched the *bloodlands* between Nazi Germany and communist Soviet Union. The people of Estonia, Latvia, Lithuania, Poland, Belarus, and Ukraine became both victims and perpetrators with nary a chance to have a say in their own fate. Between the two ideologies, no third way was possible. Nor was it possible for an individual to avoid being involved as both victim and perpetrator, which under the circumstances often amounted to the same thing, depending on the point of view. A third role, perhaps, was possible—survivor.

The story of Vilnis Bankovičs is that of a survivor in this war of annihilation. He was a nineteen-year-old, one of some 200,000 Latvian men caught in the middle of this ideological war, which their country could only lose. Latvia had declared neutrality when World War II broke out on September 1, 1939. It was a futile act. Hitler and Stalin had already carved up Eastern Europe between themselves; the Hitler-Stalin Pact of August 23 was a blatant breach of international law and treaties at the expense of a number of sovereign states. Poland was only the first victim of their aggression. Finland was next, in the Soviet attack and Winter War of 1939–40. The Baltic states stood by apprehensively, without apparent help.

As Hitler, backed by supplies of Soviet food and raw materials, invaded Western Europe in 1940 and forced France into submission, Stalin took advantage of the situation and the secret agreement to occupy the Baltic states. Ignoring all previous treaties, he created border incidents and issued trumped-up accusations and ultimatums to be accepted within a few hours. In effect, he ordered the Baltic governments to step down so that compliant ones could take their place. To ensure these changes, the governments were required to allow an unlimited number of Soviet troops to enter their countries. There was no help in sight. Changes dictated by Moscow took place swiftly: the Soviet-approved governments proceeded to dismantle the established order; Soviet-style, one-party elections chose parliaments that asked for admission (read: annexation) of their countries into the Soviet Union.

The citizens of Latvia were transformed almost overnight into citizens of the Soviet Union and subjected to totalitarian rule, whose laws had their own inhuman logic. Soviet secret services—which later came to be known as the KGB—intimidated, threatened, arrested, and imprisoned people whom they considered enemies of the state, mostly those who in 1918 had been instrumental in establishing an independent Latvia and making it work. Others, who had been politically disadvantaged, believed in the communist cause, or simply took advantage of the situation became involved in carrying out the repressions. Arrests and a mass deportation sent more than 1 percent of the population to distant parts of the Soviet Union. Families were rent apart; men were sent to Gulag hard-labor prison camps and their families to desolate areas of Siberia. The Soviets murdered or deported much of the remaining officer corps of the Latvian Army, which now had become part of the Red Army.

Soviet and Nazi collaboration came to an abrupt end on June 22, 1941, when Nazi Germany invaded the Soviet Union and occupied Latvia within less than three weeks. After a year of Soviet atrocities, Latvians were relieved despite the fact that Latvian soldiers in Russian uniforms had fought the Germans in World War I. What they had experienced under Soviet rule made them suspend their historical distrust of the Germans—for a while at least.

Though posing as liberators, the Nazis had no intention of allowing Latvians to reestablish their own army, even less—restore their state. It was the Nazis' war, and they didn't want help from those they considered racially inferior. They had other much less noble uses for those who wanted to avenge Soviet atrocities. The worst of these insidiously criminal uses was the involvement of Latvians in Nazi crimes against humanity, the most heinous of them—murdering their Jewish countrymen. In the second half of 1941, about 70,000 of the 90,000 plus Latvian Jews were murdered. It was not, as frequently suggested, a spontaneous and widespread killing but rather a well-organized undertaking under Nazi direction, a prelude to the "final solution" that was supposed to look like a local undertaking. And so it was all over Eastern Europe—the *bloodlands*.

After initial success, the war in the east did not go well for the Germans. The Wehrmacht could not do it alone. So-called Latvian police battalions were formed by the end of 1941 from volunteers, later contract soldiers. Some units fought at the front; some were used for the "dirty" war behind the lines.

After the defeat at Stalingrad, Hitler in February 1943 ordered the establishment of a "Latvian SS Volunteer Legion" under the aegis of Heinrich Himmler's *Waffen SS*. The only correct word in this cynical phrase is "Latvian." Himmler was creating an array of such Legions of foreign "volunteers," including French, Belgian, Dutch, Scandinavian, and eventually even Russian. Despite gradual racial upgrading in the Nazi scheme, Latvians could not be and were not proper SS members. They were not really "volunteers" either as attested by draft notices that plainly stated: "You are hereby drafted into the Latvian SS Volunteer Legion." And the Legion was not an independent fighting unit. Its two divisions and other units fought under the command of the Wehrmacht and except for one occasion were dispersed at various sections of the front.

Latvian men could not easily evade the draft notices, though many tried. On the other hand, they remembered and were reminded of Soviet atrocities. What were they fighting for? Certainly not for Hitler's New Europe. By 1943, they knew that Hitler had lost, but they remained under the control of the losing side that had declared total war. Having no real choice, they hoped that the Western allies would not allow Stalin to claim their country after the war and that the old European order would be re-established at war's end. That vain hope later also fed Latvian resistance fighters in the forests and swamps, who continued their partisan struggle into the 1950s.

It is noteworthy that, as early as August 1941, Stalin too had "allowed" the Latvian Soviet proxy government in Russia to establish a Latvian division to fight against the Germans. This unit was based on the small remnants of the former Latvian army and recruits. The decree had also provided for the creation of partisan units to fight against the Germans behind their lines. Thus, as the war assumed ever-increasing intensity and inhumanity, Latvians were more and more often facing each other both at and behind the front lines—enemies against their own will.

Vilnis was caught in the midst of these forces. He had been born and brought up in independent Latvia. He was a student in a teacher seminary in Soviet- and then German-occupied Latvia. The defeat at Stalingrad had just been recognized by Hitler when Vilnis and his fellow seminarians were ordered to a recruitment center. The choice was clear. Those born in 1922 had to join either the Legion or become "Wehrmacht aides," performing support and supply duties behind the lines. Those born in 1923 and 1924 had a third choice, the *Reichsarbeitsdienst*, the German Labor Service. *Better to perform labor service in Germany*, Vilnis and some of his fellows thought. So after a summer working without particular effort in a peat bog, they were sent to Germany and enrolled at a paramilitary training camp. No lounging here. It was "Los! Los!"—strict German discipline without allowances.

In early 1944, however, all pretense of labor service was dropped. Vilnis was ordered to report to the Legion, thankful for the harsh discipline that he felt had prepared him for the front lines. Fresh Legion recruits had received hardly any military training, but all were now off to the Eastern front.

His mother sends him off with her wish not to aim and shoot at anyone directly. As a good son, he obeys. "I never aimed and fired at anyone, but I have fired often in the enemy's direction, mostly to reassure my comrades. Maybe some of my bullets found their mark," Vilnis states in his memoir. And bullets are flying all over; certainly, they kill, intentionally or not. Vilnis does not engage in detailed battle descriptions and, least of all, heroics. But what are Vilnis and other Latvians fighting and dying for in this war?

His first combat experience is just east of the Latvian border. He takes part in a fierce battle in late March 1944, which has become legendary in Latvian war lore. It is the only time the two divisions of the Legion fight side by side under Latvian command. Latvians were indeed heroic, and heroism is stressed in Latvian lore, but Vilnis comments on the death of his friend Olǵerts: "Who ordered untrained boys to the front? Who ordered lives to be sacrificed in the interests of a foreign power?" The list of his fellow seminarians killed in action keeps growing. Vilnis survives.

In the summer, Vilnis is ordered back to Germany for noncommissioned officer training. In late fall, he feels lucky when he and a number of other Latvians are selected ostensibly to be sent back to Latvia, where the western part, Courland, has become a major enclave defended by a large German force, including the Legion division to which Vilnis belongs. The other division, having suffered heavy losses, is being reconstituted in German-annexed western Poland. Instead of being allowed to boarda ship to rejoin his comrades, however, Vilnis becomes a squad commander in the other division.

The Soviet offensive toward Berlin is launched on 12 January 1945. The *Wehrmacht* begins to disintegrate under the onslaught. The command structure falls apart. Retreating army units mingle on the roads with refugees fleeing from atrocities committed by Soviet soldiers. Both are mowed down by Soviet planes and overrun by tanks. Food and shelter are scarce. Discipline has broken down. German gendarmes hang suspected deserters along the roads. The main part of the Latvian division suffers heavy casualties but sticks together as it retreats by fighting rearguard battles and evading encirclement after encirclement.

Vilnis is not among them. His company and his squad are ordered north and end up in East Prussia, which, for the time being, is bypassed by Soviet forces on their way to Berlin. By the end of March, East Prussia's time has come. Danzig (today's Gdańsk) is in Soviet sights. Vilnis and his men, guarding advanced positions, suddenly find themselves abandoned by their German comrades and surrounded by Russian soldiers.

Surviving war may be a matter of chance. In this war, surviving captivity is sometimes even more of a chance. Timothy Snyder describes how the Germans allowed thousands upon thousands of Russian prisoners to die of exposure and starvation. They needed *lebensraum* – space – not people. The Soviet treatment of German prisoners of war was no less barbaric. It had become a war of extreme hate. All conventions of restraint were cast aside. "Name, rank, serial number" no longer meant anything. People died without any of them. Even graves were a rarity.

A few days after capture, Vilnis and his fellow prisoners are ordered to dig what looks like a mass grave. He has witnessed just a few hours earlier a Soviet interrogator, in a fit of drunken anger, shoot a fellow Latvian prisoner next to him. He has every reason to think the worst, that is, what he had heard about the Jews who were ordered to dig their own graves. His mother's parting words flash through his mind. "But now I was before the judgment of God."

But the grave is not meant for them. They are spared, only to begin a long stretch of deprivation and suffering that brings Vilnis closer to death than any of his combat experiences. Prisoners of war become common prisoners and experience a stark preview of the hard-labor prison camps of the Soviet Gulag.

Vilnis spends the first six months of his captivity in assembly points in Poland. The prisoners are kept in subhuman conditions. They are malnourished, mishandled, and humiliated. They die of hunger, of disease, of maltreatment. In the first assembly point, the crowded cells are first thinned by lice-carried typhus. The boy sleeping next to Vilnis is dead one morning. So are hundreds of others. Survival is for the fittest and the luckiest.

In early October, Vilnis and other survivors are loaded into freight wagons, 40 to a wagon. Release is a vain hope that vanishes when the train heads into Russia, carrying a truly European mix of nationalities. For three months on the way to the Gulag, hunger, thirst, extreme cold, and disease take the weakest. The bodies are unceremoniously dumped in ditches by the tracks. Nature takes care of them. Vilnis becomes very sick and is almost given up for dead, until the high fever miraculously subsides. On New Year's Eve, the train stops in the middle of snowbound, frigid taiga near Vorkuta, north of the polar circle—the Gulag.

But there is no camp. Vilnis did not dig his own grave in early captivity. Here, he builds his own prison camp, almost the same. In the midst of the primeval forest, the prisoners fell trees and build the first barracks for the guards, the next for themselves, and finally a barbed-wire fence to keep them from escaping to nowhere. Weakened by insufficient rations that do not replace the calories lost in hard labor, beset by disease, driven to exhaustion, and threatened by a hostile environment, prisoners die. In the daylong subarctic night, the bodies are stacked outside the fence. The wolves take care of the burial. Vilnis survives it all—barely.

Much of what Vilnis Bankovičs tells is replicated in many accounts of the Gulag—hunger, hard labor, deadly diseases, death. There are variations that all confirm the rule; release for many is only a faint hope, survival almost a miracle. Yet hope survives the longest.

On August 12, 1946, an announcement is read that, thanks to the generosity of the genial Josif Vissarionovich Stalin, some of the prisoners have been freed. It is Vilnis's twenty-third birthday. Quite a birthday gift, except that nothing really changes. The guards no longer guard them, but the prisoners lack documents and have nowhere else to go. In September though, the Baltic prisoners start their journey home. This time, it is a faster trip, but the rations are nearly as meager as on the outward trip; the men are just as hungry and emaciated, but now they are on their way home—they think. Two years earlier, Vilnis had hoped to get to Latvia as a soldier in a German uniform to defend the remaining stretch of the Latvian coast against the Soviet Army, hoping that the Allies would come to help. Now a newly released prisoner, he believes he will finally be home in his own land, if not the state he fought for in his heart. Think again.

In Narva, the historical border city between Estonia and Russia, those born in 1922 and before can go home; the younger ones must atone for their service in the German army by becoming soldiers in the Soviet Army. Three years earlier, Vilnis had been able to delay immediate service in the German army because of his birth year, 1923. No such chance now. He and his fellows are not given guns. They are assigned to rebuild the destroyed city of Narva. From "los! los!" to "davai! davai!" No questions asked. Vilnis's service in the Soviet Army, however, is relatively benign. His skills obtained in helping surveying crews in Latvia turn out to be of use here. However, only in 1950 can he return to his homeland. The war for him is over but only formally. "The reality is that those ten years of war and postwar life have not really ended for me or my comrades," he writes. Nor have they ended for Latvia. Seventy years after the war formally ended and twenty-four years after the country regained its independence, that war and the life under oppressive Soviet rule still resonate divisively in the memory and social discourse in Latvia today.

Vilnis Bankovičs is a survivor. Survivors are almost always a little suspect. Why did they survive when others did not? Vilnis does not try to reason out or to make amends for his survival, to make sense out of what happened to him. As he began his service in the Soviet army, he summarized: "Today I open a new page in the colorful story of my life. But I doubt I am really the page turner. I'm really a pawn, pushed by the will of others. Was it the will of Hitler and now Stalin's will? More likely it has been a game played by a higher power." He is a survivor, and surviving is the ultimate sense in a senseless situation. And yet his book is about trying to make sense.

Commenting on his memoir, Vilnis has expressed regret that he didn't write it forty years earlier. Well, maybe it's better this way. Forty years earlier, it would have been a story with a different coloring, certainly more valuable as a document because closer to the original experience. But it would have been dangerous to write and impossible to share under the circumstances. Only the full renewal of Latvian independence in 1991 made it possible to open the floodgates of suppressed and oppressed memory, including this memoir. And there is value in the patina of retrospection and reflection that forms on the surface of experience as time passes. It grows on and seems to hide the bottom layer of immediacy but at the same time informs later generations better than raw experience can.

There is no overblown heroism, no dramatized suffering, no self-justification, and no self-flagellation. Vilnis tells his story matter-of-factly, with touches of ironic self-reflection, wonderment, and humility about his own survival in the midst of omnipresent death. He remembers with empathy and sorrow fellow soldiers and prisoners who were not spared on the killing grounds of the war and its bloody aftermath. His memoir thus becomes a written memorial for those who did not come back.

Timothy Snyder concludes his *Bloodlands* with this plea:

> The Nazi and Soviet regimes turned people into numbers . . . It is for us as scholars to seek these numbers and to put them into perspective. It is for us as humanists to turn numbers back into people. If we cannot do that, then Hitler and Stalin have shaped not only our world, but our humanity. (p. 408)

Some estimates put the number of dead Latvian soldiers at up to half of those enlisted in a foreign war in which Latvia could only lose. Nobody knows how many of them died in Soviet captivity. Historians are still trying to find out the numbers and put them into perspective. Snyder is right: turning numbers back into people is necessary and much more important. At the same time, it is much more difficult. Historians and humanists cannot do it by themselves. The dead can do it only in retrospect. Only the survivors can testify—the survivors of the Holocaust, the survivors of the war, the survivors of the Gulag, the survivors of the Bloodlands.

Vilnis Bankovičs has testified—for himself and for those who no longer can. A little bit of humanity has been restored, a little miracle in the midst of the immense inhumanity of World War II. A few numbers have been turned back to people. Many more, perhaps too many, are still waiting to be laid to rest. Humanity would have done well to listen to the mothers. Maybe someday it will.

Valters Nollendorfs
Board Chairman—Museum of the Occupation of Latvia, Rīga

Author's Preface

The tramp of foreign soldiers' boots has left a deep imprint on our country's soul. Still, after the devastation of the First World War, Latvia was able to rapidly achieve a leading position in the economic and cultural life of the Baltic states. After the Second World War, however, we were left in the unenviable role of envying our neighbors. The heroic people of Finland courageously stood up to the mighty USSR, the Estonians with chilly reserve received their eastern "visitors," and the Lithuanians refused to give their sons for slaughter to Hitler. Latvia is home to many talented and creative people and can be proud of the most beautiful folk songs in the world, yet the Second World War robbed my generation of a vital conviction—that we are a nation that cannot be bent to others' will. There have been too many foreign influences, too many worthless preoccupations, too little defense of our own values.

Perhaps my wartime memories will reveal some of the sources of our current malaise and throw a spotlight on the times when uninvited guests decided the fate of our youth.

About My Family

My parents came from the Ogresgala district (southeast of Riga, on the Ogre River). As a child, I heard many exciting stories from my parents about the roaring of the Daugava River near the power station at Ķegums and the beautiful inlets of the Ogre River. These places of my childhood are naturally the most beautiful and most dear for me, and they are also the haunts of my youth. My younger brother and sister and I spent our summers herding animals on my aunt's farm and helping with other chores. Our parents made sure we were always suitably occupied.

My father, an elementary school teacher, worked for almost twenty years in schools in Zemgale (southern province of Latvia). In 1940, he transferred to a school closer to Riga, intending to take a closer hand in educating his own kids as well. In her youth, Mother wanted to become a doctor but had to interrupt her schooling to take care of a growing family. She stayed in the medical field in support positions throughout her career. Both our parents were industrious and did their best to teach the habits of hard work to their children. All my adult life, I have been thankful to my father and mother for their ethical clarity and personal integrity, for their unselfishness and love.

On the eve of World War II and during the war years—all the way up to 1944—our family lived in Ķekava, some seventeen kilometers south of Riga. After completing grade school there, I heeded my parents' wishes and enrolled in the Teachers' Institute in Riga, which would provide my high school courses along with more advanced subjects focused on teacher preparation. Mother favored this choice because it included a free musical education, Father because it provided stronger discipline than the high schools, as well as the ability to acquire a profession in six years, even if one did not continue studies at the university level. Still, observing the constant piles of student work awaiting review on Father's desk, I found it difficult to summon enthusiasm for the job of a teacher.

And so I enrolled in the Riga Teachers' Institute in 1938. That fall, the institute moved to Cēsis (a regional center of the Vidzeme province); in the summer of 1940, after the first Soviet occupation, the facilities were commanded for Russian troops, and our school was transferred to the institute in Jelgava (about forty kilometers southwest of Riga). Harsher winds began to blow.

Author on fifth birthday, August 1928

Schooldays in the Shadow
of War and Terror

In September 1939, at the Teachers Institute in Cēsis,[2] we hardly noticed that the Second World War had started. There was a war somewhere, but Germany, Poland, and Russia were far away, while our assignments in the chemistry-physics Lab were immediate. Our parents, having lived through the First World War, however, followed the radio and newspaper announcements anxiously; bought extra soap, salt, and sugar; and speculated about how many weeks it would take for the Germans to overrun Poland and whether the Germans would then be satisfied and whether the war would bypass Latvia. They measured current events against their experience of twenty years before.

My classmates and I were sixteen or seventeen years old in those days. We read books and studied, we spent our free time in the coves and inlets of the Gauja River, we fell in love for the first time. There were concerts by our classmates and by visiting artists from Riga. In the summer, we watched the filming of "Zvejnieka Dēls,"[3] and watched the film on the screen that winter. My brother and I built a canoe and paddled it on the old mill pond. We traveled around Latvia with our father, who bought Mother the collected works of Knut Hamsun, and preempting the collection, I lived for a while in the great Norwegian impressionist's world.

---

[2] Town on the Gauja River in central Latvia about 50 miles northeast of the capital, Riga.

[3] The 1939 film version of the novel *A Fisherman's Son*, published in 1933 by the popular writer Vilis Lācis.

Our art teacher Ernests Ābele noticed my interest in drawing and painting and felt that a few hours of art classes per week were not enough to develop my talents. He invited me to visit him at home after school hours, where he taught me by explanation and example, both of which were very helpful. We went down to the Gauja by the Raiskums bridge to paint on Sundays. Those were days filled with rich experience, and not even the D that I earned in chemistry could bring me down. We knew that Hitler had swallowed Poland from the west and Stalin from the east, but Latvia was still peaceful, and we hoped it would stay that way. In the spring of 1940, nothing yet indicated that an end to our peaceful lives was near.

But the end was fast approaching. On June 17, 1940, while Hitler's troops were parading in Paris, Stalin took the opportunity to occupy the Baltic states. Stalin gobbled up the territories that had been drawn up on a map the previous fall.[4] The events of June 17 and the consequences deriving from them have been widely addressed in the media and in books. The consequence felt most directly at the Cēsis Teachers Institute was reflected in a newspaper announcement that our school had been liquidated and merged into the Teachers Institute in Jelgava.[5] On the way back from Cēsis to Riga, I ran into my classmate Imants ("Rūh") on the train. We talked of our regret at leaving Cēsis and wondered how things would go in Jelgava and, generally, what lay in store for each of us. Rūh was an optimist in this sense: "Neither you nor I have anything to fear from the communists. An elementary school teacher is no bourgeois but one of the working people. Let the rich tremble. They'll be feeling the pinch pretty soon."

---

[4]   In the secret protocols attached to the Molotov-Ribbentrop nonaggression treaty of August 23, 1939, Hitler and Stalin agreed on a division of Eastern Europe, with Finland, the Baltic states, and Bessarabia (now Moldova) ceded to Stalin. Occupation of the Baltics was followed by rigged elections and incorporation of these independent nations into the Soviet Union in August 1940.

[5]   District town 43 kilometers (26 miles) south of Riga and 34 kilometers (21 miles) from the Lithuanian border.

Teachers Institute in Jelgava

We felt welcome in Jelgava. This ancient town was attractive and hospitable, with a well-appointed school building and the additional benefit of proximity to Riga. Still, we never stopped longing for our familiar haunts in Cēsis and the staff and faculty we had come to know so well in our two-years' residence but who were not wanted or needed in Jelgava. The newly appointed institute director Flūgins was an idealist who opened our reception to the school with words of strong conviction: "Until now, the self-proclaimed, so-called Latvian patriots thought only of their own good. The name of Latvia meant nothing to them. We are going to change that. We will now work for the benefit of Latvia and the Latvian people, without seeking any personal advantage." I think he was sincere but soon became disillusioned, like many idealists of those days.

If Flūgins was an intelligent idealist, then the Moscow-appointed *politruk* (political instructor) Žubītis was a closed-minded idealist, since the convictions of this comrade never changed despite the events of 1940–41, the war, or the evacuation.[6] Since his youth, Žubītis had been

---

[6]   The 1940 occupation and annexation, the 1941 deportations, the German invasion, and the evacuation of the Soviet regime to the east.

wired to move in only one direction. Still, both the director and the political instructor were decent men.

Among the rest of the faculty, I liked the art teacher and artist Kārlis Baltgailis best. He was energetic, unpretentious, and helpful to us students. We developed a friendship of sorts, and I was an active participant in his drawing group. He invited me to his home for extensive discussions of art and artists. His principled life, as well as his accomplished work, seemed to me worthy of emulation.

Our initial reactions to the absurdities of the Soviet regime were in the spirit of humor and satire. In the second Soviet year (1941), we began to look at things in a more political way. Our life in school and the events in the city, in the rest of Latvia, and in the world outside no longer allowed refuge in a posture of indifference. Not all of us understood what was going on, but most of us wanted to demonstrate our attitude toward recent events, to protest in some way. Āboliņš, a senior student, organized us into a nationalist cell.[7] I was a member but, because of my timidity, not an especially active one. On a few occasions, we left flowers by the statue of Lāčplēsis[8] in the railroad station square, and we carried badges in the national colors of independent Latvia. The badges were fastened to the inside flaps of our shirt pockets, and we flashed these to each other in the hallways during class breaks. We did not yet understand that we were playing with fire.

On the morning of June 14, 1941, we completed our final exams and hurried to the railroad station so we could return to our homes by evening. What I witnessed at the station has stayed with me to this day, something I cannot think of without a clutching at my heart. On many of the sidetracks stood lines of red freight cars, and from the barred windows of the wagons peered despairing faces. At first, it was hard to grasp what this all meant. The trains were surrounded by soldiers with rifles and fixed bayonets. From the wagons came sounds of children crying and women begging for water, but the guards drove away anyone trying to approach the trains.

Oppressed by what we had seen, we sat silent the whole way to Riga. On side rails in the Torņakalns station,[9] we saw even longer rows of red freight cars. The curses of the guards rose over the whole

---

[7]   That is, into supporters of an independent Latvia.

[8]   Hero of Latvian myth and symbol of the emergence of the Latvian nation.

[9]   A railroad station in the outskirts of Riga on the west bank of the Daugava River.

area, and the crying of women tugged at our hearts. We climbed out of our train in the main Riga station in shock, surrounded by the silent, sorrowing faces of the people.

When I got home late that evening, Father was not there, and no one knew what had happened to him.[10] Mother had bundled our most essential clothes in case they would be coming for us as well. The Chekists[11] had shown up twice next door, looking for our closest neighbors, the Lindes. Sleep was impossible; we sat on our bundles and waited. Around midnight, Velta[12] came by, disheveled, desperate, her face streaked with tears. Returning from school, she had found everyone gone. Her father, mother, sister, and younger brother had been taken away by the Chekists the night before, the house sealed up, and a guard left in the courtyard to keep everyone away.

None of us slept that night. In the morning, Velta and I took the first bus into Riga. She wanted to turn herself in so she could be with her parents. In every place, we asked about the location of her parents' train; we were told the same thing: If they didn't look for you, you are no longer wanted, and you can't join your parents. By then all the stations were empty, the trains on their way east. We were not able to get any further explanations. Tired to the bone, we came back home in the evening. "Now you must stay with us," said Mother. Velta said nothing. Next morning, she was gone, still hoping to find her family.

Events raced ahead. Just a week after the deportations, the radio announced that Germany had treacherously broken the nonaggression treaty and that the German army had invaded this sacred Soviet territory. The news evoked varied reactions in Latvia—anxiety and premonitions of disaster in some, reawakened hopes in others. On the evening of the *Jāņi* celebration,[13] the first German reconnaissance planes appeared, circling for a moment over our gathering before turning back west. There had been almost no reaction from the Russian side; perhaps the surprise had been too great. Only on the day of the *Jāņi* festivities did

---

[10] The author's father worked as an elementary school teacher at another location and was in transit at the time.

[11] The Soviet secret police.

[12] The author's schoolmate and first love.

[13] *Jāņi* is a celebration of the midsummer solstice, with bonfires and feasting and extensive group singing, featuring the "līgo" refrain within traditional folk songs and new variants on youthful romance themes.

we see a few Red army motorized units driving toward the west. But only a few days later, the whole Russian army was in hasty retreat. It was apparent from the first days of the war that neither the civilian nor the military establishment of the Soviets operated from any systematic or orderly approach to the crisis. The continuing radio broadcasts extolling the invincible Red army and the readiness of the Soviet state to meet any challenge took on the tones of self-mockery.

At Mother's urging, my brother and I took jobs at the digs in the nearby peat bog;[14] with this step, we hoped to distance ourselves from the threat of mobilization, since the radio had announced that all unemployed men between sixteen and sixty had to join the brigades, digging defensive trenches. The peat bog was four kilometers from our house, and we had to get up at four to be ready for work at six. The midsummer days were hot and dry and the wet strips of peat very heavy. The strips had to be carried to drying areas far from the digging machine, and we had not been used to such heavy work. We barely managed to drag ourselves home in the evenings, swearing we wouldn't go back the next day. But roused against our protests in the morning, we kept going back, taking our first steps toward learning the discipline needed in wartime.

The machine operator chuckled at our efforts. He predicted the Germans would be in Riga within a week. And indeed, our career in the front lines of the peat works ended abruptly on the sixth day, the 29th of June, when only three of us were left. The rest of the workers, having "smelled the gunpowder," had vanished into the bushes. The operator shut down his machine. "Let's get the hell out of here, boys!" he called. As my brother and I scrambled from the field, German airplanes circled overhead, and the low rumble of artillery rolled up from the west. The front was approaching rapidly.

At home, Mother prepared a bundle of clothing and food for each of us, and we took off for the home of a forest ranger, an acquaintance of hers, five kilometers away. The expectation was that defensive battles would be waged by the Daugava River, and staying home would become dangerous. People still remembered the battles of the First World War, when the front held at the Daugava for a long time.

---

[14] The dried peat was used for heating and as fuel for heavy machinery in industrial concerns.

The ranger's house in the forest was quiet and still, a good distance from the main roads. There was no radio for the news, but we speculated that the Germans had been stopped near Jelgava and so decided to go back home. On the morning of June 30, we were walking along the highway back toward Riga when we ran into the war at first hand. Two Red army trucks full of soldiers were approaching from the direction of Riga, while a squadron of German soldiers on motorcycles rode toward them from the opposite direction. Shots rang out, and the bullets flew over our heads as we dove into the roadside ditch. The action lasted only a few moments, and we still hadn't grasped what had happened before the German soldiers disappeared in the direction of Riga.

When we dared to raise our heads again, we saw one of the Russian trucks crashed into a telephone pole. The other had evidently managed to turn onto a side road and escape. A few dead soldiers lay in the back of the crashed truck. The rest of the soldiers had been shot, leaping out of the truck to run away. They lay by the roadside and in the ditch. The Fritzes had not spared their bullets. We kids saw dead soldiers for the first time in our lives. On many occasions later, I saw the bodies of the slain and those who had starved to death but never felt worse than in this first experience of sudden death. "They have mothers too," said our own mother under her breath.

Soon after the first reconnaissance unit came the next. The Germans sat on their motorcycles confidently, smiling, with sleeves rolled up on their blue-gray uniforms. Some wore their helmets; others hung them around their necks, their automatic pistols cinched to their belts. They looked like soldiers on parade. They ignored us and other civilians at the side of the road; if we didn't get in their way, we could stand there or go elsewhere. The victorious Germans were hurrying to Riga. The gear scattered by the Red army, and the bodies left behind, meant nothing to them.

On the last leg of our trip home, we saw neither of the combatant forces. The Russians had fled; the Germans had not yet arrived (not counting the reconnaissance group that had broken ahead). So for a few hours, we lived in a vacuum—without any foreign power over us. We witnessed what happens when the restraints are removed from people's basic instincts. People came running out of stores carrying large boxes of food, boots, bolts of cloth. We heard shots; these must have been reckonings with the supporters of the Year of Terror,[15] carried out by those who had not been able to otherwise complete their revenge. In this time of dramatic reversal, confusion was also a threat. It was possible to get a bullet in the forehead for little more than being in the wrong place at the wrong time.

The confusion was evident in the efforts of the exhausted, wounded Red soldiers trying to find their units, which had fled east or been destroyed. The marooned soldiers didn't know which way to look; some went toward Riga, others in the opposite direction. Mother gave one of these "lost" soldiers some bread and meat and urged him to go east through the forests to avoid German patrols. The soldier thanked her repeatedly and murmured something about Moscow and Berlin . . . and Stalin . . . and God. It had all run together in his head. He just wanted to save his life now, nothing more. He knew that a warm welcome was unlikely if he found his unit but that it would be preferable to a German prison camp.

Later in the day, the power vacuum had ended. Large numbers of trucks filled with German soldiers passed by us toward Riga, followed by a heavy-weapons caravan and Red Cross vehicles. In the evening, a whole company of the Wehrmacht (German army) drove into our courtyard, parking their vehicles in a neat row. Some of the soldiers came inside, greeted us politely, and asked to buy some *eier, butter, und speck*.[16] The soldiers paid for the food with their aluminum pennies, whose value we did not know; what they offered had to be sufficient. The Germans seemed bent on a precise order in everything: the dust-covered soldiers washed, shaved, cleaned their weapons, and then ate supper. Laughter and loud German voices sounded through the house and yard. What a difference from the recently fled, shabbily dressed, unfed Red soldiers. These Germans seemed like nice fellows; they did not try to frighten us, did not brandish their weapons, did not rob us. Having paid for and eaten their food, they gravitated toward discussion of their families, showed pictures of their wives and children, and boasted that they would be back in the *Vaterland* in a month. "We took Poland in three weeks," said one. "We'll take Russia in five." And in the first days of this war, almost all of them believed in this prediction.

---

[15] Collective term for the Soviet occupation, the arrests and executions, the annexation, and the deportations.

[16] "Eggs, butter, and bacon."

They did not rest with us that night, however. At ten or so, an officer gave a shrill command: *"Alles auf!"* (Everybody up!) Motors fired, gas mask canisters jangled, and the soldiers leaped back into their trucks. *"Los, los!"* (Hurry, let's go!) They were quickly gone, along with our eggs and butter. They had to be in Riga by morning. Everything had been precisely reckoned. Everything.

It must have gone hard in Riga though.[17] All night, the northern sky stayed bright, with occasional flashes of brighter light and the roar of cannons. The radio came back to life on July 1,[18] and for the first time in several years, we heard the Latvian anthem. People cried tears of joy, and our mother responded to the call to display the Latvian flag. Unable to quickly retrieve the flag I had hidden the previous summer, she tore a Soviet flag lengthwise and sewed the white stripe between the pieces,[19] borrowing the end of my bedsheet for the patch. Using some red paint, I covered the yellow hammer and sickle. This was enough for the first day, and I mounted the flag in the tower of the community center, in the highest, most visible spot in our region. (The church was locked, and I wasn't quite brave enough to scale the church tower from the outside.) And so our flag was one of the first to wave proudly in the clear blue sky on July 1, filling people's hearts with joy and nourishing their hopes.

---

[17]   The city center was extensively damaged and bridges blown up during the attack by the Germans and the retreat by the Soviets.

[18]   The radio had been silent the day before, as the Russians fled.

[19]   The Latvian flag colors were, and are, red-white-red, with a horizontal white stripe between the red sections.

Riga Old Town ruins, fall 1941

Our exhilaration was brief, however. Ten days later, the German authorities published the new regulations for their conquered province of *Ostland* (Eastern Territory), and the Latvian national symbols had to be removed. The local police officer climbed up the tower and took down my flag. Still, he couldn't take away our initial euphoria for the restored freedom of July 1. That feeling still resonates in me today.

The first week of German occupation also cast light on the atrocities perpetrated by the previous regime. In their last days of power, the communists had murdered victims without investigation or trial, simply on the basis of suspicion. In the courtyard of the Central Prison in Riga, the mangled face of Arnolds Čuibe, our institute's beloved algebra teacher, stared lifelessly at shocked viewers. There were hundreds of victims like him in Riga and who knows how many in all of Latvia. These discoveries were propagandized and exploited for their own purposes by the new occupiers in *Tēvija*,[20] in newsreels, in radio broadcasts. These media asserted that the Russians were all Asiatics (i.e., not Europeans), that all communists were murderers, that all the Jews were communists. "Down with the Jews!" they cried.

---

[20]   The German-approved wartime Latvian newspaper in Riga.

Incited by this propaganda, many Latvians—especially those whose family members or friends had been victims of torture, murder, or deportation—turned into insatiable revenge seekers. Volunteer groups were hastily formed to comb the forests and assist the push at the front. They were ready to serve the Fritzes in all things now, when in 1939, they had called after the departing Germans: "Let them leave quicker and leave for good! They've sucked our blood for 700 years."[21] With the change in power, the dark side of our people showed itself. The Year of Terror revealed not only the fragility of our nation's existence but also how the moral character of our people could be degraded by personal failings, exposed in the sweep of great events.

That summer, two weeks after the German entry into Riga, I started working for the surveyor Mazpolis on land surveying projects. The Russian occupation had interrupted the major land surveying work begun during the independence period, and the Germans allowed this work to continue in order to gain a complete map of the country, which could be used for local tax administration, as well as for military purposes. Mazpolis settled in our region for the whole summer, and since I had worked the previous summer as an assistant for the surveyor Baumanis, I was offered similar work now, which I accepted gladly. Working a few months for Baumanis, I had earned enough money to set some aside for school and to buy a new Ērenpreiss bicycle[22] (which unfortunately was stolen a week later).

Both Baumanis and Mazpolis saw that I enjoyed the surveying process, and they taught me some of their craft. At first, I carried a surveying rod but later got a chance to work with the plane table and the maps. I learned to measure, calculate, and draw layouts on a map board, at first in pencil, later in ink. It felt like an honor, and I tried my best to live up to their expectations. I had no idea then that surveying would help me get through the war and serve me in peacetime afterward.

---

[21] The German presence in the Baltic states dates back to the early 13th century, when the Teutonic Knights fought the Baltic tribes and established colonial institutions that lasted till the 20th century. At the end of 1939, some 50,000 Baltic Germans left Latvia in an agreement between Hitler and the Latvian government to repatriate ethnic Germans to the Third Reich. In retrospect, it seems clear that Hitler wanted to remove his countrymen before the occupation of the Baltics, foreseen in his "nonaggression" treaty of August 1939.

[22] Manufactured in Latvia by Gustavs Ērenpreiss, popular in Latvia during the 1930s.

With the front somewhere by Leningrad and Moscow, the schools resumed their work in November. I went back to Jelgava. In the 1941–42 academic year at the Teachers Institute, our sympathetic and intelligent director Flūgins was replaced by the Nazi-oriented Kupčs, whom no one could stand and whom everyone feared. At first, we did not really notice that from one laughably stupid occupation, we had landed in another—a refined, cunning, evil occupation.

In the first Russian year, I had lived in the Institute dormitory on Dobeles Street. The noisy, roughhousing atmosphere interfered with my studies and homework, so I found a classmate of similar disposition for a move off campus. Jānis Mednis (Džonītis) and I pooled our funds and rented a small room in a teacher's home. We got along well with each other and with our landlord. By sharing resources and cutting a few corners, we minimized the effect of wartime restrictions and rationing on food, fuel, and clothing. The needs of young men are not great anyway.

Jelgava lacked the romantic aura of Cēsis but had its own Zemgalian[23] charm. During the Christmas holiday, we walked to Riga and back. The passing German military vehicles often picked up the girls, but we boys had to spend half the day hiking. But it was not difficult then. We were young and healthy and glad that the war had rolled over Latvia so quickly and that we could go back to school.

The German rationing system yielded results insufficient for our schoolboy appetites, and while our parents' food parcels helped, these were quickly consumed, and we ultimately turned to self-provision. In the Tērvetes hotel, we could buy a cheap *Stammgericht*, a dish of rutabaga, carrots, and potatoes that helped fill us up. Our parents also provided the ingredients and advice for our own culinary efforts. My father furnished some good birch firewood and a sack of potatoes, while Džonītis brought a slab of bacon from home. We sliced the potatoes and layered them with slices of the bacon and set the combination in a saucepan over the glowing coals in our stove. In an hour's time, the tantalizing aroma from the saucepan turned into the most delicious meal we had ever enjoyed, then or even later.

Our landlord, Mr. Oga, gave us a chance to earn a little in his private business as well. He was finishing thin plywood boards and using a hot needle to carve some ethnic Latvian designs and sayings

---

[23]   As in Zemgale, the southern province in which Jelgava is located.

into them. Then he painted and varnished the boards and sold them to the Germans as souvenirs. We didn't know how he found his clients, but his business was brisk. Džonītis and I quickly picked up his method and became a part of the operation, for which he reduced our rent. All in all, we liked rooming with Mr. Oga, where it was quieter and less regulated, leaving more free time for us. In the fall and spring, we took our paint boxes down to the Lielupe River or the Pils Park to draw with charcoal or watercolors.

Daugava fishermen (author's sketch, 1941)

Our drawing group, headed by the art teacher Baltgailis, set up an exhibition in the spring of 1942. Mr. Aistars, an Institute staff member, liked one of my drawings. I wanted to give it to him as a present, but he insisted on buying it and pressed a few marks into my hand. Džonītis and I spent these notes quickly, eating *Stammgericht* at the Tērvetes hotel. Baltgailis urged me to enroll in the Art Academy after finishing the Teachers Institute. He was reassuring about the war's effects: "Things that look bad often turn out well." A prophet he was not.

By the same token, though we were serious about school, Džonītis and I were not always model students. On one occasion, Džonis had fallen ill, and I had a physics test next morning for which I was unprepared. We cooked up a scheme. I called a city doctor for my sick roommate, and the doctor came and wrote out a medical excuse for the patient—in my name. Džonis then went to the Institute doctor and obtained an excuse from class for himself. We were so pleased with our hoax that his temperature went back to normal the next day. We did make up the missed work later.

My most serious act of disobedience involved an attempt to help a classmate improve a failing grade in algebra; failure in this class would mean a bad report card and possible expulsion from the Institute. We decided that I would filch our class grade book from the faculty office early in the morning, while he stood watch in the hallway. We would write in a grade of A next to his latest D and put the grade book back. As I was walking out of the office with the grade book under my arm, I was startled by the voice of our director, Kupčs. (Who knew that he arrived so early?) "Where to, young man? Come into my office." My lookout was nowhere to be seen. I blushed and stammered that I had wanted to see my grades. The director remained calm. "Let me have the grade book. Go report to the disciplinary officer. We'll decide what to do with you later." The upshot of the affair was that my classmate received his D in algebra but an A in behavior, while my grades in the subjects were all good, but my behavior grade was reduced to a C, which in those days was a potential barrier for aspiring teachers. An explanatory note added that the grade had been reduced for violation of school regulations.

A more principled rebellion occurred in the fall of 1942, when our 5B class managed to observe Latvia's Independence Day.[24] On the 18th of November, we awaited our pedagogy instructor, Baltkājs, in hopes of a class discussion of the events surrounding this anniversary. But his address to us was a disappointment: "Get ready. You're going to write a class essay on your assignment." No, we will not do that, we resolved. Though there had been no prior organization, we decided to hand in blank pages with only our names and the date November 18. The message would be clear. The idea inspired us, and except for a few hangers-back, we all handed in blank pages. Baltkājs seemed not to understand our gesture and took the pages to the school director, Kupčs, who penalized us for "communistic agitation" and lowered our grades for behavior. Two of our protest leaders were expelled from school but only temporarily because of intervention from Latvian officials in Riga. Since this incident, Kupčs was not only feared but hated.

---

[24] Celebrated on November 18, commemorating the 1918 founding of an independent Latvia. Such observations were forbidden during both the Soviet and German occupations.

Despite its cruelties and privations, the German occupation period of 1941–44 was also marked by an effusion of cultural, musical, and artistic expression. Besides the officially approved books, journals, and brochures denouncing communists and Jews and praising Germany and the German army's liberation of nations, there were also real books in the fine arts, literature, art, and other genres. Because of the wartime restrictions on paper, colors, and other materials, the print runs were not large, and Jelgava featured only a modest share of these. We hunted for new books in Riga in a spirit of competition, adventure, and risk.

In both Jelgava and Riga, in school auditoriums and art museums, we attended poetry readings and lectures on philosophy and the arts and visited art exhibitions featuring classical works and new works by current artists. I joined the studio of Leo Svemps,[25] hoping to learn a lot from the master, but the difficulties of coordinating studies in Jelgava with art lessons in Riga were too many to overcome. The trains were reserved for the military; the buses required special passes, which I tried my hand at forging but could not sustain. I went back to Baltgailis and his drawing group.

My passion for music and theater intensified in this period as well. The concerts in Jelgava, the opera in Riga, even the recitals in our own Institute auditorium were memorable for their heightened intensity in a time of war and uncertainty. These performances have stayed in my memory to this day.

We knew that the war was terrible, but only theoretically. We knew that along with the Germans on the Eastern Front, Latvian soldiers were dying. We knew that a Jewish ghetto stood in a section of Riga and that the Salaspils concentration camp[26] held military and political prisoners, that the German civil authorities were plundering our country, and that their vague promises that the Latvian people would also have a place in the "New Europe" were worthless. We had heard of these things from others but had not yet experienced them on our own skins. We were young and green in most things, and we wanted to experience life in all its variety today, even in wartime, without thinking too far ahead.

---

[25] Expressionist/modernist artist (1897–1975) based in Riga, later faculty member and dean at the Latvian Art Academy. Svemps had studied in Paris before the war and was very popular in Riga at the time.

[26] Built by the Nazis outside Riga in 1942 as a prison and a forced-labor camp, housing mostly political prisoners.

In the summer of 1942, Velta and I rode our bikes from Riga to Džonis's house in northern Vidzeme to celebrate *Jāņi*. We covered the 140 kilometer distance (85 miles) in one day and came back a day after the celebration. The trip was exhilarating, and my friend's family welcomed us with real sincerity. We celebrated in the true Latvian style, visiting all the neighboring homes and singing the *līgo* songs till the break of dawn.[27] We took some of the oak leaf crowns worn during the festivities and gathered armfuls of waist-high *Jāņi* grasses—sweet flag, cattail—and took these back to Riga on our bicycles, to the delight of the city inhabitants.

Toward fall, Mother decided that I needed a new overcoat for the next winter. She had obtained some beautiful gray wool cloth and used a slab of ham to entice a Riga tailor to work on the project. The work dragged out over several months, however, and for every fitting, we had to bring along another ham for the tailor. He was not only a good practitioner of his craft but an even better psychologist and businessman. Depositing a final wedge of ham, I finally took possession of the finished product and showed up at home proudly wearing the expensive and much delayed coat. It was my first and last showing in this fancy winter garment.

In the following winters, the coat was worn by my brother. Assuming responsibility for clothing me were the builders of the "New Europe." I stayed in their care for a long time.

---

[27] Country celebrants of *Jāņi* often visit neighboring homes to serenade the inhabitants.

In the Peat Bogs at Baloži

In February of 1943, all the young men between 18 and 22 were called up. Students at the Teachers Institute were no exception; all of us had to report to the German army draft office in Jelgava. Upon medical clearance, the 20-year-olds were given the choice of "voluntarily" enlisting in the newly formed Latvian Legion or joining the Wehrmacht helper battalions. The 18- and 19-year-olds were offered yet a third choice—joining the worker battalions of the *Reichsarbeitsdienst* (RAD), the State Labor Service.

Artūrs, Vosinš, Džonītis, and several of our other classmates had to join the Wehrmacht helper battalions. All the younger boys, including me, chose the RAD, hoping to reach the war's end in Germany with a spade in our hands, rather than on the Eastern front. We all understood that our chances of survival would improve at a greater distance from the front, even though in Germany you could also die in the airplane bombardments. For all that, digging ditches in the RAD appealed to us the least. We clung to the hope that the medical commission would throw us out; we were just skinny students, while the Fritzes loved the powerful and the strong.

We remained together for the time being, but our premonitions of coming events were on the gloomy side. Soon afterward, we went through the medical examination, or *musterung*, at the Jelgava castle. We were all declared fit for service. We would become builders of "the New Europe." They released us for the time being, until the enlistment notices came. Would they let us finish school?

We continued our studies. But not all of us; those consigned to the Wehrmacht helper battalions were soon sent to the Leningrad front, completely untrained and unarmed. These "helpers" were assigned to

German units to carry munitions from the rear to the fighting lines. Later, they were drawn into the fighting itself. So some of our boys were introduced to the pleasantries of the front sooner than they had expected.

At the beginning of May, the boys assigned to the RAD were trucked directly from the Institute courtyard to the Baloži peat bog, bordering the Riga-Jelgava highway. There, we would be trained for future Wehrmacht duty (though the reality was that the peat operation lacked cheap labor, and we were perfect for that role). We worked almost four months in the bog, until the end of August. With us were students of the appropriate age group from the Jelgava high schools and several trade schools. We were a considerable force of noisy, undisciplined boys. The Institute students were a bit less rowdy, but we all took part in the general unruliness.

From left: Arnolds, Imants, and Vilnis, summer 1943

We lived in barracks on the edge of the bog, slept in bunk beds, and ate near the kitchen in one of the barracks. We worked eight-hour days at a collection point for the machine that dug out the peat. The machine was similar to one I had been familiar with since 1941. The work was more difficult back then since we had to carry the heavy, wet strips of peat to a distant field for drying. Here in Baloži, we were able to take turns digging the peat, which was the most unpleasant task. With the frequent shift changes, we were also able to rest.

Not that we really strained ourselves. Helping boost our morale were the jokes, laughter, and mutual razzing meant to allay our anxieties. After work, we received "military" training, learning to march in tune with our songs to the nearby Riga-Jelgava highway. The songs were in a martial spirit, some on the improper side. They sounded good, and we didn't need encouragement since they were basically Latvian songs—in the words if not the melodies, which came from elsewhere. Our military trainers were selected from the young men who had already completed their RAD service. Our camp leader was a 20-year-old boy named Straus (half-German, conversant in both languages), attended by two helpers. All three were nice fellows but great drinkers. We seldom saw them sober, since they could get liquor in unlimited quantities and indulged the possibility in full.

Given the wartime conditions, we were fed reasonably well. After a strenuous day in the peat fields, our appetites were strong and the portions generous. The food quality could be overlooked. On one occasion, there were fleshy white worms swimming in the soup, and we raised a ruckus. Reluctantly, the work supervisor ordered another meal prepared. We met with no problems after that.

For our work gathering the peat, they calculated a salary, but almost all of that was held back for our upkeep. Those who outperformed the quotas could earn premiums in liquor and cigarettes. In the evenings, shortly before work ended, our group's premiums were carried out to the peat machines in the field. In theory, the liquor was to be divided individually according to performance: 50 grams for 100 percent fulfillment of the plan, 100 grams for 110 percent, and so forth. In practice, a bottle or several of them were handed out to our work leader, the "brigadier." He let the bottles go from hand to hand and let each worker drink as much as he wanted. I noticed that the biggest drinkers were the brigadier, the master mechanic, and his helper. Trying hardest to keep up with these old wolves were the trade school students, less so the high schoolers, and least of all we Institute boys.

So it went in the first weeks. Later on, the students held back less, in face of the merciless kidding from the experienced drinkers. Cigarettes, however, were distributed more in accord with individual work performance. The heavy smokers consumed part of their bounty on the way back to the barracks, the rest after supper during free time.

Several young men here learned for the first time to drink and smoke, not wishing to remain the butt of their comrades' jokes. For most, no lessons were needed, and some were at an advanced level already.

One evening, as usual, old Kļaviņš brought out the premiums. He divided these according to the official list and declared that he had come to the bog for the last time; he was going for medical care. "Which of you do not drink or smoke?" asked Kļaviņš. There were several such boys in my class: Arnolds, Sergejs, Rūh, and others, including myself. I happened to be standing closer to him than the others, and Kļaviņš told me, "Come by the office this evening, and we'll see if there's a job for you."

Next day, I became the assistant to the warehouse manager. My duties were to distribute tools to the workers, calculate the premiums and draw up a list of premium receivers, carry the basket of liquor bottles and smokes to the fields in the evenings, hand out the premiums, and then settle accounts with the warehouse manager. Old Kļaviņš left the hardest job for himself: to drive the liquor and cigarettes from the base in Riga to the warehouse in the peat fields. I learned that Kļaviņš himself was not among the teetotalers, to put it mildly, and he offered me a share of the booze as well. However, I had not yet learned to drink and smoke and so found it easy to decline the offer. For that, the old man respected and trusted me, and we got along well.

Kļaviņš hated the Germans and awaited the return of the Reds. That summer, the English[28] landed in Sicily and later took Rome; Mussolini was imprisoned, and the Allies revitalized their offensive. All this heartened the old warehouse manager, and he wished the Germans and Italians a quick demise. The Germans had prohibited listening to Western radio, but Kļaviņš was listening to Moscow broadcasts, since he did not know English. I wonder if he didn't drink himself into a stupor before the return of the Russians to Latvia; after our departure from the peat fields, he was once again responsible for distributing the "firewater" to the workers, the supervisor, and to himself, despite his poor health. "I promised the doctor I would stop drinking," he'd say, "but he can't see me now, so one little drop shouldn't hurt."

Thanks to the warehouse work and the premiums, my time in the peat fields in the summer of 1943 turned out easier than it did for others. A few days after my promotion to the ranks of the "clean-handed," the

---

[28] The invasion was a joint campaign of English, American, and Canadian forces.

supervisor told me, "I need someone with good German skills to work with documents in the office."

"Yes, I know someone," I said.

Next to my bunk in the barracks slept Sergejs, beyond him Arnolds, then Rūh. I offered the office job to Sergejs, but he turned it down. "I have to get tougher," he said. "We have hard days ahead of us. I'll stay by the peat gathering machine." *Good for you*, I thought, having admired his strong resolve since our first school days together. I offered the job to Arnolds next, who accepted enthusiastically. Later, we finagled a place in the office for Rūh also. The "bookworms" were together again.

On Sundays, when the peat factory lay idle, we were under the supervision of Straus and his helpers. They were generous with passes, and all of us who wished could set out on the walk to Riga—for the girls, for the movies, for whatever, with midnight as the return limit. Arnolds and I combined funds for our mutual interests: the operas and concerts available in Riga. We understood that soon these programs would be unavailable to us and devoted all our free Sundays to the arts.

The Riga excursions were a pleasant change from the monotony of the peat fields, and these brief vacations have remained in pleasant memory for me. After many years, Arnolds and I were able to share recollections of all the exhibitions and concerts and the discussions we had on the return trips. We agreed that the best times in those days were the walks to Riga on Sunday afternoons and the evening returns after our immersion in the joys of music.

The *Jāņi* holiday arrived. On the Līgo evening, we found a festive table with cheese and beer set up in the courtyard—gifts of the factory administration to us peat gatherers. We began festivities with the *līgo* songs. As the evening advanced, liquor bottles mysteriously appeared on the table, and the high spirits grew. The *līgo* singing ended in the early morning with some ribald soldiers' songs. Straus and his helpers, along with a good number of the high schoolers and trade school students, kept on drinking till the next day and evening and fell asleep finally where they were. Not surprisingly, the next day's peat-gathering norms remained out of reach for our group.

An even greater drinking jag was achieved at the RAD farewell ball in the Lesser Guild Hall[29] in Riga. The ball was organized on a

---

[29] One of several auditorium buildings constructed during the sixteenth and seventeenth centuries by the merchant guilds in Riga.

classic model that featured bountiful spirits but little to eat. Then the level of drunkenness reached new heights among our guests from the RAD staff and among our peat bog boys. Could the farewell to private life have been any different? When we finally asked for our summer's wages, we learned that we had eaten and drunk up much more than we had earned.

Reichsarbeitsdienst recruits, fall 1943

Released from the peat bog in the second half of August, we were free for a month as we awaited induction into the RAD, expected by mid-September. Our main goal in those days was to delay the trip to the front. This meant finding a way to travel west rather than east. By reports, life in Germany would not be easy (the boot camp regimentation, the Allied air raids), but the chances of staying alive still seemed greater. So we agreed that the RAD was the best option. The likely alternatives to dodging this service were a punishment battalion at the front or, less onerously, the Latvian Legion. Given the strict regulations of the Germans, we were not tempted to flee or hide. Newspaper and radio warnings about desertion were frequent and stern.

On departing from the Baloži peat fields, we received railroad passes for travel to our homes. I asked for a ticket good for traveling around Latvia. Juggling the dates, we managed trips to Jūrmala[30] and Ogre[31] and together with Velta and Arnolds to his home on a farm near Mārciena. The trip through central Vidzeme was wonderful. For a few days, we forgot the war and the fact that soon we could become cannon fodder in that war. In my last month as a civilian, I worked on many drawings in charcoal, ink, and pencil. By the time I left Latvia, there were no unused pages left in my drawing book. I left the sketches with Velta. Never before or since did I experience such a strong desire to study and work and achieve something in art.

My free month went by so quickly. At the end of September, I received the notice to report to the RAD headquarters in Riga. There, I was given a pass for travel to Jelgava and induction into the ranks of the RAD service. The formal donning of the uniform took place in the Jelgava palace, followed by a march to the railroad station. I remember climbing aboard the red freight cars and the noisy singing of my comrades as the train rolled away in the direction of Lithuania. The boys were hiding their departure emotions with a forced bravado reflected in the rowdy words and the loud, out-of-tune singing. Most of us were traveling out of our homeland for the first time.

---

[30] Resort area on the Baltic coast.

[31] Town on the Daugava River in central Latvia.

Basic Training in Neustrelitz

Our mood was not especially solemn, since we were schoolmates and acquaintances from the peat bog, and we carried food from home, along with an assortment of home brews. With songs and stories filling the air, it was almost better traveling to Germany than cramming away at school.

After crossing the former Polish border, we were transferred to passenger cars, and travel became more comfortable. I remember that we didn't go through Berlin while crossing Prussia and northern Germany. Our destination, of which we learned after disembarking, was a small town about 100 kilometers north of Berlin. Rolling along, we viewed the German countryside with interest; it differed from that of Latvia and the fields and towns of Lithuania and Poland. These fields were unbelievably clean—no weeds, ditches well maintained, the crops neatly gathered. Large areas were planted in pine, the trees in straight rows like soldiers, with no dead branches, no brush border zone. Brick buildings surrounded by mature leaf trees, order and cleanliness everywhere. That was our first impression of Germany.

We had left Jelgava on October 5, 1943. We reached Neustrelitz, our next duty station, in three days. It was a town of mostly one-story buildings, with stands of aspen in the center, the streets paved in neat patterns of cobblestone. The main street from the station led uphill and down, past the arching trees glowing in fall colors. A kilometer beyond town, on one side of the road was a navy camp with the sign *Kriegsmarine* (Navy). Our RAD contingent was assigned to a similar camp on the other side of the road.

We were joined by a group of German boys, called into service from the age of 17 to spend their first year in the RAD, then a year in the Wehrmacht, and finally in specialized military units. In other words, they were subject to military service till the age of 20, if not beyond. The best recruits were offered further service. Courses, noncommissioned officer schools, officer schools, and academies were spread like a thick net over the country. It was held as self-evident that no one had ever outdone Germany in the art and science of war. In wartime, the required service lasted until victory or a wooden cross. We understood that this principle would also apply to us.

Because the German boys were two to three years younger than us, they did not display the characteristic German superiority complex, making our own service easier. This distinction did not become apparent until later, however. Both Latvians and Germans were lined up in the courtyard by height and then divided into groups. In our group, formed first, no one stood below 185 centimeters (about six feet, one inch), with the tallest—Pekka—at 192 centimeters (over six feet, three inches). Our first squad boys were all Latvians (Pekka, Vilsons, me, Ziedonis, Grīnbergs, the rest Jelgava high schoolers). The shorter German boys were divided among the second and third squads. All squads were introduced to their commanders, who quickly became our closest direct superiors.

Jutrzenko, our first squad commander (or *Zugführer*), was a Party old-timer as attested by the swastika pin on his chest. He was a middle-aged man of average height, fairly intelligent, but dour and unsmiling. Jutrzenko also served as chief political indoctrinator to the camp. His German punctuality and sense of superiority, radiating everywhere from his cap brim to his mirror-bright boots, failed to gain our allegiance.

The second squad commander was a small Austrian of advanced years and even disposition whom we called "Gailītis."[32] He was the direct superior of Arnolds, Sergejs, Rūh, and the other second squad boys. Gailītis was quite fearful of being sent to the front and worked to stay on the good side of his superiors. While Jutrzenko never descended from his heights to consort with his charges, Gailītis was happy to initiate discussions during rest periods. He was interested in the market prices in *Ostland*[33] (being unfamiliar with the name Latvia) and happily described his beautiful Austria and his large Alpine village family. He was an accomplished yodeler and, in the absence of the other führers,

---

[32]   Or bantam rooster in Latvian.

[33]   The German term for the territory of the Baltic states.

gladly demonstrated his singing skills. He stood well apart from the National Socialist ideology; his aim and hope was to last out the war here in the backwaters of Neustrelitz and then return to his vineyards.

The third squad leader was a brutal, confrontational type whom we called "Bull" or "Boxer." He was of medium height and athletic build, with a thick neck and red face. We couldn't understand how such a healthy specimen had managed to elude the front. In all weathers, Bull drove us unmercifully until he lost his voice from the constant yelling.

Of our various health checkups, the strictest was the *Feldscher* (field medic) Franke's. His slogan was *Fur Letten nur Tabletten.*[34] Actually, this portly "doctor" treated us not with medicines but with disciplinary drills. Franke's alpha and omega were *ordnung und sauberkeit*[35] in the highest degree. Another colorful personality was the supply officer who was unwilling to change our ill-fitting clothes without a contribution of cigarettes: *"Du siest doch wie ein Konigssohn aus! Was willst Du den noch?"*[36] The clothing we had received in Jelgava was severely mismatched, so the supply officer's pockets filled up with our cigarettes.

We were subject to many commanders, whom we had to salute smartly, even from a distance. This was the first duty drilled into us. Military bearing above all. The camp commander Lohse walked around like a baron, with a big shepherd dog at his side. The dog didn't leave his master's side by a step and marched around, looking as severe and indifferent as Lohse himself. The Germans knew how to train soldiers and dogs equally well. Toward his officers, who were afraid of him, Lohse was more attentive.

Zugführer Jutrzenko, his glasses gleaming above his well-fitting uniform, always began drills with a ringing command: *"Ein Dolmetscher hierher!"*[37] Hustling forward was Cers (son of a teacher, later mayor of Tukums), our best German speaker, who immediately translated Jutrzenko's most complicated statements into clear, precise Latvian. All the commanders and RAD inhabitants esteemed Cers's translation skills. But already on the train, we had agreed to pretend we didn't know any German at all. This ensured that our communications

---

34 "Only pills for the Latvians" (a way of saying Latvians were not worth more specific or appropriate treatment).

35 "Order and cleanliness."

36 "You look like a king's son. What more do you want?"

37 "Let's have a translator here!"

were handled with translator assistance and allowed us, as well as the translator, to gain time for answers. Eventually, the Germans smelled out our "diplomacy" but lacked clear confirmation of the ruse.

On the first day, after division into squads, each assigned to a room in the barracks, we selected our bunks, learned to hang our clothes in wardrobe cabinets, and lay them out on stools at bedtime. Then we learned the geography of the camp; the other barracks contained the dining hall, the storerooms, the classrooms, and finally the toilets. We were also introduced to our work site, an abandoned building plot about half a kilometer from camp, masked by a stand of pines. Our duty would be to cart peat from one valley to the other. Once again in the peat, we laughed. This kind of work didn't scare us.

After supper, the supply officer checked our equipment and solemnly handed each of us a four-cornered spade, warning us that this was the instrument for earning honor and reputation and that we must guard it like an eye in our forehead. We soon understood that a spade was the weapon with which Germany had buried the paragraph in the Versailles treaty forbidding rearmament, began to form an army, and prepared its youth for the next world war. All the holds and movements made with a spade lined up with those made with a rifle. In the visible foreground were the spades but behind them everything necessary for a new recruit to become a soldier. Spades were our RAD version of rifles, and we had to clean and polish them as intensively as our belt buckles and boots.

Every room in the barracks held six two-level bunk beds. The rooms also contained a wardrobe cabinet with twelve subdivisions. Each man received a blanket, a nightshirt, and a set of bed linens, that is, two checkered, blue-and-white cotton bags—the larger in place of bedsheets, the smaller for a pillowcase.

Before bedtime, we had to clean the day's clothes and fold them over our four-cornered stools so that the clothes covered all the space without overlapping the stool edges by even a centimeter. On top of the clothes, we were to lay our caps and belts, with the buckles pointing to the right. At the same time, the stools had to form a perfect line at the foot of our bunks. At first, we couldn't meet these requirements and endured repeated drills to bring us into line. After we had crawled into our bunks for the night, the watch officer would kick over our stools and scatter our unevenly piled clothes, giving us three minutes to reassemble and line them up again. If the results still didn't meet regulations, as they often didn't in the first weeks, the stools would go flying again . . . and again. Often, we lost an hour of precious sleep in these drills. But with time, we learned our lessons. After a month, we no longer had to crawl out of our warm beds at night. We were able to fold our clothes and line up our stools in a few minutes, climb under the covers, and drop off to sleep right away. Discussions and friendly insults died away in midsentence after the day's labors. Making up our beds in the morning was also subject to regimentation. The blankets on our beds had to be drawn tight, without the slightest wrinkles, and lined up perfectly across the room. For some reason, we learned these tasks more readily than the evening's obligations.

All this sorting of clothing and bedding has stayed in my memory in full detail as a classic example of pedantry—the arbitrary adherence to rules and forms. We sweated mightily in the name of cleanliness and order, until the rules and forms became automatic, there at our fingertips even with eyes closed. This German precision attended every step and every action. It was regimentation meant to wear away a person's individuality and personality. Once the uniform was on your back, you were handled like an animal. At first, we felt like rebelling against the pressure. But we came to understand that obedience without extra emotions was easier and that disobedience was pointless. The regimentation of the German army had evolved over the decades, and all the objections had been resolved long before.

Every day at the RAD unfolded the same way. At seven in the morning, the whistle would sound, and the watch officer would throw open the doors and bellow, *"Alles auf!"* (Everybody up!) By the time of the command, we had to be out of our beds. If the officer was ill disposed toward a squad, he would sound the whistle and run into the room at the same time. So we quickly learned to leap from our beds at the whistle's sound and to await the *"Alles auf!"* standing on the floor. At the next command, *"Achtung!"* (Attention!), we came to attention in our nightshirts, and the squad leader informed the officer that the squad had risen.

After that, regardless of rain or snow, we pulled on our exercise clothes and dashed out into the courtyard for the morning exercises, mainly running. On command, we jumped over a ditch, on command paused to relieve ourselves (*Pinkelpause*), and then resumed our trot up the next hill. We were quickly covered with sweat and often had to end our hill climbs standing in a sharp wind, yet no one fell ill or even caught a cold. After ten minutes or so, we ran back to the barracks to finish our morning routine. The time for washing and breakfast had been reckoned to the minute. In the first few days, we couldn't manage to wash and finish breakfast in the allotted minutes and had to leave our portions on the table. But we quickly learned to finish our meals, though we remained hungry all the time. (The smallish cubes of margarine, artificial honey, and processed cheese did not measure up to even the wartime food norms in Latvia.) The Germans had learned to get along on these rations and did not complain. We learned to get along as well.

After breakfast, the whistle summoned us to form in the courtyard for military training. In this case, we Latvians were not complete beginners—we had learned some of the basics of military drill in the institutes and high schools in Latvia. The German boys did not have these preliminary lessons, and so we were all treated as beginners.

A few weeks into the training, we were lined up in front of the barracks to await the arrival from the German squads of a short, roly-poly, and decidedly good-hearted soldier named Sharf, who never seemed able to keep up with our squad. Often, we were already heading out the gate when Sharf, still buttoning up, caught the end of our line. At first, they punished him with runs and commands to drop to the ground and quickly rise, but nothing worked. Asked why he was late repeatedly, Sharf calmly answered, *"Einer muss doch der letzte sein."*[38] Over time, the training staff got used to Sharf, but when we were visited by higher-ranking officers, Sharf was hustled out of the way to work in the kitchen.

The days in the RAD camp were all the same: marching drills, work, weapons training, and off-road training. In the marching drills, we practiced the same moves every day—marching individually, marching in step, marching in parade formation—with and without our spades. Most often, we practiced the parade goose step, which took a toll on our feet from pounding the cobblestones for several hours. The trainers understood this well and, if they wished to impose extra punishment, ordered the goose step.

Even better punishment was the command *"Marsch, marsch!"*— to run—which we dreaded the most. But we learned to fight back somewhat. Having run a good distance, we no longer "heard" the

---

[38] "Someone has to be last."

command to turn around and run back. We continued on our way, forcing the drill instructor to run after us to bring us back. Brought to a halt, we maintained our innocence. The instructor's explosive curses quickly added to our knowledge of German.

Once, we rebelled against our squad leader's cursing reference to us as *blödes volk* or stupid people. "How do you reconcile calling us stupid," we asked, "while training us to fight shoulder to shoulder with you for the 'New Europe'?" It was a small but definite victory, since we were no longer addressed as idiots. We continued to learn other new words from his salty language, which actually helped us withstand the rigors of soldiering. But no one has been able to outdo the Russians in cursing as we learned a few years later.

After the morning drills was lunch, followed by a short rest. Afternoons were for weapons training. We learned to break down and then reassemble the infantry weapons we were learning to shoot. The method again was rote learning—we repeated the moves endlessly until we could do them in the dark or at night. On the same principle of repetition, we donned and removed gas masks and practiced marching and running and even singing with gas masks on. Peering through the fogged-up glass, short of breath, we wondered if we would survive. On special occasions, we learned to march to RAD and German soldiers' songs. Marching was easier when we sang—without the gas masks, of course.

Our off-road training usually took place within the campgrounds, which were circled by a barbed-wire fence of more symbolic than practical value. Fortunately, the grounds were located on a clean sand base, rather than clay or muddy earth. Cleaning our uniforms was easier after we had fulfilled the repeated commands to hit the dirt and spring up again. These commands came fast and furious. We had not finished hitting the dirt properly before the order to get up sounded. Often, this sustained jerking around (twenty to thirty times in a row) was directed individually at a clumsy or rebellious soldier, allowing the rest of us to catch our breath lying on the ground. The victim was in dire straits meanwhile. If he tried to resist, he was driven mercilessly till he couldn't even eat or sleep. An added punishment was the order to clean the latrines in the dark while the rest of us slept. The orders did not spell out how quickly the "get down—get up" commands had to be carried out, though the victim was constantly ordered to do it "*schnell – schneller*": fast – faster! So we drilled every day for several hours. "When they bark at me like dogs," said Pekka, "and stretch my body beyond its limits, I'm reminded that the Fritzes have been enemies of the Latvian people for centuries." The rest of us were in complete agreement.

Most characteristic of the RAD life were the inspections (*appell*). Everything had to gleam and shine as order and cleanliness reached their apex. First and foremost, not a grain of sand was to be found on your spade, which had to shine like a mirror. It was our weapon of honor after all, though we went to work with other spades that were more like scoops than digging tools. Our clothes, from the caps down to the boots, also had to sparkle. The belt buckle had to be slathered with shoe polish and then brushed till it shone as much as the boots. All the nails in the soles had to be in their places, the heels reinforced with cleats. Our laundry was done communally, but the white collars for our dress uniforms we washed and ironed ourselves. We also had to sew on and mend all the hooks, buttons, collars, and patches ourselves. Every evening, we had to check our dress uniform, work uniform, exercise clothes, dress boots, work boots, and exercise shoes. This amounted to a lot of clothes, but we also had to care for our belts, gas masks, two kinds of spades, and the one rifle assigned to each squad. All items had to be perfectly clean and in working condition.

Every evening, including Sundays, we put together a display of gear for inspection by the duty officer, who allowed only the fellows from a room judged to be fully clean and in order to go to bed. In these inspections, we stood by our bunks, the squad leader notified the duty officer that our room was ready, and the officer tried to show his eagle eye by finding traces of dust even where there weren't any—on window ledges, in the farthest corners of the bunks, under the wardrobe, wherever he could imagine dust. Inevitably, after the other checks came the turn of the clothes folded on our stools. A swift kick, and you were sorting and folding again and again. When *Heilgehilfe* Franke was duty officer, no one from any of the rooms went to bed after the first inspection round. Generally, staff personnel like him were the most exacting, trying to show the line officers what they were missing by leaving them in subordinate positions. One evening, our squad was still awake after the third inspection round, Inspector Franke bending and twisting his rotund body to find the last trace of dust under the wardrobe. The old tyrant was keeping himself from bed by keeping us awake. Finally, after midnight, well into the fourth round, sweating profusely, he overcame himself and yelled good-night on his way out the door. Clearly, the man had tortured himself more than his victims.

There were times when the spotless conditions under the bunks were an advantage. During the frequent bombing alarms at night, we had to rush to the shelters at the other end of camp, but one of our boys, Kārlis Grīnbergs, would crawl under his bunk instead. "Wake me after the recall sounds," he said. "If the bombs really fall, it won't matter whether you're a hundred yards in one direction or another." He was right. The RAD shelters would not have withstood a major hit.

On many nights, the British bombers passed overhead in unhurried, precise formation on their way to Berlin. In the morning, the ground was covered with shiny foil streamers discarded by the bombers to disrupt the ground locators. Most impressive was the gigantic British bomber flight on Berlin the night of November 22, 1943. For an hour, the uncountable numbers of bright birds passed overhead with their deadly cargo. The air vibrated from the roar of motors and the howling of the German sirens. A scary sight, but Neustrelitz felt no bombs; they were all for Berlin. We could imagine how the pitch darkness of night turned into a firestorm a hundred kilometers to the south.

The American tactics were different. They flew during the day and in clear weather and dropped their loads precisely, in sectors previously identified to the Germans, evidently for humanitarian reasons. By the summer of 1944, the German air defenses were no longer a barrier to the vast numbers of the American planes. This was shown tragically in the February 14, 1945, destruction of Dresden. In the RAD camp, we were bypassed by the American bombing flights. They flew further south, and our northern sector was in the "care" of the British aviators.

"*Ordnung muss sein!*"[39] These words should have been written above the gates of the RAD camp. Every day began and ended in the spirit and letter of this phrase. We were warned while still in Latvia that only by surviving all the obligations of cleanliness and order would we become real soldiers. Discipline was drilled into us from morning to bedtime in the same way a hundred times. If you are sharpened like a knife blade down to the spine, down to your boiling temperature, then your nerves are being tested to the limit. And so they were, in full measure. Yet without the physical and psychological toughening we received in the RAD, we would not have survived all that awaited

---

[39]   "There must be order!"

us in the days to come. Today I think these trials were in some ways a blessing. We did not think so then.

In Neustrelitz, in the district of Mecklenburg, we felt the differences in climate from Latvia. Here, a golden fall could be felt not only in October but also all of November, with a fairly warm December still to come. A wet snow fell around Christmas but only for a few days. Letters from Latvia told us that December had been buried in snow and cold there. In my recollections, Neustrelitz remains wrapped in the glow of fall colors, fog, and silence—a markedly clean provincial town.

We forgot the rigors of training on Sunday afternoons. After a thorough inspection of our uniforms, complete with white collars, we were handed a few marks and a pass to town—good until supper. Three or four hours' leave was our reward for a week of drill. We almost did not feel the three kilometers to town, walking freely without commands or formations. We strolled the streets, turned into a few of the stores (to look, if not to buy), and sat on a park bench to observe, to our minds, the lucky civilians and the peculiar German architecture. It was all so interesting to us after the rigors of the barracks. We saw largely women and children, since all the men capable of carrying weapons were far away at the front. If a man came by, he was clad in the RAD or naval uniform. Soldiers from other military units appeared only on leaves from the front or on recovery from wounds. The young women were also in uniform (usually of the Red Cross). The streets were relatively empty, and the civilians regarded us with sympathy, since in every German family, a husband, son, brother, father, or newlywed was far from home in uniform. And the sorrow news kept coming...

The plan had been for us to spend a year in training, but we ended up at the RAD camp only three months. At Christmas in 1943, we received the news that twenty-year-olds would be enlisted in the army. The front had neared the Latvian border, losses had been heavy, and the recently formed Latvian Legion had to be quickly reinforced. The front needed fresh blood.

The days after Christmas passed under the import of this news. On New Year's Eve, we drank our issues of warm red wine and said good-bye to our commanders. In the afternoon of New Year's Day, we shook hands with our younger comrades, gathered our belongings, and handed in the weapons and spades. With all of us formed in ranks, the supply officer even took away our suspenders, which actually had not been handed out to us on the trip from Jelgava. Then we marched again down the main street of Neustrelitz to the station. We remembered that other walk over the fallen October leaves to the RAD camp three months before. Today's brisk pace over a light snow cover showed that we had learned a bit about discipline and order in our time here. Did that mean that the mindless drilling of *"Hinlegen–Auf! Marsch, marsch!"* and all the other commands had done us some good? On one hand, we were sick to death of this regimen and glad of the change we were being called to. On the other hand, the front was not the change we had hoped for.

The return trip to Latvia was similar to our October arrival trip, just quicker. We left Neustrelitz in passenger wagons and switched to freight cars at the German border. The only prolonged pause in our journey was in Bromberg, where a couple of our more enterprising fellows managed to find a *Puffhaus* (bordello), while the more innocent of us spent our time buying trinkets at the penny stores, intending these as souvenirs from abroad for those at home. In the afternoon of the second day, we crossed the Latvian border at Meitene.

On January 5, 1944, we disembarked at the Dubulti[40] station and were driven to the high school, where we spent the night. In the school auditorium, in the half-light of the wartime blackout, we laid out straw beds and prepared for rest after a long journey. In the straw nearby, I heard the voice of my classmate Olģerts Musts: "I've never seen the sea. It's so close here. We should go look at it." I joined the excursion, which also included Arnolds and another Institute classmate. Our quartet set out late at night through the pines in the direction of the sounding sea. There was little snow but a strong winter wind. We got used to the dark, and the dunes sheltered us from the fiercest winds, but from the top of the dunes, we beheld an elemental scene. Great waves were pounding against the ice concentrations; the sea was roaring, the wind howling, the pines giving off their soughing sound. Scudding clouds roiled the gloom.

Likely under the influence of all he saw and heard, Olģerts caught my hand and murmured, "Awesome…" That was the last time I felt his sopping wet hand. No one then could foresee that Olģerts—the best organist in our class, the hope of our teacher Kalnājs, our quiet, sincere classmate—had only two months, eleven days to live.

---

[40] A seaside resort town, about 22 miles from Riga.

We walked a while along the drift ice-littered shore and the beach clad in its light coating of snow and looked out to sea, where the dark water merged with the cloud-whipped sky. Then we turned back for the auditorium. This excursion touched us all deeply and so remained unforgettable. In our beds, we talked over what we had experienced and looked happily forward to our three weeks of leave. Olǵerts said he would be spending every free day at the organ in the Ēvele[41] church. We tried not to think of what lay beyond these three weeks.

Next morning, we spiffed up our RAD uniforms for the last time. After the mid-day parade formation, we were addressed by a RAD officer, then by a Legion officer in the uniform of the former Latvian army,[42] who spoke in Latvian about the critical need to replenish the ranks of defenders as the enemy neared our borders. We received our enlistment orders into the Latvian Legion. A medical examination would be conducted on the 29th of January in the war college in Riga. We had to return our RAD greatcoats in Jelgava, where we had left our school uniforms three months earlier. While some delayed returning the coats in order to enjoy the privileges of the uniform on trains, in theaters, and in movie houses, every RAD veteran hurried to get home as fast as possible.

---

[41] Small town in northern Latvia.

[42] The Latvian army had been born in 1918 and fought the war for Latvia's independence. After the occupation of Latvia in 1940 and the incorporation of the country into the Soviet Union, the army had been disbanded, many of its officers arrested, shot, and deported. During the German occupation, a Latvian army was also not permitted. That a speaker on this occasion was allowed to wear the Latvian army uniform suggests that a special effort was being made to motivate the young men in the audience.

In Transit in Riga

On a gray January evening, coming from Jūrmala, I rode once more into the old capital. On the steps of the train station, I was greeted by Velta and by Džonītis in his Wehrmacht helper's uniform. It was a welcome reunion for all of us. Džonis had just returned to Riga from the Eastern front, to await orders to a new unit forming in northern Vidzeme. Learning from Velta that I was coming through today, he'd quickly decided to meet his old partner in crime at the station. So we were happily reunited after nine long months.

We celebrated our reunion at Velta's. Džonītis had brought a supply of *knäckebrot*[43] and Velta brewed tea, for which I could furnish only a few saccharine tablets. These were our best wartime provisions, but the most bountiful table could not have made us happier than this chance to spend an evening together. Džonis told us about funny incidents at the front (staying away from the tragic events), I related my RAD adventures, and Velta brought us up-to-date on her high school at Draudziņi. (The Germans had moved the school to another location and set up an infirmary in the former site.) Our few hours passed all too quickly. The barracks awaited Džonītis; for me, nothing could be more wonderful than the trip home to parents and family.

---

[43] Crisp, dry bread.

Velta, 1943

My January 1944 home leave between the donning of two different uniforms seemed to be over as soon as it began. I arrived on the appointed date at the book bindery on Lačplēsis street for the medical examination. A few RAD comrades were already there, along with many other inductees, mainly from the high schools of Riga. In Jelgava, we had been examined only by German doctors, who measured and probed us to sort the Aryan from the non-Aryan and so avoid importing members of the "lower" races into Germany. Now next to the German officers sat two Latvian doctors, one of whom again wore the Latvian Army uniform. Likely, they had instructions to disqualify only the completely hopeless candidates. Both doctors asked me if I had any complaints.

What complaints could I have other than that I was freezing, having waited a half hour naked by their table. "No complaints," I answered, and a check was entered by my name in the register. "*Gut, weitergehen*,"[44] said a German official. Clearly, if I was suited for duty in the RAD, I was even more suitable for the Legion, and the front. In my group, all were declared qualified, but I later learned that a few others had managed to evade service. A few were genuinely unsuited for such duty, a few others had friends in high places, others had resorted to bribes, and a few others had smoked all the pot they could manage before the exams. The trenches were no longer calling to anyone. The volunteers of 1941–42, with their zeal and enthusiasm for battle, were long gone in 1944. Everyone was ready to defend Latvia, but no one wanted to die for Greater Germany.

In recent months, the front had "straightened" several times. Most people no longer believed in a German victory. The men were constrained from trying to escape duty by the expected consequences to their families, for as everyone knew, the Fritzes lacked a sense of humor, and the war tribunals worked quickly and lethally. A hope persisted that soon we would see a repetition of the World War I outcome; first, the British would defeat the Germans, then smash the Russians, and finally, our own national army would…. Unfortunately, these rumors and hopes did not reach the Allies. No one saw the white ships of Sweden in the Bay of Riga, and "Uncle Joe" had grown very close to Roosevelt.[45] As the writer Uldis Ģērmanis has said, "Wishful thinking fills a vacuum."

On January 29, as ordered in my induction notice, I arrived at the war college on K. Barona street, carrying Mother's knitted wool socks and a jar of my aunt's honey in a handbag. There were plenty of new recruits and a few familiar faces. There was a bravado atmosphere in the reception hall among the experienced recruits toward the "greenhorns." The former had already smelled the powder, some only theoretically perhaps, but who knew which. The new recruits, for their part, tried to show that induction was proof of their manliness, that they were not to be taken lightly. We RAD shovel soldiers felt more secure than the high schoolers and country boys. Three months of training had

---

[44]   "Good, let's continue."

[45]   A number of imprecisions can be noted in this summary of the outlook from 1944 Latvia: the identification of the Allies largely with Britain; the contradiction in expecting Britain to attack its ally, the Soviet Union; and the simplification of Roosevelt's relationship with Stalin. There was, of course, no "national army" anymore, and Sweden, whatever else might be expected of it, had worked hard to remain neutral.

left their imprint on our bones and in our minds. Yet under everyone's mask of bravery burned the same desire—to return as soon as possible to civilian life. It was one thing to stroll before the girls in your new uniform, another to arrive in that uniform at the front. Heroism was a declared goal only in group-drinking bouts, never when alone or sober.

New recruits gave up their passports for the soldier's personal ID, the *Soldbuch*,[46] and a number to hang around their neck. At the next table, we received the blue-gray uniform of the German army, with the Latvian Legion distinction—a Latvian flag shield on the sleeve. We took possession of a clothing and equipment package and a 98k rifle with a few magazines of training bullets. My greatest satisfaction was to receive a pair of well-fitting leather Hessian boots that overcame the sizing problems typically created by my big feet. I wore these splendid boots proudly until the fateful day of March 24, 1945. I had converted from a civilian to a Legionnaire in an hour's time. Then farewell, private life, and in Byron's words, "Farewell, and if forever, then forever farewell."

In the twilight, we lined up in the courtyard in our new uniforms, loaded like camels in the desert—rifles on our shoulders, gas masks at our sides, and ammunition, bayonet, eating bowl, and bread sack at the waist, with full field packs supporting rolls of blankets and camouflage dress. We marched out the gates singing *"Div dūjiņas gaisā skrēja"*[47] in the wintry dark of Riga. We marched through the city to the barracks in Samārina street, where they divided us into units. Our newly formed battalion consisted of three companies, formed from the merged remains of the Latvian troops from the front, then the newly conscripted RAD men, and various reservists. We were enrolled in the first company, first battalion of the 44th regiment of Kociņš.

We lined up by height again. In my company, only four of us Institute boys remained: Arnolds, Oļģerts, Laimonis Vilsons, and me. We learned that the newly formed battalion included only men with last names from A to O. The other RAD graduates, with names from the other side of the alphabet, were sent to a reserve battalion in Jelgava. This included Ziedonis and left several others (Sergejs, Juris, and others) for later induction because of current health problems.

---

[46] Essentially a military passport, with basic identifying information along with training received and rank achieved.

[47] Latvian folk song "Two Doves Rose in the Sky."

About half of our newly formed units consisted of high school, trade school, and Teachers Institute students, the other half country boys. Later, they added some previously inducted older men, along with veterans from the front. We could not explain why Vilsons ended up in our battalion, rather than on reserve in Jelgava. But ours was not to reason why....

After heavy fighting around Volkhov in late fall of 1943, the 19th division[48] was moved south of Ostrov in the Velikaja River region.[49] The decimated 44th regiment needed to replenish nearly all its units; its most battered battalion—the first—had to be recalled to Riga and reformed completely from medical units and newly inducted 20-year-olds. Our 44th regiment commander Kociņš was an old soldier, from all appearances knowledgeable and capable, but the First battalion commander Grunte remains in my memory as a good-hearted middle-aged man but coarse and a heavy drinker. There was little evidence of his skills as combat commander, though he was well served by a socially adept adjutant.

We saw little of the higher commanders at first. Our immediate responsibilities were military drill and marching in formation. Compared to the severe demands of the RAD, these Legion training sessions were a joke. We were barely able to contain ourselves. The familiar drill commands spoken in Latvian sounded awkward and were not suited to quick, precise fulfillment. We were divided into squads, and each squad was trained by someone who had been at the front. These veterans were worthy of honor and respect, but they were wholly unsuited to lead military drill in the German manner. Their life at the front had been totally different. They began with the observation that "You can march all you want here, but that will be worthless in the trenches. There, you'll need guts and a good shooting eye."

---

[48]   Of the Latvian Legion. The other Legion division was the 15th.

[49]   Volkhov and Ostrov are towns in western Russia, near the border with Estonia.

Inspector-General Bangerskis reviewing Latvian Legion

Since we had already spent three months in this kind of drill, we readily took on the outlook of our guides, that is, we spent time standing around, gabbing, listening to war stories, smoking, and keeping an eye out for a commanding officer. We were supposedly being prepared for the front but picked up little military knowledge or skill. If we knew something, it was only because of our RAD training. We never shot any of our training bullets but did practice cleaning our weapons, over and over.

After a week of such desultory activity, our battalion was formed up in ranks, and the commander's adjutant announced that specialists were needed: tailors, shoemakers, locksmiths, and others. All these positions were quickly claimed. Commander Grunte came by. "We also need a draftsman to prepare topographic maps. If you qualify, take a step forward." Next to me in line, Vilsons whispered, "What are you waiting for? Step up." I stepped forward somewhat unwillingly, not sure I wanted to leave the relaxed training regimen we had graduated to. A soldier from the second company also stepped forward. "Only one is needed, Adjutant," said Grunte.

Turning to both candidates, he asked, "What was your education?"

"High school" and "Teachers Institute" were our replies.

"Let's take the schoolmaster," said Grunte. "Those selected report to the staff office to register."

So unwittingly, I became a "headquarters rat" of the First battalion. But first, I returned to the same drills, since there was as yet no proper office, or maps, or instruments, not even a table. So I was not yet able to demonstrate the skills and knowledge in topography I had gained over three summers. All that came later.

In late February, the First battalion was transferred to the barracks by the Krusta church. These were elegant quarters compared to the rough facilities on Samārina street. A small room was set aside for the staff office. I succeeded to a desk, maps, and to what then seemed most important, the forms for granting leave. For this privilege, I had to thank our newly installed battalion scribe and head of the staff office, Corporal Edgars Vīķis. He was the husband of my elementary school teacher, and we were from the same district. Before the war, we had met frequently in school, at the community center, in church, at dances, but the age and interest divergence kept us from closer friendship. Now we were in a different situation; our shared geography and common fate in the military drew us closer. I doubt if Vīķis gained much from a greenhorn like me. I had yet to see the trenches at the front. His relatives had been deported on June 14,[50] along with Velta's parents and other family members. Soon after the German invasion, Edgars joined the volunteer forces that were quickly sent to the front. He traveled a difficult road from the environs of Leningrad to Volkhov to the Velikaja River. Together with Kociņš, he had returned to Riga and been assigned to the First battalion. So we met again after many years. I gained a lot from his friendship. He helped me learn the ins and outs of the trenches and never spared his advice if he felt he could be helpful. It's possible he even saved my life on the fifteenth of May that year. More on that later.

Corporal Vīķis became my closest direct superior. My first assignment was to prepare the leave permission forms for the battalion—a pleasant duty that, in which I did not forget myself and friends. And so, for a whole week, every evening after duty hours, I hurried with others to the trolley stop by the Krusta church to ride to the city center. My route led to Lazarete street, where the temporary quarters of the Draudziņa high school had been established. Velta was a student in the second shift,

---

[50] In 1941, a week before the German attack on the Soviet Union. These deportations, along with the depredations of the Soviet secret police, the Cheka, were a major reason for the enthusiastic welcome initially extended by Latvians to the invading German army.

but she was quite willing to play hooky for the last two hours. Thanks to my uniform, we were always able to get tickets to a Zarah Leander film, to "Maria Stuarta" at the Dailes theater, "Falstaff" at the Drama theater, or "Ieleja"[51] at the Opera house. We both admired the acting of Lilita Bērziņa, Alma Ābele, and especially Jānis Osis; and we loved the singing of Milda Brehmane-Štengele, Mariss Vētra, and Ādolfs Kaktiņš. Some evenings, we didn't go out but sat on a bench in Ziedoņa park and shared the same wishes—for a quick end to the war and no trip to the front. We both wanted to live. I was twenty, Velta eighteen.

Near the end of February, rumors of a move to the front intensified. Officers hustled around nervously, sorting out personal affairs, canceling leaves, posting a reinforced guard at the gates. Vīķis asked if I knew a likely man in our battalion who knew German; there was a good position working for our German bookkeeper. I recommended Arnolds for this additional "headquarters rat" position and phoned Velta that we were leaving Riga, asking her to let my family know.

In the evening, they checked our equipment and passed out ammunition for our still unfired weapons, dutifully smeared with Vaseline. The supply officer distributed felt boots (meant for guard and trench duty in extreme cold). Food would be passed out on the train. Despite Grunte's order to lay off alcohol, several of the boys had found liquor, and a bottle had been opened. Grunte, of course, did not feel that the order applied to him as well.

Meanwhile, Grunte's adjutant introduced Vīķis to a chubby 18-year-old apple-cheeked boy named Alberts, who was offered to him as a staff liaison. Pointing to me, Edgars said, "We already have a liaison."

"He'll be busy with the maps," said the adjutant. "We don't know how long our sector of the front will be, so you'll have both reporting to you."

And he added, "We don't discuss orders." We learned later that Alberts's appointment was a favor to a friend of the captain, when the friend had been unable to keep the boy in Riga. This was meant to keep him somewhat behind the front trenches.

---

[51] *Tiefland* by Eugen d'Albert (1864-1932).

We marched through Riga that night without singing, to avoid disturbing the sleeping population. The thud of our boots echoed in the streets, along with occasional clanging of gas mask canisters against rifle locks. It would be hard to describe our emotions as we traveled from our barracks to the Šķirotava station. We walked silently, and even the drinkers found no reply to their exclamations and so fell silent as well. The heavy backpacks and rifles pressed on our shoulders. Likely, we all posed similar questions in our minds: *When will we return? Will we return at all?* By the Vidzemes market, we turned off Brīvības Street (at the time named *Adolf Hitler Strasse*)[52] and moved down Matīsa street. As we walked under Velta's windows, I gazed upward but saw nothing in the darkness. Is she sleeping or not at home? And then we were past her building.

Dawn is breaking as we arrive at Šķirotava station. A long chain of red freight cars sits on the auxiliary tracks, without a locomotive at either end. We are assigned to cars and given partial rations, which the more carefree polish off right away under the principle "Eat while you can." We lay out bedding; food is loaded on the kitchen car, ammunition boxes on another, along with antitank weapons, machine guns, and other heavy weapons. Officers with lists in hand walk by the cars, checking provisions. Time passes slowly as we wait to see if family or friends or a sweetheart will come by. We wait anxiously and wait still. There's no sign of imminent departure, as the train still lacks a locomotive. Kettles are brought up from the kitchen, and warm food is promised in a few hours.

The first visitors appear—mothers, fathers, wives, sisters— hurrying up alone or in groups, with or without packages, as managed in haste. Riga inhabitants have reached the station more easily than the country folk, not all of whom have means of transportation, even a horse or bicycle. All the faces are solemn. After a few drinks from the smuggled bottles, smiles and even laughs break out here and there.

---

[52] Brīvības, or Freedom, Street is the main avenue through central Riga. During the late Russian empire, it was called Alexander Street, for the Tsar. Renamed Freedom Street with the gaining of independence in 1918, it was renamed again for Hitler during the German occupation, and then for Lenin (complete with a Lenin statue at the northern terminus of the street) with the Soviet reoccupation in 1945. One of the first acts of the new government in the 1991 restoration of independence was to pull down the statue and restore the name of Freedom to this fabled thoroughfare.

The day turns toward evening. The adjutant walks around and warns everyone to stay in place, but few heed the order, walking out to say good-bye to loved ones, some as far as the bridge over the tracks. If the train were to start moving now, some would be left behind to face the courts-martial. I'm eating my soup when I hear Mother's voice. The family are all here—Mother; Dad; my brother, Alnis; my sister, Ata. The kids have come to say good-bye, but my parents find that a hard task. This is the second war in their lifetimes, and they understand that this leave taking could be permanent. I walk them back to the railroad bridge, where we struggle to find words, till we are interrupted by Velta, who hurries up overheated and out of breath but glad she is in time. She makes parting from my parents somewhat easier, for in her presence, as a soldier, I cannot shed tears. We walk back to the wagon, where the presence of others also helps us say good-bye.

"Till we meet again."

"Oh, yes, till then."

"Why are there tears in your eyes?" I ask.

She whispers something but has no answer, walks away along the track. The darkness swallows her quickly and for all time.[53]

We could start rolling now, but the locomotive is still missing. The boys sing their sad and also defiant songs. An accordion sounds from one of the wagons. It's played by Ikvils, my friend-to-be, who sings "*A boy from the river.*" A few girls are still in the wagons, threatening to come along. Shortly after midnight, the command sounds, "Everyone in the wagons! Doors closed! Squad commanders, take the roll!" A whistle, the train shudders to life along its whole length, and we are rolling—in the night, in winter, to somewhere on the Eastern front. We've heard about the partisans blowing up bridges and derailing trains. If so, we have to accept our fate. We are still in Latvia, among our own people, in our own land. No one sleeps before we reach the border in Abrene. As we cross into Russia, we sing "*Dievs, svētī Latviju,*"[54] singing almost without sound, more in our thoughts than our voices. The anthem sounds subdued, but it sounds true.

---

[53] The author learned three years later that Velta, along with her brother, had escaped in a refugee boat to Sweden in March 1945. The Soviet army had taken Riga in October of the prior year. Years later, Velta married in Sweden and still later emigrated with her family to the United States.

[54] "God Bless Latvia." This is the national anthem.

ON THE EASTERN FRONT: BY THE VELIKAJA

In the early morning light, we disembark in the deep snow somewhere south of Ostrov. I have a map but can't see a station to help pinpoint our location. When we have unloaded the wagons, the train reverses and rolls off toward Latvia again. We're surrounded by the snow, with only a strip of forest visible in the distance. There's nothing to fix your sight on, and the area looks uninhabited as well. No sign or sound of the enemy either. We eat a warm lunch, get organized, and march off in the afternoon toward the east. On the way, we cross two highways filled with vehicles bearing war materials and supplies in both directions.

We reach the western bank of the Velikaja River in the evening. Here, we can hear cannon fire and know that our eastward march is nearing its goal. A worn-out horse plods by pulling several wagons of wounded German soldiers in the other direction. During the day, we have seen no civilians, likely because the Germans have sent them farther to the rear so they can't support the partisans. We spend the night dozing by the river's edge. It's quiet, with only an occasional rocket lighting up the distant sky.

At first light, the First battalion crosses the Velikaja on foot. The ice is shot through here and there but otherwise thick and firm. In a valley on the right bank of the river, Captain Grunte assembles the troops and gives orders to the company commanders. Moving on from there, each company steadily nears the front lines, with the staff personnel following close behind. After a runner confirms that all three companies have replaced the German units in the first trenches and the company commanders have been briefed on the situation, Captain Grunte asks Vīķis to set up the staff headquarters in a suitable location. We move into three snow-choked bunkers. Grunte chooses the largest of these for himself, his adjutant, and his runner. The next largest bunker is for the medical staff, and the smallest, about 100 meters closer to the trenches, is reserved for Vīķis, our runner Alberts, and me. Our bunker leans into a hillside and has a narrow door and a tiny window to the west. The other three walls are swathed in layers of earth topped with sod. Several plies of logs and a half-meter thick crust of earth lie on top of the bunker, as we learn later, after the snow melts off.

Our first impression was favorable; the Germans had built these bunkers solidly and with expertise the previous fall as possible second and third line fortifications. In the following days, I also looked over the trenches on the east side of our hill. These were fortified only around the machine-gun nests, but the ground had frozen through, and the trench walls held up well. The lines of sight to the east were quite good, overlooking a broad, shallow valley. With binoculars, you could see the first Russian lines in the next hill. Our commanders concluded that surprise attacks were unlikely here. Grunte was more worried about the strength of our second lines in the rear, feeling our reserves were insufficient.

Our bunker held a narrow and uncomfortable three-level bunk bed, but we were just glad we didn't have to sleep in the snow. Vīķis chose the middle bunk and Alberts the bottom, leaving me on top. We soon learned that the floor is always cold at night, but as long as the stove is going, the top is hot. Because of the smoke, we couldn't use the stove very often, especially on clear, quiet nights. Also, finding wood for the stove was not an easy task for Alberts and me. We found no remaining wood around the bunker and had to search in the rear. Trips to more distant fields, however, ran the risk of attracting the attention of snipers. We risked the scavenging trips for the sake of getting warm. The outside temperature ranged from minus 10 to 15 degrees Celsius (14 to 5 degrees Fahrenheit), and the unheated bunker typically stood at zero (32 degrees Fahrenheit).

We slept in our clothes, removing only our kits and helmets.When the stove was burning, I didn't crawl up to my bunk, where I would only sweat and gasp for air, and then sometimes have to go stand guard out in the wind. I caught a few winks on Alberts's bed instead. Sleep in the normal sense of the term is really not possible in the trenches;

Bunker at the front, near Velikaja River

it was more a fitful dozing of longer or shorter duration. We were all starved for sleep, and I can attest that this is as debilitating as starving for food. While we were entrenched by the Velikaja, our field kitchen fed us regularly, in this respect upholding the German reputation for efficiency and order. We experienced delays in food delivery under battle conditions, of course, but nothing was lost unless the bullets struck a food container or thermos jug or even the person carrying the food (an occasional, though rare, occurrence). In our first weeks on the front, we never went hungry but were hard-pressed to overcome the sleep deficit. In time, we learned to sleep on our feet and even steal a few catnaps marching along.

When the snow had been swept from the bunker, kindling provided, snow melted in the boiling pot, tea consumed, munitions checked, and when Vīķis had clarified the duties of both subordinates—then guard duty began. We changed shifts every two hours. When Alberts was with the commander or in the trenches, I stood guard in his place. Our guard duties covered all three staff bunkers, with the commander, the adjutant, and Vīķis not participating. That left six of us lower-ranking soldiers with fairly light duty—four shifts of two hours each every 48 hours. Such was the plan, but in practice, our additional duties often upset the schedule and created a need for adjustments.

Beginning our reconnaissance of the area gave me a chance to show my surveying skills. I got various instructions from the adjutant, but Captain Grunte only listened and smirked. Battlefield topography is not the same thing as surveying, he suggested. Fortunately, the front was quiet at first, perhaps because the enemy was also reorganizing. I traversed the front lines, fixing them on my maps. Our battalion was assigned to a large defensive perimeter, but our soldiers were mostly untrained recruits, in the trenches for the first time. *God help us if the attack comes directly in our sector,* we thought.

Creeping around, inspecting the trenches, I meet acquaintances, among them Velta's cousin, a high-spirited squat 35-year-old man. He asks about Velta's brother, Roberts, and about Vīķis and promises to look him up once "the Ivans"[55] have been smashed. He's no Johnny-come-lately here, having spent two years in the trenches already. "I've been traveling a paved road in the marsh," he laughs. "Not even a

---

[55]   A term denoting the Russians, as "the Fritzes" stands for the Germans.

Heimatschuss[56] to get home on, see the girls, eat some home cooking." I notice he's often humming a song and feels cozy and relaxed even in these conditions. *Wish I could be that way*, I think, *Why am I so timid?* In parting, Velta's cousin says, "I'm not afraid of the Ivans. Let's just hope we hold up our end."

In a bend in the trenches, I run into Vilsons. We say hello but don't have time to talk. I'm looking for Oļģerts but am told he's been rotated elsewhere recently. I crawl forward. After visits to the second and third companies, I am sweating profusely. It's not easy to move like a turtle. I could walk around without stooping at night, but then I couldn't see anything to add to my maps. I crawl back into our bunker completely drenched in sweat, in part because of the rubberized camouflage suit I'm wearing, which admits no water or air. Even with the suit turned white side out, we remain good targets for the enemy snipers. They shoot very accurately, and we have to stay on guard at all times.

The Russians seem to be ignoring us at first. A few flares, some shots right and left of us, but nothing in our sector. The First battalion's housekeeping unit has set up in an undemolished Russian village a kilometer behind our lines. I'm carrying a letter from Captain Grunte to the 44th Regiment's commander, Kociņš, whose headquarters are well beyond the village. The adjutant advises me to take somebody from the housekeeping unit along, since the area is crawling with partisans. Meeting Arnolds, I invite him to come along. I stash the letter, chamber a cartridge in my rifle,[57] and we are off. It's a clear, starry night, with the moon showing us the way. It's the beginning of March but still winter, with no sign of spring. The snow crunches beneath our boots in the surrounding silence, broken by occasional rifle cracks in the distance.

The regimental headquarters is five kilometers away, but the road is straight and clearly visible. Yet our feeling is that an enemy could leap at us from anywhere, from any bush along the way. We felt safer in the front trenches, when we clearly knew the direction of the enemy. To dispel anxiety, we talk about home, about music, topics that are not suited for the bunker. We reach our goal without incident, and I hand my letter to Colonel Kociņš. Waiting for his reply, we warm our hands by the cooking stove. A large Russian bread-baking oven takes up the

---

56   A wound allowing him to convalesce at home.

57   From the five-cartridge clip held in the 98k carbine.

center of the room, with sleeping places ranged around it. The room is warm and cozy, and the feeling is that the Russians are far away. Signs of wartime are present only in the covered windows and the soldiers' aluminum bowls on the overheated stove.

We remain undisturbed all the way back. No sign or sound of the partisans. Arnolds goes back to the bookkeeper he works for; I keep walking east. I'm back in our bunker at dawn, with an hour of sleep left till my guard duty shift. Sleep falls on me like a stone. After this trip, I don't see Arnolds for almost a month. Our trips to the rear are over.

We have not removed our boots or taken our clothes off for nearly two weeks now. Sleep has been relegated to intervals between guard shifts, but it's not really sleep, not even proper dozing. And it's a wonder we haven't been infested with lice yet. One day, returning from the housekeeping unit, the runner says he's noticed a sauna on the edge of the village. Vīķis receives the news with joy. "Boys, we need to go wash up and change clothes, or the fleas will eat us with our boots on." The runner and I go investigate. The sauna is undamaged, with stones piled on the firebox and a hole in the roof for the smoke. There's a barrel for the water, even something like a ladle. Finally, clearing the snow away, we see an ice-covered pond.[58]

At noon on a cloudy day, we go fire up the sauna. A hole is chopped in the pond ice; we bring water and a birch broom—it's all as in peacetime. The silence on the front assures us that we will finally be able to switch ourselves and wash up. The battalion commander and his adjutant go first and then Vīķis and a medic, with Alberts and me next. We have to save the remaining warm water for the two men following us. It's wonderfully warm in the little room. We get wet and soap ourselves. It's twilight outside but totally dark in the sauna, so we work by touch. For some reason, we have started whispering, despite the distance to the Russian lines. We only have to rinse off, dry off, and then put on our clean shirts.

Suddenly, a mortar round is howling and lands somewhere near the sauna and, a moment later, a second one, a bit farther off. They've spotted us. We both drop naked to the muddy, slimy concrete floor. The

---

[58]   These are the components of the wet sauna common in these parts. The stones are heated and water thrown on them to raise steam, while the bathers soap up, rinse off, and switch themselves with birch branches or brooms to open the pores. Finally, the bathers run outside and plunge into a snow bank or, in this case, a pond to close the pores.

washing fever has left us. My only thought is to get dressed, not to die naked as though it made a difference to a dead body. At the moment though, it seems very important. Some five or six more rounds explode in the vicinity, though farther away than they feel to us groveling in the mud. Just as quickly, the bombardment is over, and all is quiet again.

The sauna experience was over as well, leaving us not much cleaner. Our soapy, muddy, soot-covered bodies hastily wiped down in the dark and then dressed in clean clothes undoubtedly made us look pathetic. But for both of us at the moment, our appearance mattered little. We had managed to get dressed and stay alive, earning almost a double victory. Even today, I don't fully understand why we were so fearful of departing from this sinful world naked.

The mortars that had been fired on our sauna rang in some hard days and nights. A major enemy attack began the next day. It was March 16, 1944, a significant date in the battle history of the Latvian Legion. It was also the first clash with the enemy for our newly created band of soldiers. The full shock of the attack was borne by men in the first lines; the impact was less in the second and farther lines, but no one in our sector was left untouched by this first taste of war.

For almost two hours, the artillery shells blasted our lines. Since the roof of our bunker would be unable to withstand an artillery round, we crouched in a dugout in front of the bunker and awaited orders. If our lads in the front trenches withstood the Russian attack, we would remain in place. If the lines were breached, we would be sent forward to fill the gap. Strangely, I was consumed by fear and trembling at the start of the bombardment but later reached a state of near indifference, as my senses were completely numbed. Whenever a round roared in nearby, I dropped down against the dugout wall automatically, without emotion. The shells at first fell on our front lines and then in our vicinity, dazing us but leaving us uninjured. Later, the deadly cargo began to fly over our heads toward the rear. Each blast tore another hole in the snow-covered ground, and soon the hillside was unrecognizable.

Red Army offensive

The artillery bombardment prepared the way for the infantry assault. Vīķis and I couldn't see the attack from our positions, but from the rifle fire, we could guess that the action was intense in the first lines. We waited several hours for orders, but none came. Uncertainty about the status in the front trenches tore at our nerves. I saw Edgars raise and lower his automatic pistol, aim it right and then left, his hands trembling slightly. He was tightly wound, ready for an attack at any moment, hardly able to wait for the flare that would signal that we must move forward.

When the battle noises shifted slightly to the south, we received both the good news and the bad. The Russians had attacked in large numbers over the empty field between our lines, providing good targets for our men. (We knew that the Russian commanders did not spare their troops but drove them forward even in hopeless situations, with the *politruks*[59] threatening the unwilling with a bullet in the back. Thus, some of the more fearful Russian soldiers achieved a "hero's death" with the help of these comrades.) A number of the attackers had nevertheless reached our trenches, and our boys had engaged them in hand-to-hand combat. Many were dead and wounded on our side as well, but our lines had held.

---

[59] Political officers attached to the Soviet units.

As darkness fell, the battle noises gradually died down. Realizing that they could not drive us from our strategic hillside positions, the Russians withdrew to their own lines, leaving many dead on the battlefield. We spent a sleepless night, as sporadic bursts of enemy rocket fire lit up the torn battlefield. Under cover of darkness, both sides brought up additional troops and ammunition. Everyone understood that the battle was not over. The Russians needed our hill as a base for future attacks; we needed it to hold our sector of the front.

Next morning, the bombardment resumed with even greater force, again followed by an infantry attack. Alberts brought back news from the front trenches: the number of attackers had been greater than the first day, and the number of casualties greater as well. Our Latvian boys held firm this day too, and the hillside remained in our hands. The enemy retreated again with no gains.

After another sleepless night, our runner brought the list of each company's dead and wounded. Among the first casualties were Olǵerts Musts, also Velta's cousin, and many more. Olǵerts had died on the 16th of March, how, I could not learn. I never saw him again. That same night, the dead had been collected from the trenches and, along with the wounded, sent back in sleds. Evidently, the dead had been buried together in a shell crater, since the ground was still frozen. If a memorial of some kind was left on a group grave, the Russians would later tear it off and level everything with the ground. The Soviet army did not think of their enemy as human.

Olǵerts—aspiring musician, organ virtuoso, quiet lad from the Ēvele church area—fallen in his first battle, having lived only 20 years, leaving his dreams unfulfilled. Who was next? Who ordered untrained boys to the front? Who ordered lives to be sacrificed in the interests of a foreign power? He fell for Latvia, they'll say, yet Hitler had not promised Latvia anything, except that we would later need to be Germanized, if we stayed alive. Pity and anger overwhelmed me when I learned of Olǵerts's death.

After that, we waited for the next Russian attack. Our companies needed replacements. The trenches had been thinned out, and it was doubtful if we could hold our sector with the remaining forces. Grunte phoned Kociņš to ask for more troops but received a disappointing reply. Reserves had been promised, but the Germans were in no hurry to send their units, having weighed the situation and wanting to avoid spilling their own blood. Grunte slammed down the receiver and let off a string of curses. "If the Russians resume the attack tomorrow or the next day," said the adjutant, "we are done for." Yet the Russians mercifully gave us two days to recover and reorganize. This was not out of pity, of course, but because of their own need to recuperate and bring up reserves.

On the 19th of March, the earth and sky were in uproar again, as the second major battle for our hill began. By now we knew the Russian tactics of starting with artillery and following with infantry charges—the first lines in a row, the rest in a disorderly mob. This time, they brought something new. After the artillery bombardment, which was longer and more intense than those of March 16 and 17, we suddenly saw them—five or six Russian tanks. As they neared, the roar of their motors grew louder, freezing the blood in our veins. After each tank ran a dozen or so infantry. But our boys had brought antitank weapons[60] with them. To use these, they had to let the tanks get right up to the trenches. This was a difficult task psychologically—to let the monster crawl nearly upon you and then aim and shoot at the right moment, when advancing right behind was a group of the enemy firing automatic weapons at you.

And yet two of our *Panzerfausts* had found their marks. The tanks stopped, burning like torches, thick black smoke billowing around them, while our mortars continued to fire. Both tanks burned up, likely with their crews, while the soldiers behind them tried to hide in the black smoke. A third tank reached the crest of the hill, rolling over the front trenches, and fired at our bunkers. We hugged the ground. Bullets and grenade fragments flew over our heads, along with rocks and huge chunks of mud. The remaining tanks, their crews sobered by the fate of their comrades, turned back. Our antitank weapons were no longer able to reach them in pursuit, and our rear artillery fire was not accurate.

The tanks vanished, but the battle was not yet over. With shouts of "Hurrah!" a band of advancing Russians had already reached the base of our hill. Had our lines been breached? "Get the grenades!" shouted Vīķis. With trembling hands, I gave one grenade to him and crawled down the trench with the other toward the machine-gun nest. Suddenly and inexplicably, the attack was reversing and the Red soldiers running back toward their own lines. Perhaps conditions in other sectors had

---

[60]   These were the hand-held *Panzerfausts*, or "tank smashers," weapons effective to only about 33 yards.

changed, and the offensive in ours no longer made sense. We held our positions until dark, when the runner arrived with news that the enemy had retreated to their own lines, and we could return to our bunkers.

There were many dead and wounded again in this March 19 battle. Among the fallen was Laimonis Vilsons, a blond, rosy-cheeked boy, not especially diligent in his studies but determined to become a singer. (He had a good tenor voice as yet untrained for lack of a voice coach in high school.) Standing in the ranks in Neustrelitz, I had Ziedonis Purvs on one side and Laimonis Vilsons on the other, and in the RAD barracks Laimonis's bunk was next to mine. We had been together three months and got along well. In free moments, he often sang the Cavaradossi aria *"E Lucevan le Stelle,"*[61] with its line "And never was life so dear to me as now." My question after Oļģerts's death—who would be next?—had been answered. But in war, the list of the fallen is never final, and I wondered again, *Who will be next?*

In a two-week period, the First battalion had lost two-thirds of its men and was no longer battle-capable. Colonel Kociņš reorganized the battalion and in the process merged our housekeeping unit with that of the Second battalion, transferring Arnolds to them as well. I was the last of the Teachers Institute students left with Grunte. I don't know how Grunte was able to maintain a staff, but it remained intact even after the 44th regiment was shifted to a new sector in April. The front had been held, but the regiment had been reduced by half.

In the middle of April, a command came down from the upper echelons to shift the bloodied 19th division from the Ostrov region south to the Opocka sector for rest and rehabilitation. Our move took several days. We recrossed the Velikaja River, by ferry this time, to reach the Ostrov-Opocka highway. We crossed quietly and with no casualties, glad to be leaving this harrowing place, looking forward to the promised rest.

The broad but unpaved highway was mired in mud, though it had somehow escaped the surrounding destruction. The heavily wounded had previously been evacuated to the rear, and the lightly wounded rode in trucks, while the rest of us walked the 70 kilometers (42 miles) to Opocka. Among the marchers were our battalion commander, Grunte, and his adjutant. The "battalion" now consisted of 30-40 exhausted men. All of us who remained—along with the fallen, the wounded,

---

[61] The aria from Puccini's *Tosca*, "When the stars were brightly shining…"

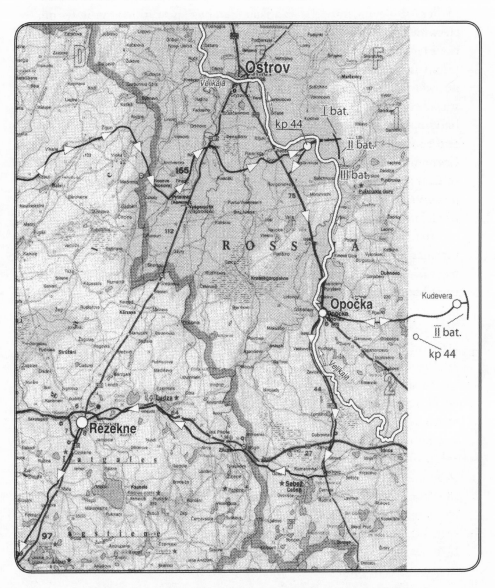

Eastern front near the Velikaja River, March to May 1944

and those assigned to the Second battalion—had left Riga on March 1, filling a long line of red freight cars.

On the second day of our march south, Russian reconnaissance planes drove us into the roadside ditches, now filled with spring snowmelt. With no place to hide, the truck drivers and passengers faced their fate out on the road, but fate was merciful, since the machine-gun bursts from the planes hit no one. Facing no further attacks from the air, we reached Opocka in the evening of the second day. The village was undamaged though empty of civilians. We spent the night on straw bedding in the empty rooms of a large house. We hadn't slept so well and so long for seven weeks. The next morning, we dried our soggy clothes, ate a good breakfast served by the field kitchen, cleaned and oiled our weapons, and gulped down as many beers as possible in the improvised canteen.

Thus refreshed, we marched off to the east. The going was not easy, the road softened by the spring weather and deeply rutted by heavy German vehicles. But the day was sunny and our mood light, for we were heading for rest. It was some 50 kilometers to the front lines. We were happiest for the total absence of any battlefield noises.

A Respite in Kudevera

Late in the evening, we reach the village of Kudevera, still a good distance from the front. It's an area of brush-covered hills and small valley lakes dotted with rundown villages made up of rough log houses, sheds and barns, and tiny garden plots. Next to the houses stand oversized gates but without fences or yards, since a gate touches right on the wall of the next house. All the houses are lined up along the road, with nothing more to break up the sameness. Life here must have been similarly gray.

The area around Kudevera reminds me of Latgale,[62] except there are no forests or birch groves here that so richly adorn our Latgale. And in further contrast to the grayness and poverty here, every house in Latgale has a flower garden and a well-kept courtyard. The Kudevera soil is sandy clay, which should have been productive for farming, so the poverty here might stem from the apathy of the inhabitants and the oppressive demands of the Soviet system. Of course, three years of war have also left their mark in the German invasion and its brutal treatment of prisoners and in the harsh counter activities of the partisans.

Once the spring sets in and everything turns green, even this place will be beautiful, I'm thinking. If they would only let us alone for a week or two. And the wish was granted, since the Russians did not attack in this region until mid-June. Besides some localized fire fights and clashes with patrols, nothing serious took place. While the headquarters staff crafted their grand offensive plans, the soldiers in the trenches and

---

[62] The easternmost province of Latvia.

support areas basked in the feeling of peace—so long hoped for, so necessary after the battles in March.

The snow melted away quickly, osiers bloomed, and on the southern slopes, new grass sprouted from the thatch. We felt this awakening of nature in our own revival. It's amazing how quickly a person can shift from one extreme to the other. Someone found a stock of hidden moonshine, someone else a supply of sauerkraut and potatoes (likely left by the hastily evacuated civilians before us). Then the feast began in earnest. With the blessing and participation of the battalion commander himself, we threw decorum out the window. My friend Ikvils was finally able to use his prized accordion, which had traveled in the supply wagon with us all the way from Riga. He had a good ear and played well, though his repertoire did not reach beyond the common Latvian and German drinking songs. But what more could one wish in this time and place? We listened to his singing only at the start. Once the home brew had gone to our heads, which it did quickly, we launched our own melodies in our own tempo, with no thought of the enemy or the presence of death.

The front stayed quiet, since the Russians also needed rest. The main reason for the pause was the spring thaw that had limited the movement of men and materials. It was clear though that the German forces were in decline while the Russians were growing stronger. Soon we would see more "straightening" and "tightening" of the front lines. We suppressed our doubts, though we knew that the Red Army had the upper hand now, that the Latvian border was near, and that the final peace, if we saw one, would be terrible for us legionnaires. So we tried not to think of a tomorrow we no longer had. Peace and honor to the fallen! For now, let's sing *"Zilais Lakatiņš"*[63]—no, something wilder and crazier.

At the beginning of May, we finally received mail, and the parcels forwarded by the "People's Aid" committee. These contained food items like bacon and bread, wrapped in the mittens, socks, and scarves knitted by our mothers, wives, brides, and sisters. Some of the parcels included letters to unidentified soldiers (passed out to those with no family or friends at home). Reading these messages from home touched our hearts and brought tears to the eyes of many a tough-talking soldier.

---

[63] "The Blue Scarf," a Latvian folk song of lost love.

A week passed in relative quiet. Some of the braver, or more foolhardy, boys reconnoitered the area and came across the materials for brewing our own moonshine. The apparatus was primitive but yielded the prized beverage. The distilling went on without official sanction, but once a bottle of the finished product appeared on a commander's desk as a present, the regulations went up the chimney. The staff, the moonshiners, and all the men not on guard duty gathered in the large office of the former village elder. Ikvils raised the accordion to his chest, the mice ran to their holes, and the festivities began again. I was still officially a nondrinker but, I must confess, only officially so. It was not easy to be the "white sparrow" in the flock, to stand out as though accusing others, so I drank my share as well.

On the first of May, Russian biplanes dropped flares to remind us of their holiday.[64] At times, the flares turned night into day, twisting the shadows every which way. It was a game and a display that heartened the Russians but warned us that major battles were ahead. From this, our boys took the lesson that the drinking should be intensified while the Ivans hadn't yet chased us off to poorer pastures. We would not be able to haul the still very far, and if we ended up in the next world, there would be no drinking anyway. So the idea was to use up the alcohol now, before it fell into the enemy's hands.

After a month or so, we received the accumulated mail that had been delayed by our transfer here. I had three letters—from home, from Velta, and from Džonītis. My parents wrote of their everyday work activities, but I understood they were more concerned with my situation at the front. Velta wrote about the visit of Andrejs Eglītis[65] and the painter Arijs Skride to her farm, events at school, and the new poetry and art books and films she had seen. It all felt so far away to me. How different our lives and interests and opportunities were now. Though I had not taken part directly in the battles of March 16–19, the experience would never let me be the person I was before those days exploded around me.

On a visit to the housekeeping unit, I looked up Arnolds, who shared his last month's issues of the newspaper *Tēvija* and the journal

---

[64] May Day was an important Soviet holiday celebrating workers.

[65] Latvian poet, who was also inducted into the Legion in 1943. Working as a war journalist, he was visiting Velta's home on an island in the Daugava River to observe local fishing practices.

Laikmets. Reading these, I felt within arm's length of Riga. Nothing could be gleaned from the political and military news, but the periodicals insisted in one voice that Latvia would never fall to the Bolsheviks again as guaranteed by the Latvians, the Germans, and the other peoples of the "New Europe," who would stand like a wall in defense of their culture.

The first weeks of May passed in the best possible way for us, in peace and quiet. The Kudevera village "garrison" brewed a new batch of moonshine every few days, and we let the chimney smoke away without fear of being targeted by artillery. We were happy that we didn't have to squat in the trenches, that we could sleep under a roof in the straw. The past two months would have seemed like a bad dream if we weren't still thinking of the many comrades we had lost. I still thought of Olģerts.

On the 12th of May, the battalion received an order from 44th regiment headquarters: Send us three slim, orderly, educated boys for noncommissioned officer training courses. Our "troika" of Grunte, his adjutant, and Vīķis discussed candidates. Vīķis nominated me, and the others agreed. They drew up a list, and then Vīķis gave me the written orders. I was visibly unwilling, but Vīķis overrode my objections: "*Befehl bleibt befehl!*"[66] he said. That clinched the matter, though I remained strongly opposed. In my three months of RAD training, I'd had enough of the German military drill, and I hated the thought of going through this again and of leaving my friends here and the comfortable life we were leading now that the front was so quiet. Since I couldn't reverse the decision, I comforted myself with the thought that at least I would be farther from the trenches and the fateful bullet when it flew. Yet Germany was no safe harbor. Everyone knew of the increased bombardment of German cities and the thousands of military and civilian deaths it had caused. You could not escape your fate, either at the front or behind the lines.

---

[66]   "Orders are orders."

In Training Again
at Lauenburg

Four of us from Kudevera—two high school grads, one Institute student, and a soldier suffering from viral hepatitis—travel to regimental headquarters on May 15, where we are joined by six more of the "intelligentsia." From there, we undergo a wild ride to Opochka, clinging to each other in an amphibious vehicle a bit small for our numbers. The sky is bright blue, the spring sun warm, lark songs fill the air, and best of all, we hear no battle noises. It feels like a ride out of an oasis. On the way, we are overtaken by two trucks carrying instructor trainees from other Legion units. We form a group of thirty or so.

In Sebezh, south of Opochka, we climb on the familiar red freight cars for the ride west. Our mood is lifted when we cross the Latvian border again and travel through Rēzekne,[67] hoping to go on to Riga, but the train turns south again toward Daugavpils.[68] Our ride through Latvia lasts only six hours, and then we are at the Lithuanian border, headed for Vilnius. The train sits a long time in Vilnius, where they hook on more cars but don't let us disembark. The more enterprising among us start bartering with the Lithuanians. Some German marks and a spare pair of boots pass through gaps in the wagon walls; bacon and vodka materialize in return. The bartering lifts our spirits again, after the disappointment of not seeing Riga.

While we wait, I manage to write letters to Velta and to my parents and ask a railwayman to drop them in a mailbox. The train resumes its

---

[67]   A district town in eastern Latvia.

[68]   Second largest city in Latvia, on the Daugava River in the southeastern corner of Latgale.

southwestern course through Lithuania and eastern Prussia until we reach Königsberg.[69] Here, we are finally released from the wagons and offered a buffet meal by girls in neat *Arbeitsdienst*[70] uniforms. They bring a sparkle to the eyes of our trench-crawlers, but we quickly understand that a distance must be kept. We are offered instead *ein bisschen* (a bit, a little) bread, *ein bisschen* margarine, artificial honey, and a cup of substitute coffee. When we're seated, they bring us some powdered pea soup. It doesn't seem like much in our empty bellies, but it's something, and the service is so pleasant. We had forgotten such things at the front.

There are several former RAD men in our group, and we chuckle at the reaction of the newcomers when they see the tiny cubes of margarine and honey. They will have much more to wonder at, though the Germans have long stopped wondering how Hitler, for ten years now, has managed to provide them with cannon in place of butter.

We learn that we are traveling to Lauenburg (wherever that is) and that we are in total 60 Latvians and 40 Germans, almost all with combat experience, many hung with medals. In that respect, I'm the "white sparrow" among them, neither this nor that. Königsberg is a large, beautiful, and exceptionally clean city. There are few good-sized towns in that part of northern Germany, but they are all clean. You see the difference as soon as you cross the border from Lithuania or Poland. Because our train will depart only at ten that night, we get a chance to explore the city. Especially noticeable are the varicolored ceramic tiles that cover not only building facades but also parts of some streets, fences, and small courtyards. I had not seen tile used this way before, either in Latvia or in Neustrelitz, and it lends a richness of tone to the city. When I saw Königsberg again ten years later, it was unrecognizable. The place—now called Kaliningrad—was one vast pile of rubble, the destruction more complete than in Berlin, Dresden, Jelgava, or Narva.[71]

We return to the train that night and in the morning head west again along the Baltic coast, through Danzig[72] to Lauenburg, which turns

---

[69]   The provincial capital of East Prussia, annexed by the Soviet Union in 1945 and renamed Kaliningrad.

[70]   Work service, the female counterpart of the *Reichsarbeitsdienst* (RAD).

[71]   Cities in Germany, Latvia, and Estonia that suffered from heavy bombing in the war.

[72]   Today's Gdansk.

out to be a small town in the former Polish Corridor,[73] 60 kilometers beyond Danzig and 25 kilometers from the sea. It's a level, quiet place that looks like it has never seen the war and never will. What a contrast to our last posting on the banks of the Velikaja.

Riding through East Prussia, we were often hailed by German women waving kerchiefs. They all had loved ones at the front, whom they hoped to welcome home one day. We never saw German men in the fields, only laborers impressed from the occupied areas, predominantly Poles, Ukrainians, Belorussians. These workers never saluted our passing train, reckoning matters within their own accounts. We understood both sides.

In Lauenburg, we marched from the railroad station to the camp, singing Latvian songs. The German women by the roadside looked at us as exotic beings never seen in this small town before. It's a good thing they did not understand Latvian, as the words of our songs were not always refined. From there, the setting unfolded just as in Neustrelitz— the wire-enclosed camp on the outskirts of town, the wooden barracks, the training grounds to one side. Almost everything was familiar to us shovel boys from the RAD. These kinds of camps must have been all over Germany in the hundreds, perhaps thousands—the same pedantic orderliness, cleanliness, and soullessness. There were differences too. We were no longer in the drab field uniforms of the RAD but in the blue-gray of the Wehrmacht, with a Latvian flag shield on our sleeves; here too, the eighteen- to twenty-year-olds were augmented with some older men, and our RAD shovels had been replaced by rifles, automatic weapons, gas masks, and antitank weapons. We occupied the familiar two-level bunk beds and received new uniforms, kits, weapons. Ranged by height again, we were divided into squads and companies.

My first surprise next day was to see Ziedonis Purvs. He and Pekka and several other RAD trainees had been inducted into the Legion with the rest of us but ended up in reserve in Jelgava (because their last names fell in the second half of the alphabet), where he and his companions enjoyed a loose regimen that allowed plenty of free time in the town and little instruction or drill. He was very satisfied with his months there. He had visited our former school and the classmates who, for health reasons or because of age, had been able to continue

---

[73] A strip of land separating East Prussia from Germany and giving pre-WWII Poland access to the Baltic Sea.

their studies. The male proportion had shrunk considerably though, and the Teachers Institute had almost become a girls' school. Ziedonis's friendly relations with his unit commander had helped him get passes every few days to Bauska[74] to see his parents and his girl. He would have liked to continue serving this way till the end of the war, but the order to all Legion units to send candidates for instructor training had terminated his idyll.His Teachers Institute background had contributed to his selection from the reserves.

Like me, Ziedonis was happy that we would be able to spend some time together. We were not as closely situated as in the RAD—I was in the first, he in the second squad—but we often met in the evenings. Ziedonis soon gained access to an accordion, and Pekka had brought his guitar along. We formed a quartet dedicated to singing in harmony. Our sessions took place Sunday afternoons during the free hours. On weekdays, we drilled from 6 am to 9 pm, so intensely that our only wish in the evenings was to crawl into our bunks and shut the world off. Looking back, the RAD experience now seemed like preschool. The summer of 1944 in Pomerania was very hot and dry, and we were driven to exhaustion. The carefree days in Kudevera seemed like a lost Paradise.

The tempo and mood of our activities was set by the trainers. As in all armies, especially the German army, the company first sergeant is God Almighty to the soldiers in the barracks and on the training fields. To gain the proper respect, these supermen use their throats to full effect. In German, the company first sergeant is called *Spiess* ("Sarge"). The word *Spiess* is also related to *spiessig*, which means "limited." Our company's *Spiess* was a limited type indeed and, to our minds, also a degenerate. Whether from fear of being sent to the front or from just a sadistic desire to demonstrate his power, he tormented his charges endlessly, who cursed him behind his back and promised him a bullet should they be together at the front. These words came back to Spiess's ears, and the rigors of our drill intensified.

He was a large man with a face reddened by drink but with soft, almost girlish hands. When he bellowed his commands, spit flew from his mouth, often to a distance of a meter or more. We never saw him calm or quiet, even in his sleep, which was dominated by his powerful snoring. When he saw an officer, *Spiess* grew pale, froze like a statue,

---

[74] A small town south of Jelgava, near the Lithuanian border.

and let out an *"Achtung!"* (Attention!), shrill enough to frighten every creature within a hundred meters. His reports to officers were just as loud as his orders to subordinates. He was incapable of normal speech. Recalling my RAD days, I concluded that *Zugführer* "Boxer" was a meek lamb compared to this forty-year-old "Bull."

More than anything else, *Spiess* hated intelligence and directed his most inspired curses toward any signs of this trait. He had completed only a few grades of elementary school, and his civilian job had been delivering beer barrels as he proudly told us. In the barracks, he spent a long time slowly reading and deciphering the written orders from officers, and no one was allowed to disturb him at these times on pain of extra duty cleaning the latrines. His other free time activity, of which he never tired, was looking at pornography. Those were times of peace and quiet for us, without the sound of his bellowing.

At one end of the barracks, *Spiess* had a small private room, which had to be cleaned and straightened by the soldiers on duty. Three photographs were pinned on the wall above his bed. The caption of the largest said, *"Unser Fuehrer Adolf Hitler,"* shown in a dress tunic. The next photo included a matronly woman and two kids in *Hitlerjugend*[75] apparel standing behind a seated *Spiess*, who was successfully imitating the Führer's arrogant expression. The third photo showed a naked model in an expressive pose, with an army hat cocked jauntily on her head.

Instructor training in Lauenburg

---

[75]   The Nazi Hitler Youth organization.

In our first lineup in the courtyard, we received information on the rules and regulations of the camp. Then each trainee was asked to call out his school or occupation in civilian life. In my naïveté, I named the Teachers Institute as my school. The name had saved me from the first trenches in the past; now it condemned me to the special notice of *Spiess*. "*Du, Flasche, bist ein Student? Also, gut, sofort meine Stiefel putzen! Los, los!*"[76] And so several of us "students" earned extra duty cleaning the barracks and completing other onerous tasks. On the training field, *Spiess* singled out the former students and high school grads for additional rounds of "*Hinlegen! Auf!*" (Hit the ground! Get up!). Why did he dislike the educated so much? Inferiority complex? "I promise you, I'm going to drive all these idiotic notions from your stinking heads and make you into real people! And if you don't like that, you can kiss my ass!" To me, *Spiess* was the quintessence of the National Socialist Party stalwart, the perfect example of the Führer's "New Europe" denizen—unthinking, obedient, and aggressive.

We enjoyed the off-base training most because it took us away from *Spiess* and the drilling program generally—usually for a few hours but sometimes, during maneuvers, for twenty-four hours or more. It was great to be outdoors in the balmy summer. But on hot days, a ten-kilometer hike with a machine gun on your back was no picnic. At the shout of "Gas!" we would quickly don our gas masks and march along while the sweat flowed and breath came in gasps. On the return trip to the barracks, we usually heard the command "*Ein Lied!*" (A song!) If the song didn't please the commander, we would hear, "Gas masks on!" followed by "*Ein Lied!*" again. So our hours of physical training were capped off by marching along wearing gas masks, carrying full packs and weapons, while singing loudly enough to please the instructor. Yet it was due perhaps to this ferocious drilling that I was able to save my life in the next year. Those who had not been toughened died like flies then.

Unlike the pleasant breaks we enjoyed in the RAD training, the Lauenburg routine provided few moments of rest. After formation drills, weapons training, and off-base activities, we were so exhausted that, in the few free hours on Sundays, we could only manage to write a letter, wash or mend some clothes, and lie in the grass next to the barracks. We went to town a few times, but there was nothing to see or

---

[76] "You're a student, you bottle? Good, then clean my boots! Hurry up!"

hear. Lauenburg was not truly a German or a Polish town, but it was certainly more bleak and empty than Neustrelitz.

A hospital had been established in the largest four-story building in town, and it was filled beyond capacity. Next to the south wall of the building, the sick and the maimed warmed themselves in the summer sun. A strong medicinal smell hung in the air. The Führer was hoping to fix up some of the wounded and return them to the meat grinder, but the sick and the crippled longed for a quick end to the war. Each with his own hopes. On the training fields, you could still hear the bravura martial songs "*SS marschiert in Feindes Land*"[77] and "*Wenn wir fahren gegen England.*"[78] But in the hospital courtyard, they sang the sad songs like "*In der Heimat, in der Heimat, da gibt's ein Wiedersehen*"[79] and "*Lili Marleen.*"[80] They were running out of room for the bravura, as the front continued to be "tightened" and "straightened."

On the night of June 6, 1944, alarms sounded all over the camp. We had to be out on the training field in formation with full combat gear in ten minutes. *Spiess* ran through the barracks, bellowing as always, his threats slowing rather than accelerating preparations. Lined up in formation, we were informed by the school commandant that, at the moment, the English and Americans were landing in France from the Channel and so opening up a second front in the west. An order had been received to transfer part of the trainees closer to the new front. "Volunteers first of all, three paces forward!" I saw that Ziedonis had stepped out from his squad. What to do? As usual, I could not decide on the spur of the moment and stayed in line. I wanted to remain closer to Latvia anyway and to my loved ones. No western front for me.

Lacking enough volunteers, they assigned additional soldiers, registered all the departing, and passed out extra weapons, ammunition, food, and medical supplies. All the equipment was loaded into trucks and the soldiers herded into other trucks. It all went with amazing smoothness. Undeniably, the Germans organize things like no one else. When I was later introduced to the Russian *system*, I always remembered the exemplary discipline of the German army, especially in the *Waffen*

---

[77]   "The SS marches in the enemy's land."

[78]   "When we go against England."

[79]   "We'll meet again in our native land."

[80]   German love song written in 1915, which became popular in World War II.

SS[81] units, at least until February 1945 and the onset of the German
army's collapse. The commandant looked at his wristwatch and, when
the designated moment came, called out *"Los!"* (Go!) All the trucks
started up at the same time and drove one after another into the
street. It was German precision at its best. And perhaps this case also
illustrates the rationale for the unquestioning obedience taught in the
drills. Starting with the *"Hinlegen! Auf!"* routine, you can quickly get
to rearranging the map of Europe, with everyone shouting in unison,
"Heil!"

Since we were still in formation, I wasn't able to say good-bye to
Ziedonis, but as his truck drove by, I called out, "Don't worry, and
say hello to the Yanks!" That was all. *Spiess* yelled to our remaining
contingent, "Everyone to bed, hurry!" My last thought before falling
asleep was *It's too bad they didn't take the Spiess along. It's time he smelled the
powder too.*

So the invasion in the west, perhaps the most important event in
the war after Stalingrad, began while I was in Lauenburg. We remaining
trainees continued to be schooled in the arts of war by experienced,
knowledgeable officers but still under the thumb of *Spiess*. Many came to
regret the decision not to volunteer for the western front. A determined
Spiess drove us even harder, hoping that would keep him from the
trenches. Every day was equally wearying. The weather held at hot
and dry. We were sick of it all—the weapons, gas masks, the sweating,
the shouted orders. Then a few weeks later, in the middle of June, the
men sent to the French coast all returned, whole and healthy, including
Ziedonis. They hadn't seen any second front but had spent a pleasant
summer month in southern Denmark, near the German border. Food
rations had been ample, and our comrades looked well fed.

We envied the returning "Danes," especially for the upgrade in their
rations, since the artificial honey, margarine, and mustard we received
here in their miniature portions did little to satisfy our developing
bodies. But we couldn't complain, having made the choice ourselves.
Ziedonis described Denmark as a quiet backwater far removed from
the war, the Danes leading their lives as in peacetime. They had no
love for the Germans but remained sympathetic to Latvians, he felt.
He and the other trainees had been sent back when the situation at

---

[81]   "Weapons SS," the combat arm of the *Schutzstaffel* (Protective Squadron), a force
distinct from the regular army.

the front stabilized. (Maybe the commanders also feared they would try to escape to the English and Americans.) I was regretful as well that I hadn't seen the fabled rivers of milk and mountains of butter of this land. Soon these regrets were forgotten, under the force of new developments.

The Eastern Front moved in the middle of July. This was serious. Suddenly, the front could not be held at Kudevera, Opochka, or along the whole Latvian border. The Red army was advancing irresistibly. The Germans hastily withdrew their dislocated units. To avoid encirclement, the Latvian Legion's 19th and 15th divisions also had to retreat to the west, leaving the Latvian border open to the enemy. The poet Andrejs Eglitis has caught the essence of the next ten months' events in his laconic song title, *"Dievs, Tava zeme deg!"*[82] There was no truer way to say it.

We received the bad news by radio and later by mail from home. While events on the eastern front did not change our training routine, an air of anxiety was apparent among the officers and staff of the camp. Everyone understood that the school would be closed soon, and we would get a chance to show our new skills in practical operation. The Red army's offensive in the Center area of the eastern front was very effective. In the period from June 20 to August 20, the Russians reached the border of East Prussia, pausing there. We feared the interruption of mail service to and from Latvia, but the letters kept coming, though with major delays.

In the afternoon of July 20, another alarm called us into formation in combat gear to await orders. A vile assassination attempt, it seems, had been directed at the Führer. The bomb had exploded at his feet, but he had survived. ("By the will of God," said the *Spiess*, while we Latvian boys were thinking, *Too bad.*) Training was interrupted, ammunition passed out, and we were ordered to await further orders in the barracks. The alarm was lifted after two days of uncertainty. The assassins had been caught and executed. The Führer had dealt with his enemies quickly and mercilessly. One has to wonder how the war would have ended if these brave men had been successful. As it was, the 20th of July decided the fates of millions.

Life in the camp returned to the familiar rhythms, unchanged even by the situation at the front. At the end of July, ten kilometers from

---

[82] "Lord, your land is burning!"

town, we played some "war games." We began, in fact, in an actual sandbox, where we analyzed several variants, and then proceeded to maneuvers in the countryside, including nighttime activity and the participation of a real tank. A general from Berlin was present as inspector. It looked like *Spiess* would crawl out of his skin to show himself in the best light before the commanders. With less than three months of training under our belts, we wondered if we would be going to the front after this field inspection. In the present situation of the war, it was impossible to predict anyone's future.

We moved across a hilly, brush-covered, uninhabited area, shooting our training ammunition at each other. We shivered at night and sweltered in the 30-degree Celsius heat (86 degrees Fahrenheit) of the days. Still, maneuvers are more enjoyable than the training field because of the periodic absence of the instructors. The best thing in the middle of the day is the *Feldflasche* with *Sprudel*,[83] which we were generously supplied with. Our high-ranking visitor was evidently pleased with the maneuvers and our demonstrated skills. After he had climbed into his automobile and left the area, we could see the broad smiles of our officer-instructors. As a reward, we were allowed to return to the barracks walking in free step. In the canteen back in camp, each soldier received a stein of beer and five cigarettes and, best of all, a free afternoon. We slept like the dead for fifteen hours straight.

The next stage of my training ground to a complete halt. I had contracted bronchitis during the maneuvers, and now my chest wheezed like an organ, and all the strength had left me. I held out a few days but then stayed in my bunk even after the morning whistle. The *Spiess* cursed himself out but then sent for the camp doctor, who sent me to the hospital. So I exchanged my bunk in the barracks for a soft white bed and the luxury of complete quiet. The German doctor and a Norwegian nurse took good care of me, the food was good, and the time I spent in the infirmary seemed like a holiday. Moreover, on my birthday, I received a combined package of Latvian delicacies from my mother and Velta, along with letters. Though I didn't know at the time, these would be the last items I would receive from Riga. Letters sent from Latvia after that all disappeared in the confusion of war.

I wanted to stay in the hospital as long as possible to regain my strength. Friends from the company told me that the training would

---

[83] Field canteen with mineral water.

be stopped on August 18 and our unit divided, sending one half to the front, the other to antitank courses in Czechoslovakia. I wished I could be sent back to Kurzeme,[84] where I would find my regiment. I was fed up with training in the German manner and happy that I could remain in the hospital for the time being.

Thanks to the bronchitis, my vacation lasted three weeks. It's possible that the stay was extended at the behest of the German doctor and the Norwegian nurse (a real beauty, with movie star looks). There had been few patients in their department (internal medicine and respiratory ailments) that summer, and the doctor worried he would be transferred closer to the front, having to leave his nurse behind. I could see that they were in a personal relationship. Once, the nurse asked me why I, a Latvian, was serving in the German army. "And why are you not in Norway today but here?" I retorted. We smiled at each other in unspoken recognition; we both knew something about circumstances.

I was discharged on the 23rd of August and returned to the barracks to find my unit already gone. In the office, I picked up my previously issued *Marsch befehl* (orders) for Beneschau, south of Prague, where the antitank courses would be held. Fate had decided for me once again, without my participation. I stuffed my belongings in my backpack, signed a document attesting that I was not in debt to the camp, and walked to the train station. *Why worry about it?* I thought; it will be a new experience to travel through Germany and then see Czechoslovakia.

---

[84] Westernmost province of Latvia, where Latvian and German units held out against the Soviets till the war's end.

TANK SCHOOL IN NEVEKLAU
(AND OPERATION DEUTSCHKRONE)

In her last letter, Velta wrote that if the Russians kept advancing, she would not stay in Latvia. After all she had suffered in 1941, I could understand this decision completely. I wondered also what my parents would do if the front pushed to the gates of Riga. They had never been involved with politics, worked in routine civil service jobs,[85] had few possessions. It would seem that they were not slated for repression if the Russians came into Latvia again. On the negative side, their oldest son was serving in the Latvian Legion, but he had been conscripted straight from the classroom, just like thousands of other young men his age. Would it be possible to repress a large part of the Latvian people who only wanted their freedom? Later events proved that far more terrible actions were possible.

At the time, I thought that my father, who loved Latvia so much, would never leave. He had crisscrossed the whole country on foot— by himself and with his students (whom he had taught geography, history, and the Latvian language for twenty years). With his friend Jānis Grests, he had collected rocks and assembled collections and visual aid displays for schools. All his hopes were for the future of Latvia. No, my father would never leave Latvia of his own free will. If they couldn't stay home, the family would find temporary shelter in Kurzeme. Maybe I could also get there by a sea route. Would I get back to Kurzeme after my training was complete or be returned to Grunte's

---

[85] The author's father was an elementary school teacher, his mother a midwife employed by her district.

74

battalion, nearly destroyed in the Velikaja battles? Who could tell? In wartime, you just had to be thankful about every day you stayed alive.

Such thoughts occupied me as the train traveled through the former Polish Corridor and farther west toward Stettin[86] and then to Berlin. I saw little of the darkened capital, arriving at night and changing trains at the same station for the trip south toward Dresden, also conducted in darkness. The Germans scrupulously observed the blackout regulations in the cities, as well as the countryside. I don't know how travelers by car were able to stay on the roads. I dozed along with the other passengers, all soldiers or other army personnel. There were frequent requests to show our travel documents to the gendarmes (military police), who were aggressive and nitpicky. They would shine a flashlight into your eyes and then down at your documents. If something was not to their liking, they didn't bother listening to explanations. You were off the train and on your way to the prefecture as happened to several of my companions in Dresden.

The gendarmes paid less attention to travelers going in the other direction, toward the front. My travel orders required me to report to the control office at each stop—in Berlin, Dresden, Prague, and Beneschau. These checkpoints were intended to eliminate side trips and dawdling along the way and to ensure that the destination would be reached in the shortest and quickest way. Still, the reality was that the process could spring some leaks, and these were quickly exploited.

I disembarked in the early morning sunshine in the pleasant little town of Beneschau and reported to the control office, where I received further orders to proceed to the village of Neveklau twelve kilometers away. The area was beautiful—hills, forests, quick-flowing rivers within steep banks, everything bright and glowing in the late summer sun. It was my first time this far south in Europe, and it looked like the setting from a real fairy tale. With all of Europe at war, the peace and quiet here in the very center of the continent seemed like Paradise.

I stopped to rest and drink from an icy stream, where I refilled my *Feldflasche*. The whole way, I did not meet anyone, civilian or military, though I passed through several villages, each made up of ten to fifteen neat, well-cared-for houses along the roadside. Behind the houses and utility buildings usually stood five or six apple, plum, or other fruit trees and bushes, but no inhabitants could be seen. Later, I learned

---

[86]   Today's Sceczen, on the Baltic coast.

that the area had been emptied of its residents a few months before. The German authorities had ordered the Czechs to clear twenty square kilometers so they could establish training fields and artillery ranges. The Czechs had been forced to leave their homes with all their animals and seek shelter in the surrounding parishes.

We met some of the displaced people about four kilometers south of Neveklau, where we had gone to buy bread. While they refused to sell anything to the Germans, they were glad to trade with us once they learned we were Latvians, as long as we proved our nationality by speaking Latvian or Russian. A Czech loaf, about 30 centimeters (nearly one foot) in diameter, is round with a large hole in the middle. It tasted delicious after the "sawdust bricks" we had been eating in the barracks. The Czechs didn't want our *reichsmarks*, preferring to trade the bread for possessions, if we had any. After a satisfactory trade, the baker would shake hands and pronounce, "*Lettland und Tschechoslowakei*," while giving the V for Victory sign in hopes that the Germans would soon be defeated.

To wind the film backwards a little—to my arrival in Neveklau—the sign above the entryway of a large two-story building said "*Panzergrenadier Schule Neveklau*."[87] The building—once part of a baronial estate—was set in a small park with utility buildings behind it, the roads neatly laid with paving stones, the buildings well maintained. No one was around at the moment, probably out on the training fields. I went inside and reported to the duty officer, who said the school supervisor and company commander would be back after a few hours. I could rest for now and look around.

Those were my last free hours before I resumed, for the third time now, the mind-numbing Germanic drill I had grown so tired of. The boys told me that the duty here was just as bad as in the last three months but with some advantages: there were few Germans in total; the school supervisor, a youngish German, was a decent sort, having served at the front rather than climbed from a privileged position in the Party. The *Spiess* was also German but incomparably better than our Lauenburg "Bull." The school was made up of three companies: two Latvian units with Latvian commanders and one Estonian unit with an Estonian commander. Commands were delivered in the languages

---

[87]　Tank Grenadier School of Neveklau. The term *grenadier* refers to infantry soldiers with additional duties, in this case operating and servicing tanks and, alternatively, learning to destroy them.

of the respective companies. The theory taught in the classroom or out in the "sandbox" was presented in German or Latvian, depending on the nationality of the lecturer. The same principle applied to field maneuvers.

A second advantage: all the empty villages in the area had ripening fruit orchards. Our Sunday afternoons were devoted to raids, targeting as many apples, pears, and plums as we could carry and consume. Yet this was not enough for us, and every evening after retreat had sounded, we sent two soldiers with sacks on their rounds. Thus, we ended up stealing not only fruit from Czech orchards but also several hours from our night's sleep—waiting for the raiders to return, dividing the spoils, and consuming the booty.

My turn to go on a raid came only a few weeks after my arrival. It gets dark earlier in the Czech lands than in Latvia, and it's dark early in September. As a result, we crawled along in the grass and tried to fill our sacks by touch. If there weren't enough fallen fruit, we shook the lower branches of the trees; and if visibility improved, we climbed up after the fruit. Fortunately, all the dogs had left the area along with their masters, and our forays were not interrupted. Getting back into the barracks was not as easy, however, and often required leaving part of our haul with the duty guard. It was the only time during the whole war that we ate as much fruit as we wanted. We didn't think anyone else in Greater Germany,[88] other than the Party elites, were so privileged.

After the daily training rigors, with the familiar *"Hinlegen! Auf!"* and the singing in gas masks and similar exercises, we were exhausted by evening. Yet the craving for the juicy plums and apples kept us from sleep. We sat on our bunks and quietly traded anecdotes to chase off sleep. The weaker among us lay back on their bunks and instantly fell asleep, missing a chance to fill their bellies. At first, we tried to save their portions in backpacks, but these "storehouses" were quickly discovered and the fruit confiscated, putting an end to this contingency plan. Our main campaign continued through September as long as we were able to find fruit we could reach and get to. Surprisingly, no one got sick or suffered from the runs from all this overindulgence.

With the end of the fruit season in October, we switched our sights to potatoes. Planting their crop in the spring, the Czechs could not have

---

[88] *Grossdeutschland*, consisting of Germany and the lands it had conquered or occupied.

imagined that someone else would harvest it in the fall. In the dark
of night, we burrowed in the potato fields like moles. A supply shed
provided shelter for our hidden stockpile. Then on Sunday afternoons,
the yard looked like a gypsy encampment, with smoke rising from
campfires and twisting around the hunched forms of the soldiers.

There was no recreation available in Neveklau. For five kilometers
in any direction from the school, you wouldn't find a movie house, a
drinking place, or any kind of society. We were located on a beautiful
green island. Weekdays, we heard commands and training explosions;
but on Sundays, all was quiet, without the sound of voices, barking dogs,
or lowing cows. You could get some beer but little else in the school's
canteen. So we developed our own ritual for Sunday afternoons. After
cleaning our weapons, we boiled potatoes in our field kettles in a corner
of the yard. These went well with the beer and the mustard available
from the canteen. We set up a barrel for the mustard and spread it
liberally on bread and the potatoes in place of butter, eating our fill.
After the feast, Ziedonis would play the accordion, Pekka the guitar;
the rest of us sang along, and so for a few hours every week, we felt
great. We tried not to think about the future, which we could not alter
or improve anyway. Everything would happen as it had to.

The war in the east was certainly taking its unalterable course. In
the summer of 1944, the Red army began a major offensive along the
whole German front. The Germans retreated, understanding that they
could not hold such an extended front. On July 10, on the orders of the
German high command, the Latvian Legion began to pull back from
positions in the Opochka area toward the Latvian border. We learned
only later that the Legion had retreated across all of Latgale, fighting
rearguard actions, and that the remains of the 15th division had been
sent to Germany for rebuilding, but the 19th division had settled into
defensive positions by Lake Lubāna and the Aiviekste River.[89] In face
of stronger Russian forces and the pullback of German units, the 19th
division had retreated across all of Vidzeme in September, with heavy
fighting by Cesvaine and More (towns in Vidzeme), turning south
before reaching Riga and in October crossing the Daugava River and
then digging in again at Džūkste (southwest of Riga). I could only
speculate on what had happened with my regiment.

---

[89]   Areas on the western border of Latgale.

At the end of July, the Red army had broken out of Lithuania with superior forces, reaching Jelgava and temporarily even Tukums in an effort to reach the Bay of Riga and isolate Kurzeme. The Germans were able to hold off the attack and push the front back a bit, allowing them to evacuate Riga. The Red army entered Riga on October 13. Now all of Latgale, Vidzeme, and most of Zemgale were in Soviet hands, but a redoubt—the "Fortress Kurzeme"—formed in the northwestern part of the province, maintained by still strong German forces and the decimated 19th division of the Legion.

The Red Army had taken Estonia in September and in October reached Palanga (Lithuanian town) on the Baltic Sea, cutting off Kurzeme from German forces in East Prussia. That meant we could reach Kurzeme only by sea, if even that route remained open. No one had expected such a rapid collapse, though we had long understood that Germany could not win this war. Now the Russians were on Germany's borders, irresistibly driving west. It seemed absurd that the Germans could still hope for victory. The fabled wonder weapon had not materialized, the Americans were allied with the Russians, and there was no solution, though the speculation continued without pause.

Back in Neveklau, we sometimes wondered why the word *Panzer* had been attached to our school. Viewed from a distance on the training field, a couple of plywood structures did resemble tanks but not so at close range. We danced around these "tanks" in the training sessions, toting *Faustpatronen,* laying mines, carrying out the officers' orders. But we did not gain a realistic knowledge or skill in combating tanks until we returned to the front and experienced the terror of waiting for a real tank to rumble nearly upon us before we could fire our weapons. The school's obligation was to teach us and keep us hustling, ours to temporize and wait for the war to end.

Field training in Neveklau, September 1944; author shown in top row

I can't say how my family obtained my address, but I received news at the end of October that they were traveling as refugees in eastern Germany. Earlier in the month, they had been driven out of their home because the Germans wanted to set up defensive positions in the outskirts of Riga. My parents had to decide what to do on the spot. They borrowed a horse and wagon from neighbors, tied a cow to the wagon, and headed in the direction of Riga. The neighbors had talked about Kurzeme; the Germans urged them to go to Germany. In Riga, the Germans were seizing men from the streets and driving them aboard ships to go work in Germany. A few days before the arrival of the Russians, feeling the general panic, my parents had boarded a ship in the Daugava, which took them to Danzig, and then to several refugee camps in Prussia, until they ended up in a small village called Deutschkrone.[90] Like other refugees, they were totally bereft but in

---

90   Town in West Prussia, today called Walcz, in Poland.

good health and all together. If for nothing else, I was glad we were closer together and all on the same side of the front.

The rains came in November. In our field training on fortifications, we smeared ourselves with mud to such an extent that we had to spend all evening cleaning, patching, and ironing our clothes and oiling our weapons. The weather grew cold, and we had no winter wear. There were no more fruit either, and we had eaten our way through the potato reserves. We felt the full bleakness of late fall. Then we heard that a ship was being organized to transport troops from Danzig to Liepāja.[91] It was a chance to get back closer to home, before the Russians cut off access completely. Every trainee from the Latvian companies signed up for the trip. (The Estonians were stranded, their country completely occupied.) The school supervisor, however, told us that only half of us would be able to travel, the other half remaining in Neveklau. I was fortunate to be able to join the travelers.

On the 20th of November, we left the *Panzerschule* in four heavy trucks headed for Prague. Ziedonis and I were separated again. We spent two days in Prague waiting for a train, enjoying the delay, uncertain if we would ever have a chance to see the "Golden City"[92] again. We had all volunteered for the front and so were considered reliable. We were given passes until the next evening, when we had to reassemble in the railroad station. There were no other restrictions (nor help with the overnight stay). We felt like birds freed from a cage. Looking for things to buy in the stores, we found little there and little we could afford. We ate some bread and soup at a diner, lacking the ration coupons for more substantial food. Exploring the city center was more rewarding. We had heard of the beauty of Prague and watched films that made us eager to see for ourselves. Here was the ornate baroque church of St. Nicholas and the Street of the Goldsmiths. There was the panoramic view of the Old City from the shore of the Vltava River, then the bridge of the Emperor Charles over the river with medieval towers at the end of the bridge, and the old street leading up to the Prague Castle. In the courtyard of the magnificent palace rose the towers of the Gothic cathedral of Saint Vitus. We roamed the streets and lingered on the corners of the Old Town well into evening.

---

[91] A major Latvian port on the Baltic.

[92] *Zlata Praha* in Czech, named for its golden spires and monuments.

On the other side of the river, we viewed the town hall with its unique astronomic tower clock and strolled through Vaclav[93] Square in the city center. A massive museum building stands at one end of the square, the statue of King Vaclav in front of it. I had to agree: Prague was the most beautiful city I had seen till then.

Absorbed in the monumental scenery, I didn't notice that the other soldiers had turned off on a side street, leaving only me and Roberts wandering in the twilight. We had to find lodgings for the night if we didn't want to return to the train station. Roberts's parents had recently been transferred from a refugee camp in Danzig to a village near Prague, but he didn't know how to get there. His case set me to thinking of my own. We tried to get tips on cheaper accommodations from passersby but were received unwillingly, probably because of our German uniforms and language. We couldn't change the uniforms, but switching to Latvian, which the Czechs didn't understand but which conveyed our non-German status, did get us beds for one night. Though we had heard that the Czechs would lure German officers into apartment buildings and kill them, we felt reasonably safe as non-German nonofficers.

An old Czech woman in an old brick building led us down a series of long hallways and up steep stairs till we found ourselves in something like a bird's nest in the attic. The beds were clean but incredibly short. Having learned to sleep on our feet or even while marching, we raised no objections. The old woman spoke German poorly and probably did not understand our explanations of who we were. We showed her the flag shields on our sleeves, but "Latvia" was a word she was probably hearing for the first time. We had no weapons and decided to sleep in our uniforms. We fell asleep like twenty-year-olds—in midsentence.

Seemingly a moment later, we were shaken awake and squinting into flashlights. Two middle-aged men in civilian clothes asked to see our documents. They looked us up and down, scanned our papers, and conferred in their own language. "Why are you fighting with the Germans?" they asked. We told them we were conscripts straight from school. "You can stay with us. We'll give you some clothes and hide you till the war ends, which will be very soon, by the way. *Hitler kaput!*"

---

[93] Vaclav I, king of Bohemia (crowned 1228), also known as King Wenceslaus.

But we remained wary, afraid to fall into the hands of the gendarmes. We said we did not want to desert. "The Russians will be here soon. They will liberate all of Europe," they said.

"That's why we have to hurry home," we said, "so the Russians don't liberate Latvia."

"You're being foolish," they said, handing our papers back with the added comment, "Greetings to your Führer. Tell him we have a noose already woven for him."

"But to us, Hitler and Stalin are one and the same," we said. In the fall of 1944, this was not something the Czechs could as yet accept.

We relied on the discretion of the Czechs since, for this kind of loose talk, we could earn a bullet in the neck from the Germans. For the sake of caution, we rose early and traversed the labyrinths of the old hotel till we found ourselves out on the street at sunrise. We spent the day wandering the streets. In the afternoon, our feet dragging, we turned into a movie house to watch a Zarah Leander film called *Die Grosse Liebe* (The Great Love). For a while, we almost felt like civilians on vacation in an exotic land.

Discipline in our unit held up well, as we all showed up at the appointed time to climb aboard a train with the indicated route of Prague–Goerlitz–Frankfurt an Oder. We rode slowly through the night, as I crouched in a corner, turning over in my mind an action plan to which I gave the code name "*Deutschkrone*." If they were going to attach our wagons to another train in Frankfurt for the trip further north, there would be a delay, perhaps a chance to disembark. In that time, I had to board another train that would go through Schneidemühl or Bromberg.[94] From there, I could easily reach Deutschkrone, according to the map. The risks would be great; I could be caught by the gendarmes as a deserter. Still, I wanted to risk it because I knew it would be my only chance to see my family before I reached the front lines in Kurzeme. I wanted to hug Mother for just a moment before heading back to the war.

In Frankfurt an Oder, I learned we would have a half hour's layover before departing on Track 3. Making do with this meager information, I asked Roberts to watch over my backpack, as I was heading for the station's canteen. There, I scanned the schedule for trains, finding

---

[94] Cities in West Prussia, today part of Poland and called Piła and Bydgoszcz, respectively.

several going in my direction. Soon the loudspeakers were announcing the imminent departure of our train on Track 3, and my comrades called to each other to head down the tunnel to climb aboard. On the spur of the moment, I ducked into a restroom and waited with pounding heart for news of the train's departure. The next five minutes seemed like five hours, before the loudspeaker proclaimed that my train had left the station. I waited a while longer and then found the control office and frantically told them I had missed my unit's train headed for Berent.[95]

---

[95]   Town in West Prussia, today part of Poland and called Kościerzyna.

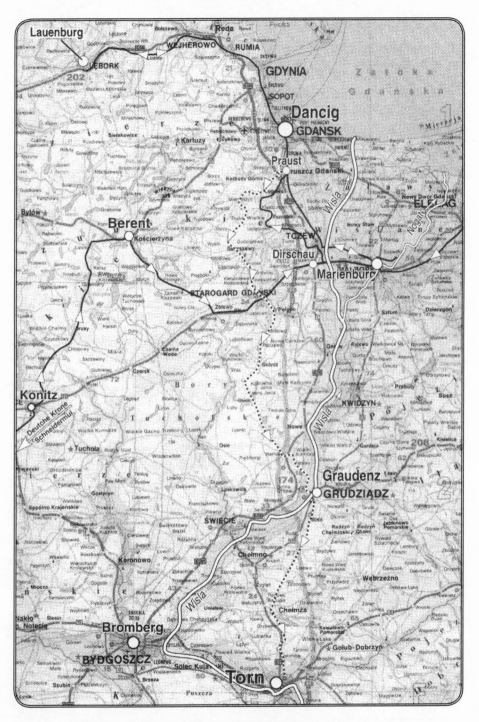

Danzig and environs

The commandant swore mightily, cursing the damned *ausländers* (foreigners) for their ineptitude but did write me a note, saying I was traveling to my unit. Fortunately, the direction of travel was toward the front, or I would have likely fallen into the clutches of the gendarmes. The commandant explained that the next train on my intended route would depart only in 24 hours. Alternately, I could leave in an hour on a route detouring through Berlin and Landsberg but would not catch up to my unit in either variant. I asked and was given a permit to travel through Berlin but without permission to leave the train there. *Good,* I thought, *the sooner I leave here, the better, before a message is received from my unit about a "deserter."* Having begun with mighty cursing, the commandant ended by writing me a requisition slip for two days of *knäckebrot* (bread crisps) and margarine that filled the void nicely, since I had left my food stores in the backpack in Roberts's care. The commandant sent me off with a hearty *"Viel Spass! Heil Hitler! Viel Spass!"*[96]

We rode into Berlin at twilight. I found my next train and, without the required permission to go outside, spent my time idling in the station. Late that night, the train took me northeast again from the darkened city emptied of its civilians, the uniformed patrols looking grim and forlorn. I went through a number of document checks without problems and disembarked in the darkness of Schneidemühl at five a.m., with no idea of which direction to take. Hearing the clang of milk cans in the distance, I found a nearby dairy, handling its first deliveries of the day. I asked the manager how to get to Deutschkrone. He said the milk driver from the village, which was 25 kilometers away, would be here soon; perhaps I could arrange a ride with him.

The morning was cold enough to cover the puddles with a coating of ice.I was shaking in my thin uniform until the manager invited me inside to warm up."Are you on leave from the front?" he asked.I told him I was traveling to see my folks in the village, which didn't quite satisfy him, though he did not question me further.I was glad he didn't ask to see my leave papers.Feeling uncomfortable, I kept to the front room of the dairy, away from the manager.

The village driver arrived and unloaded his milk cans, taking on the empties in the back of the truck.He gave my request for a ride a curt refusal.Frau So-and-so would be riding next to him, but the back was full of milk cans.In fact it was *streng verboten* (strictly forbidden) to

---

[96] "Good luck! Heil Hitler! Have fun!"

take on passengers. I offered him the best kind of wartime currency—cigarettes—and he grew more accommodating. I could sit in the back among the empties, but I had to hold on tight, as he would be driving fast over a road laid with paving stones. And he drove like a maniac, as promised, while the empty cans in the back careened in a wild rhythm that threatened to get out of control and squash me like a bug. An icy wind lashed my face, and it felt like my intestines would seize up from the constant shaking. Luckily, the ride lasted only a half hour. I crawled off the truck stiff, frozen, thoroughly battered.

It was getting light as I viewed the low-slung buildings of the village. I asked the first person I saw where the refugees from Latvia had been quartered. Almost every house has some *ausländers*, I was told. Families with children had been put up at the other end of the village. To keep warm, I trotted the length of the whole village, accompanied by the sound of barking dogs. I saw hooded lamps in a few windows, and people rising to go to work. Trusting to luck, I opened the door of a farmer's cottage to a poorly lit entryway. I knocked on the inner door and heard, "*Ja, herein*" (Come in). A moment passed, and then in the doorway stood ... my mother! We were both so shocked we didn't know what to say. It was the moment of a lifetime for both of us.

I was embraced by everyone and fed with the remains of the provisions they had carried for two months from one refugee camp to the next. We had all stored up so much to talk about that the questions and answers collided one with another. But I was back with my family. Father led me around the village to show me to the inhabitants and introduce me to the Prauliņš family with whom they had been traveling since Latvia. The day flew by, and it was time to head for the narrow-gage railroad stop and the local train that would take me to Schneidemühl in the evening. Mother did not want to part so quickly and came up with reasons for accompanying me part of the way with my younger brother, Alnis.

Just like Deutschkrone, the local train did not fit into the authorized travel limits described in my Frankfurt an Oder documents. I was very nervous the whole route, while the train stopped and started on its way to Schneidemühl. I was lucky again to escape questioning, since men my age were a rarity in Germany; those capable of carrying weapons were either at the front, in the barracks, or in a hospital. My presence in the village, the train, and the station waiting room attracted various shades of attention—benevolent, envious, and accusatory.

The three of us spent the night in the Schneidemühl station waiting room. My train to Berent departed at five a.m. but Mother's and Alnis's to Bromberg at eight. The parting was difficult, as we looked at each other and wondered if this would be the last time we ever met. It was easier to part in a rush from Father, and my sister and brother were still young, but Mother sensed that we were parting for a long time, perhaps forever. The train finally came and took me away in the darkness.

I reached Berent in three hours, some 60 kilometers southwest of Danzig. Berent was a staging area for the reserve companies from the 15th division of the Legion. The division had been transferred here in August to be reorganized and restaffed for expected duty in Kurzeme to assist the 19th division, which had also been heavily depleted.

I was met in the train station by two fellows from my squad, who warned me of possible negative consequences at headquarters.I could earn a ten-day sentence in the brig, though I could also be released without punishment. It would depend on the commander's mood and on how well I could think on my feet. I had never been a nimble self-justifier, and who could tell about a commander's mood? I was saved by circumstance: a short time before my expected interrogation about a 24-hour absence from the company, the commander was given the division's mail, in which there was a major mix-up of some sort. The commander's attention was absorbed in a lengthy telephone conversation with headquarters about the mail snafu, and I doubt that he heard or understood my explanation about the absence. I was dismissed and hustled back to my unit, determined to melt back into the troops. By next day, the event had been forgotten, and I breathed easier. Operation "Deutschkrone" had been successfully completed.

STAGING IN BERENT

Berent, a small town in the former Polish Corridor, was notable primarily as a railroad hub on the Berlin–Danzig mainline. The flat, barren countryside offered few attractions of nature. The general grayness was reinforced by the darkness of late fall, the massive heaps of coal around the train station, and the pervasive coal dust choking the streets. For us, the greatest source of gloom, however, was the war and our foreboding of tragedies to come.

Berent seemed like a town near the front, though the front was still far away. The town was filled with troops and crawling with battlefield machinery. Like all the towns in Germany during the war years, this one was dotted with multistory barracks and the training fields, infirmaries, canteens, courtyards, and guard posts that supported them. There was also a large jailhouse and a movie theater. We saw few civilians, since the local Poles and the Germans relocated here from the Baltic states,[97] stayed away from the areas designated for the military. The Poles especially kept a low profile, and their language was almost never heard on the streets. For all that, German-Polish relations were no secret. Polish hatred sometimes erupted in acts of retribution—German soldiers disappeared, a munitions storehouse burned and exploded. The German response followed predictably; they surrounded a few selected Polish buildings, arrested all the inhabitants, sent them to a concentration camp, and burned down the buildings.

We were warned from the beginning not to leave the barracks without a weapon and not to wander around at night. Latvians took the

---

[97] Some 150,000 ethnic Germans living in the Baltic states were resettled in the "Greater Germany" of Hitler in 1939–40 as a consequence of the Hitler-Stalin Pact.

warning less seriously, assuming the flag shield on their sleeves would help distinguish them from the Germans. Not always so. Passions could drive reason away, as they did when two Latvian boys were killed while out, looking for girls. The girls had lured them to their love nest, and their lovers had done the rest. After this incident, everyone grew more cautious, though girl hunting did not stop.

Berent was also a gathering point for convalescence units that drew their numbers from hospitals and recovery centers across Germany. These half-invalids had been pronounced suitable for combat again, though in peacetime they would have been rejected by the army. Now in the fourth year of the war, almost everyone was fit to be cannon fodder.

Troop deployment in Berent included a number of units from the Legion's 15th division, including groups from the eastern front, from Kurzeme, from hospitals in the south, and others. The plan was to pull these units together into a new, combat-ready force and send it to Fortress Kurzeme. There were also troops of other nationalities but few Germans available. The evolving view was that it would be difficult to form strong and stable units here, but the Latvian soldiers retained a single goal—to get back to Kurzeme. We felt that the Germans would not be able to hold the eastern front, at least not in their part of Poland, and that we could not allow ourselves to become prisoners of the Russians. We had to get across the sea to Liepāja or Ventspils[98] to defend Kurzeme. We had no alternative.

---

[98]　Major ports on the west coast of Latvia and of the province of Kurzeme.

Training march near Berent

In addition to training responsibilities, our company also stood guard duty at the barracks gates, by munitions storehouses, by the coal piles around the train station, and at the jail. At the beginning of December, the jail duty created major unpleasantness for us. One night, a leader of the Polish resistance movement escaped. The escape had been organized by a beautiful young Polish girl, who had provided the handsome young man with a German uniform (just like in a romance novel), allowing him to calmly walk out the front gate. We found it hard to believe that the escapade could succeed, but the prisoner had indeed disappeared and the girl, a prison caretaker, with him. They were not caught as far as we knew, but for their escape, our guard unit and its supervisor earned substantial jail terms themselves, while the whole company lost its leave privileges. Reckoning that the Poles knew how to corrupt us Latvians, the Germans took over guard duty at the jail themselves. It's true that we sympathized with the Poles, but we were not involved in this escape. The Poles did not trust us, perhaps because of our German uniforms. They felt degraded by the German occupation and vengeful as a result.

Shortly before Christmas, Roberts obtained a four-day pass and left for Prague to meet his parents. I let the official application period for a pass elapse to avoid calling attention to my recent 24-hour absence. I would have had to submit a letter from my parents, along with their full address. Roberts was back by Christmas Eve, and we had the evening off. We decided to explore the surrounding countryside and test the Polish Catholic tradition of treating visitors on this holiday evening. Our meager rations in a reserve unit left us constantly hungry. If we could overcome our timidity, we might be rewarded with some holiday treats. We would offer to chop firewood for the family in exchange, so we wouldn't be taken as beggars while in the uniform of the "world's best army." A short distance from town, we made our first offer to a farmer's wife in German, but she slammed the door in our faces. Our next stop, at a run-down little house, was more successful, perhaps because we spoke Latvian with a sprinkling of Polish words we knew. We were invited inside to a modest room with a small Christmas tree and a bowl of potatoes and fried rutabagas on the table. In return for the food, we gave our hostess some cigarettes. The wood-chopping offer was forgotten.

No men were present in the household. Around the table sat the old woman and her two middle-aged daughters, along with a gang of kids. We spoke in a mix of German, Russian, Polish, and Latvian, trying to explain our situation. Our hostess brought out an old map and asked us to point out Latvia. A Latvian school child could have found Poland on this map immediately, but none of these Polish women, or their kids, had any knowledge or understanding of the geography of Europe. On the other hand, they had something more important to offer us— compassion. We sang a few Christmas songs with them. On departure, the women wished us well and hoped that we could each spend the next Christmas with his own family. For our part, we wished them a free Poland. A year later, our wish for the Poles had been fulfilled; their wish for us had fallen far short of the mark.

Walking back toward town, we felt only slightly less hungry and remained alert for other possibilities. At the end of a lane bordered by ranks of leafless trees, we saw the outline of a stately house. The Fritzes wouldn't have left this kind of house to the Poles, we concluded. Driven by a strange urge to take on the risk, we approached the front door. We could hear happy voices inside, though not a gleam of light penetrated the curtained windows. Suddenly, we were startled by a very large dog barking at the top of his voice, straining against the chain keeping him from our throats. "*Wolf, was ist los?*"[99] called a woman through the half-opened door. We lost no time appealing to her sense of basic Christian values and the Christmas spirit, but the woman replied in a completely different tone. We were chewed out so thoroughly that even Wolf put his tail between his legs and crawled back into his hut.

What did it mean when German soldiers were not busy guarding the *Vaterland* but brought shame on the glory of their arms and a stain on their honor? It was because of such cowardice that the enemy was now at the borders of Greater Germany. We should be brought up before a war tribunal. If we didn't get back to our barracks immediately, then by God, she would telephone the commandant the next day (Christmas Day). Our hunger vanished, along with the holiday spirit, and we melted back into the trees, praising the darkness and the chain around Wolf's neck. At the end of the lane, we slowed down a bit, and Roberts muttered, "It's a shame we didn't yell out '*Heil, Hitler!*' before we left."

We spent the rest of Christmas Eve in the canteen drinking dark beer with our somber comrades. In place of "*Es skaistu rozīt zinu,*"[100] we sang a song well-known to all who fought for the Germans, "*Es geht alles voruber, es geht alles vorbei.*"[101] Our group singing helped us in many ways—in tempering physical problems, marching in formation, and spending time in the evenings when the longing for home was strongest. The melodies of these soldiers' songs were simple; the words were rather trite, but they were just what we needed.

We also didn't forget our own folk songs, though these were more suited to rest periods than to marching in formation. In the outdoor training in Lauenburg, our German commanders demanded we sing only German marching songs. There were so many of these, and they did help us stay in step. We learned the words for some of them quickly, not so quickly for others, and we frequently developed parodies of the songs. When we were tired and fed up with the constant drill, we sang for spite of the Fritzes and for gratification for ourselves:

---

[99]   "What is it, Wolf?"

[100]   Latvian folk song "I know a beautiful rose."

[101]   "Everything passes, everything disappears."

Mes sitīsim tos sarkanos—arvien, arvien
Pēc tam tos zili pelēkos—arvien, arvien…[102]

We assumed the Germans did not understand these words or the feelings behind them.

It was clear to nearly everyone at the end of 1944 that the war would end in the coming year and that Germany would be the loser. But at the behest of the Fritzes, we still sang the bravura lines "*Wenn wir fahren gegen Engeland*"[103] and the equally unsuitable:

Wir werden weiter marschieren,
Bis alles in Scherben fällt!
Denn heute gehört uns Deutschland,
Und morgen—die ganze Welt![104]

---

[102] A popular "spiteful" song in the Latvian Legion, whose meaning, apart from the cadence, is "We will thrash those Reds—ever and again/ And then those blue-and-grays—ever and again…" Reference is to the color of the German uniform and the symbolic red of the Soviets.

[103] "When we go against England."

[104] "We must march onward, till everything lies in ruins; today we have Germany, tomorrow the whole world."

Moving East in West Prussia

In Berent at the turn of the year 1944–45, our re-forming 15th division units are still mostly Latvian, with Latvian commanders to the battalion level but Germans in command above that. We have few dealings with the Fritzes and prefer it that way. And I'm a squad leader now. Ours, the first squad, has 13 men or, more accurately, half men. Three of the older Legionnaires have been wounded on the eastern front. They've been patched up, but one is still seriously hobbled. The rest are younger than me; they've been recently sent from Liepāja, presumably to serve as helpers in the air defense system. They've been detoured into our convalescence company[105] to be readied for their first combat experiences. Are we preparing 16-year-olds for the front lines now? Not that drastic perhaps. Currently, it's only the basics of military formations and order—breaking down and reassembling weapons, donning and removing gas masks, and other such drillable stuff. It's difficult for the hobbled men to stand in formation, harder yet to march, run, hit the ground, scramble up again. So I choose a distant corner of the training field behind the barracks and let the older men stand around and smoke, while I put the younger boys through their paces. Luckily, all nine are responsive, and our relations stay positive. Our goal is the same anyway—to make it to the next mealtime without the unwanted attention of superiors.

It's New Year's Eve. I am scheduled for guard duty at the barrack gates, since the sick and wounded have been exempted from the task. We stay awake till midnight to bring in the new year. The fellows

---

[105] A unit composed of various reserves, including soldiers who have been discharged from hospitals in a "half-invalid" condition, which would disqualify them from army service in peacetime.

have acquired rockets somewhere and will be allowed to shoot these off since the front is still distant. We buy a bottle of red wine in the canteen, heat it in a kettle, and dispense a mouthful to everyone. More wine would have been nice, but it is good enough for the fifth year of the war. At midnight, we watch the rocket trails carve up the skies overhead.

It's a relatively warm winter night with scattered, dry snowflakes drifting in the air. I stand in the guard cabin and think of my family in Deutschkrone, of Velta, of Latvia. My country is split into two parts today; the Russians have occupied all the places where I used to live and grew up. Only Kurzeme is still in the hands of the Latvians and Germans. The 19th division is on the front line somewhere near Slampe and Džūkste.[106] How are our boys doing? According to the radio, there had been major battles with major losses there at Christmas. After our evening cleanup ritual in the barracks, we had been talking about events in Latvia. We are all agreed that we need to get back there as soon as possible. We are tired of the German drill, the grayness of the Polish countryside; we want to be back among our own people to defend our own country, not some occupied foreign region.

Besides our longing for home, Roberts and I harbor a quiet desire to see our families again. His folks are near Prague, mine only a few hundred kilometers west of here. We accept the fact that these wishes may go unfulfilled. Our company commander, in his Christmas greeting, gave us strong assurances that at the end of January, or beginning of February at the latest, we would be on our way to Danzig and then by ship to Liepāja. Fortress Kurzeme was in need of reinforcements, as the Germans were no longer determined to hold this area of the front. Who would guard Kurzeme then, if not we Latvians?[107]

Standing guard, I'm grateful for my warm felt boots. The darkened city is quiet except for the rumble of trains and the shriek of locomotive whistles. It feels like the war has ended or at least is too far away to affect us. Over the whole of the past year, I don't remember any moments as quiet as this. My thoughts always turn back to the same questions: What will the new year bring? Was this the last New Year's Eve of my life? Will I see my loved ones again? And what will happen

---

[106] Small towns on the eastern border of Kurzeme.

[107] In fact, the German and Latvian units held out in Kurzeme till the end of the war, repelling six major attacks by the Russians.

to Latvia? I have no answers. The radio and the rumor mill are full of conflicting assertions. The Russians brag of their impending victory; the Germans promise to launch their wonder weapon very soon, ten times more powerful than the V-2.[108] We don't often pick up the Anglo-American broadcasts, and the Germans strictly heed Goebels's[109] warnings that listening to foreign broadcasts is forbidden. When there are only Latvians around a receiver, we listen and try to make some sense of the English words, but it's mostly gibberish to us. Our hopes of gaining support from the Western democracies have not been fulfilled thus far; the English talk only of defeating Hitler and accept the Soviet claims to the Baltics. My guard session passes quietly, and I return to the barracks. But sleep does not come; I continue to speculate about our chances of getting to Kurzeme. The morning comes.

The first of January brings a thaw. The training field is covered with coal dust and blowing trash. We slog on and get an early release to leave time to clean our clothes for inspection. I have requested a leave and now wonder where to go. The drinking crowd holds no attraction for me, and I have no close friends here. Most of the time, I'm reading old issues of "*Tēvija*" and German magazines. Once a week, there's a film, attended by everyone, though the films are old and previously seen. Tonight the Legion orchestra is playing in the canteen for officers, tomorrow night for the rest of us. That's our program: music and *Dunkelbier* (dark beer).

I use my leave to go to the nearby hospital, set up in a barracks like ours, though a bit brighter and cleaner. The hospital for the Germans is situated in a three-story building, the largest house in Berent, while we make do with a wooden barracks. I'm going to visit one of the boys from my squad, who is feeling quite chipper and confesses that if he hadn't rubbed the thermometer for a while, he'd be out of the hospital now. I'm content. Who wouldn't want to get some rest and decent food? Suddenly, a voice is calling my name from the other end of the ward. It's Vilis Roze, a classmate from my district at home. "What's wrong, old boy?" I ask. "Are you wounded?"

---

[108] A liquid-propellant rocket and the world's first ballistic missile, launched by the Germans in 1944, primarily against London. The "wonder weapon" rumored to be in development was probably the atomic bomb, which German scientists had been working on for several years as Einstein pointed out to Roosevelt in his 1939 letter.

[109] Nazi propaganda minister.

"No, I'm just sick. Dysentery, temperature 39 degrees (102 degrees Fahrenheit), getting weaker every day. But it's great that you came by!"

I was very happy to see him again. We called up memories of our years in grade school and at the Teachers Institute, of our classmates and teachers. Vilis was optimistic about the future. He'd be out in a week and join us in the convalescence company for the trip to Kurzeme. I promised to come see him every free day. But I couldn't keep my promise because all leaves were canceled on the 3rd of January. I had seen Vilis for the last time. After the war, I learned that the illness had weakened Vilis to a critical extent. Just before the entry of the Russians into Berent, they had evacuated Vilis to the west, where he had died. My parents had arranged for a memorial plaque and tended his grave until they left Germany.[110] In tending his grave, my parents were also remembering me. Vilis's brother, Visvaldis, part of my company in the winter of 1945, had unwittingly performed the disservice of informing my parents that I had been killed on the battlefield.

On the 3rd of January, we were told that the Red Army was about to launch its winter offensive in eastern Prussia. The German response, resulting from a command from Hitler, was to declare a total mobilization not only in *Ostland* but also in the *Vaterland* itself. Old men and young boys were ordered into the *Volkssturm* (People's Army) units, which were quite different from the regular army. In the hands of 15-year-old boys and 70-year-old men, not only the rifle and the *Panzerfaust* but also the shovel and the axe seemed like misplaced weapons.

On the 12th of January, a Russian offensive along the whole eastern front was announced. Reserve units were armed and sent east. Our company was given the task of guarding Berent, which was the junction for three major roads—Danzig, Gotenhafen, and Bromberg. My squad was assigned to guard the southern route from Bromberg. The company commander gave me a map of the area, indicated the approximate guard locations, and selected a runner. Carrying three-days rations, we marched out of town on a paved road lined with meter-thick oaks and soaring ash trees, which would have provided a relaxing, cooling passage in the summer. I remember this stretch of the road clearly, since a few days later, the *Volkssturm* squads began a week-long campaign to cut down these trees and sling them across the

---

[110]   The author's family emigrated to the United States in 1950.

road to form tank barriers. Many of the German women were in tears at this destruction, the men cursing under their breath, but neither of them raising an outcry against the Nazi Party orders behind it. (They were still fearful of the Party functionaries, even in January 1945 and later.) The felled trees symbolized the insanity of the war. Coming generations would have to wait a hundred years and more for trees that replaced the full-grown sentinels along the road. Meanwhile, the enemy tanks simply drove over the fields next to the road, and the pace of their attack hardly slowed.

The oak trees were still standing along the Bromberg road when our squad reached the last house on the outskirts of town. The house stood on a hill, with good visibility to the south, and we decided to set up defensive positions here. We erected guard posts on both sides of the road and dug some pits for our automatic weapons. I arranged to "rent" some rooms from the homeowner. We carried straw into his largest room and covered it with canvas for bedding.

The homeowner, a schoolteacher, and his wife and 13-year-old daughter were quite receptive toward us. The teacher was also a Party member and put in some time clarifying and affirming the messages of Goebels's speeches to us. We *Letten* were as familiar to him as Eskimos or Papuans would be to us. He thought Latvia was located somewhere above the Arctic Circle. He had never been farther east than Königsberg. Like all Germans, he was clean and orderly and spiffily dressed, of course. Though he did not understand Latvian, I warned our boys not to mention Hitler or other Party notables in his presence. His wife was not interested in politics but did ask us about the food situation in Latvia and in the Legion. She treated us with tea, and we returned the hospitality with *knäckebrot* and artificial honey. We understood that our army provisions were better than those of civilians.

The teacher's daughter, Eva, was already singing with us the first evening, joining in on the German soldiers' songs about blue-eyed girls with golden hair. She listened to our Latvian songs with open mouth. As soon as her mother knocked on the wall, Eva stopped singing in midphrase and, with a brief "good night," disappeared in the other room by her parents. We saw this as an example of the way discipline is bred into Germans from childhood.

A few days later, our schoolmaster received an induction notice. His lame leg had exempted him from service before, but now everyone was needed, so everyone was suitable. His reaction to his wife's and daughter's tears was brief: "*Befehl bleibt Befehl!*" And off he went, though not for long. Having organized his *Volkssturm* group, he stopped at home again to get an axe and saw so he could help his fellow inductees fashion tank barriers on the roads around Berent. The command to cut down mature trees in the area went against the grain for him and others, but their fear of the Ivans outweighed their reason and understanding. And of course, "*Befehl bleibt Befehl!*"

With the front still far away, we lived in peace and quiet as in peacetime, if you don't count the duty watches in the machine-gun nests. There were no Anglo-American air raids on Berent. A couple of slow Russian biplanes overflew the city a few times, raising the alarms but doing no damage. We could live like this, we told each other, till the war's end, if not for the Russians pressing on Kurzeme. Of the ultimate German defeat, we remained convinced. It was apparent in the first cracks in their obsessive pursuit of efficiency and order—if only in the massive amounts of machinery stalled in Berent for lack of fuel. There was also the continual "straightening" of the front lines, from Leningrad to the borders of Prussia. We waited for the collapse of the Fritzes but feared the Ivans' victory. Of the wild rumors concerning the other side of the front, one more terrible than the other, we didn't know which to believe.

My career as squad leader (if an invalid group can be called a squad) lasted only seven weeks. On the 20th of January, we received marching orders to gather our weapons and backpacks and return to the barracks in an hour. Eva managed to shake everyone's hand and say, "*Aufwiedersehen*" (So long), before we boarded the line of automobiles by the gate and drove off in an easterly direction. We had to drive around the felled trees at first. When the ruined parkway was behind us, our caravan picked up speed.

In Dirschau,[111] we hop off the autos, which will drive back for the remaining reservists. We assemble by companies, hearing Latvian commands for the last time, as we are integrated into German units with German commanders. (As we learn later, regular German soldiers were about half of the new battalion, the rest a mixture of various

---

[111]   A town south of Gdansk (Danzig), on the Vistula River, today called Tczew.

nationalities drawn from the Penal Regiment Kaltofen.)[112] While waiting for the kitchen utensils, we are supplied with ammunition, and each squad gets several *Panzerfausts*. Before the battalion is fully staffed, we are ordered to march off toward the Vistula River in the darkness. As we cross the bridge, air-raid sirens sound in the city. With no place to hide, we press forward on the bridge. No airplanes appear this time, but we are seeing this beautiful bridge and the splendid *Autobahn* crossing it in pristine condition for the last time. On our return trip, we will clamber over the air-raid damage and merge with the streams of retreating troops and refugees choking this main link across eastern Prussia.

We cross the Vistula and march east all night, leaving the former Polish Corridor and entering Prussia itself, as evident from the architecture and the broad well-kept fields. The company commander tells us we are going to Marienburg, just across the Nogat River.[113] He hasn't been informed of the next moves, knows only that the Red Army has launched its offensive into East Prussia and is rapidly heading in a northwesterly direction. We stop to rest in a pine grove before we reach the river. The full field packs on our backs are getting heavier with each step. With relish, we consume the pea soup served by the field kitchen and quickly fall asleep. We have learned how to sleep and rise in a moment and to collapse a civilian's eight hours of sleep into one.

In the morning, we leave Marienburg behind, marching down the side of the broad highway to leave room in the middle for the trucks carrying troops and pulling howitzers and for the trucks carrying the wounded back in the other direction. The enemy has been engaged, and we soon hear the echoes of the battlefield again. We advance another 20 kilometers before we turn left and a few hours later take up positions by a large manor house. The Germans have been living well here; the residences and housekeeping buildings are large and of solid brick construction. The high-roofed, modern barn is worth seeing by itself. Everything, of course, is tidy and in good order. The war has not reached here before, and the owners have apparently left their homes shortly before our arrival. Our German officers move into

---

[112] A penal regiment would be made up of men given a choice to serve in the military as punishment for their crimes. SS-*Sturmbannführer* Hans-Heinrich Kaltofen was the commander of one such unit.

[113] A branch of the Vistula.

the manor house (where we soon hear the tinkling of a piano), and we occupy three of the grain barns, where we spend the next night sleeping soundly in the fragrant hay, just as we once did in Latvia.

Next day, before we have time to get back on the highway, we receive orders to dig in where we are. The officers yell nervously on the telephone about the Russian tank column that has broken ahead and is advancing toward us. Someone in headquarters has decided that our job is to hold the advance and destroy the tanks. It shouldn't be too difficult to knock out the tanks with our *Panzerfausts* and stop the attack, since the bulk of the Russian infantry is still far behind. We don't think it's going to be that simple but take camouflaged positions on both sides of the road. The rumble of tanks draws near, yet the Russians aren't stupid. Their tanks are avoiding the road and advancing over the fields to the north of it. The rumble grows louder as the tanks roll over ditches and other impediments in their haste. We are too few to both hold the road and advance north to meet them. We stay in our foxholes by the road. Then the hardest moments of the encounter are upon us as we wait tensely for the first glimpse of the tanks.

Suddenly, an explosion resounds to our right, and flames shoot toward the sky. Our neighboring company has hit the first tank. It's a shock and a signal to the rest of us. All the weapons open up. Moments later, two more explosions sound, raising their gushers of fire. We see that two of the tanks have stopped, and there are blackened figures jumping down and getting picked off in the snow. One of the tanks turns back, the other stays stranded with a damaged engine. Then the motor noise grows more distant; this means that reinforcements will not be coming for now. Of the five attacking tanks, one stays stuck by a ditch, two are destroyed, and two roll back. The battle (or "incident") ends so quickly that we weren't sure just what had happened. Later, we go to look at the destroyed tanks. The charred bodies of the tank crew are terrible to see, and the foot soldiers in their quilted jackets lie spread-eagled in the snow. Eight of the enemy are dead, no casualties on our side.

February 1945 battles

Our company with their antitank weapons was lucky to stop this breakout. Easy victories such as this are rare in wartime and more often matters of chance. Our newly formed battalion was not really prepared for serious battle. If the Russians had sent reinforcements, we would all have stayed there, lying in the snow. That was my first encounter with enemy tanks in East Prussia, and the only one in the whole war in which the casualties were all on one side. No one in my squad fired a shot because the action was all in the next sector of our lines. We were in many bigger battles later, but this one has stayed especially sharp in my memory.

Confusion has crept into the German tactical orders. Commands are followed by counter-commands.

"Forward, at once!"

"No, to the rear!"

"No, let's wait!"

The day after the tank battle, we march back to Marienburg by the same road as we had come but do not reach the Marienburg bridge. The Germans have decided to take up positions on the Nogat River. The tank attack indicates a Russian advance toward Danzig, northwest of our positions. By the Nogat bridge, we are relieved by units of the Spanish Blue Division.[114] I had seen them in the streets of Riga a year or two earlier and am not surprised to see them here in Prussia.

We cross to the west bank of the Nogat, move north, and settle for the time being in a small village right on the riverbank. It's not clear what we will be guarding here, since the Nogat bridge is too far away and the ice on the river too thin to support enemy soldiers trying to cross on foot. If they blew up the Vistula and Nogat bridges, we would be in a relatively safe position, but the situation is generally very uncertain. Since the enemy crossed the German border, there's been an erosion of discipline and good sense. On command of the Führer, civilians have left the area, crossed the Vistula, and moved toward Danzig and Gotenhafen. They are likely part of a growing refugee stream.

Our squad, now led by the former company commander (who has been replaced by a German at the company level), moves into a small house on the riverbank. We can see that the homeowner, probably a fisherman, was not well-to-do but left everything he had in good working order. All the doors are unlocked, and a note on the table invites us to use what we need but not to destroy anything. It's signed Heinrich So-and-so. We observe the request strictly, wondering if the Fritzes in Kurzeme are being as scrupulous. The wardrobe cabinets are filled with clean, ironed clothing; the kitchen shelves hold neat rows of dishes and utensils; the beds are covered with bedspreads. It reminds

---

[114] The Blue Division (*Division Azul*) was a group of Spanish volunteers, mostly veterans of the Spanish Civil War, who served in the German army on the eastern front. Among their postings was the siege of Leningrad and, briefly, Latvia.

us of home. The squad leader's warnings to observe the homeowner's requests are not needed; we take nothing from the cabinets and use only the stove and a few dishes. We still have our own rations, meager as they may be.

Exploring the area next day, our boys hear a pig squealing and locate the animal in a pen in the barn. With the departure of the inhabitants, the animal has been left without food. It's not likely that a group of soldiers would deny themselves such a tasty morsel. Two of the farm boys from our squad butcher the animal, scorch and divide it, and then prepare such dishes as we haven't tasted since peacetime in Latvia. While our chefs work their magic in the stove, the rest of us have to make sure the smoke does not attract unwelcome guests— neither the Germans at the end of the bridge nor the Russians in their biplanes. Then the feast begins. After our prolonged diet of dry food substitutes, real pork tastes delicious and even better with the bottle of vodka, which the boys have obtained somewhere in exchange for a few cuts of meat. We toast to the good health of the Prussians.

We're half expecting to hear the rumble of Russian tanks crashing our festivities, but God is merciful. Our guards by the river protect us from internal and external enemies, while the rest of us indulge ourselves in the little fisherman's house. Everyone's mouth, cheeks, chin, and fingers glisten with fat, and the bottle goes from hand to hand till the last drop. Our mood is lifted, and we feel like singing. We brag about how we will hold the Russians by the Vistula and then defeat the Germans by the Oder.[115] No one can stand up to us; we will return as victors to Kurzeme. It didn't take much to make us fearless. It was the only pig roast of my military career and the only time I felt completely full. We feasted three days and shared our spoils with the other Latvian squads, but on the evening of the third day, our company was hastily transferred north of Marienburg, where the room and board were considerably less opulent, though still far better than what was to come.

---

[115] Border river between Germany and Poland.

RETREAT AND BETRAYAL

The Russian offensive to cut off Danzig and drive a wedge to the Baltic Sea began on the 10th of February. Russian radio said the drive would take a few weeks, German radio that the enemy would get nowhere because the whole nation was standing like a wall and would not allow a single Bolshevik into the holy German land. For their part, the English were only focused on the western front, where the Allies were building up for a major offensive. We gained no enlightenment from this jumble of news. One thing was clear, however; without the long-promised "V-3,"[116] we would not be able to advance or even resist, only to "straighten" the front till they drove us into the sea. The Germans had no fuel left, and the air was controlled by Russian planes, which were successfully degrading the German fortifications. This made it impossible to dig in at fixed positions. Every few days, we had to pull back from our trenches and bunkers to avoid being encircled by the enemy.

With every abandoned village and lost kilometer of ground, erosion of the once-exemplary discipline of the German army grew. The first days of the war in the east in June 1941 saw Russians deserting in large numbers; now the deserters were Latvians in Latvia and various nationalities from the German forces in Poland. For the first time, we also saw Germans deserting here in West Prussia. High in the branches of trees still standing by the highways swung the bodies of the hanged deserters with placards around their necks reading, "I betrayed my country," and similar words. The effect of the hanged men's twisted

---

[116] A V-3 supergun was in development at the end of the war. Its purpose was to bombard London from sites in northern France, a distance of about 165 kilometers. The farthest shells were fired in tests was about 93 kilometers.

blue faces, stretched necks, torn uniforms stripped of insignia, and swollen, bare feet swinging in the wind was shocking and depressing. Was the noose waiting for us as well? It would be better to fall to a Russian bullet.

We retreated to the Vistula, to the same bridge at Dirschau that we had crossed a month before, heading east. Now our course was only west. We had to wait our turn, as large numbers of troops flowed by, moving day and night, along with many wounded and many refugees, with and without possessions. During the Russian bombing runs, the bridge was closed. Gendarmes with shiny breastplates regulated the traffic at both ends of the bridge, their shouts and pistol shots echoing above the din. It was apparent they were near panic themselves. We made our crossing in the dark next morning.

Our orders were to head north from Dirschau toward the Baltic coast and to link up with some mythical antitank battalion near Danzig and dig in about 20 kilometers from the city in order to repel the expected Russian tank attack. Our march was constantly interrupted by the Russian planes, whose overflights increased daily. When the planes appeared, we dove for the ditches on both sides of the road. The planes came in lower and lower, the pilots knowing that the Germans had no means of repelling them. Our machines and equipment and we ourselves made good targets against the snow. We did take the expedient of pulling on our camouflage suits, white side out, making ourselves less visible.

We had covered some 15 kilometers by evening, stopping near a small village, bedding down in a stand of trees on a hill while the Germans occupied the nearby houses. No fires were permitted though we wanted very much to dry our clothes. We spent the night shivering and trying to sleep. With the front nearing steadily, we received orders for three companies to dig in on the south side of the hill and to finish the job before daybreak. We were able to dig down into the thawing earth readily, having gained much practice in this kind of work during our retreat. Just as we had finished, a command came in to get ready to depart. The order was quickly countermanded, and we settled down at dawn to await the enemy tanks. The tanks did not come, and we spent the day freezing in our foxholes soaked by a light rain. Food arrived on the other side of the hill, but I wasn't hungry, even when a friend brought a pot of soup. Teeth chattering, I felt my temperature rising.

In the evening, the squad leader, checking his men in the trenches, crawled up to me as well. I asked for an aspirin, and he saw that I was shaking all over. He left without a word but soon sent a replacement, allowing me to report to the company medical tent. The German doctor there, cursing away about who knows what, reminded me of the RAD camp medic and his catch phrase, *"Fur Letten, nur Tabletten!"*[117] My temperature stood at 39.8 Celsius (104 degrees Fahrenheit), and I wished there was a bottle of vodka at hand. I did get some medicine, and the orderly hung a piece of cardboard around my neck with my name, unit, and diagnosis, motioning me to a corner of the tent where several other sick bay soldiers were squatting. In the event of a battle, we would all have gone back to the trenches; only the wounded were held back, awaiting evacuation to an infirmary, if one was even available amid the disorder of the retreat.

March 1945 retreat in Pomerania

But the next day also went by peacefully. Likely, the Russians were gathering their troops for the next attack. Once there were enough of the sick, the orderly sent us to battalion headquarters over the next hill. No one there wanted to deal with us, and we continued slowly walking to the rear, carrying our official diagnosis cards. We were checked along the way to confirm that the diagnoses agreed with the

---

[117] "Only pills for the Latvians!"

notations in our *Soldbuch* and directed further north (as though anyone would be waiting for us there). Gradually, my fever subsided. I sweated and shook, but my youthful constitution, toughened in the past year's training, brought me back to health. Over these three days, we had covered a considerable distance, dried out and cleaned ourselves up in some abandoned houses, and found something to eat as well. I thought of getting back to my unit.

The general picture did not change as we traveled; the flow of refugees and wounded soldiers toward Danzig continued without pause. Moving toward the front were the old men of the *Volkssturm*, a pitiful group unrelieved by any regular army units. The roadsides were littered with damaged wagons and automobiles, broken ammunition boxes, smashed weapons, dead civilians, and dead horses with swollen stomachs and feet in the air. Deserters swung like bells from tree branches. We were as yet free of the burning smells and acrid smoke that accompanied us later in the retreat and settled into our very bone marrow. For now, the offensive action was provided by Russian long-range artillery and airplanes, with no infantry yet in sight. We retreated rapidly enough to stay out of the fire zone. There were no German planes in the air and no antiaircraft guns firing, leaving the German troops with no support whatsoever. The mood was dark as could be.

We found shelter in a barn somewhere near Praust.[118] Settling into the hay, we felt dry and warm and watched the Russian biplanes on their reconnaissance runs coming in low and steady, tossing out an occasional flare to brighten the ground beneath. We were prepared for the bombing runs too, but these did not come that night. In the event, we spent some time teaching each other how to survive a bomb blast: Wear your helmet, but don't hook the chinstrap under your chin, or an explosion will rip your head off. This was "common knowledge" for us, but we felt safer whispering to each other while we waited for the bombs in the bright winter night. If the barn had been hit, we would have burned up along with the fuel tanks hidden beneath the hay (as we discovered later). But it was not our turn yet.

The allowed term of sickness indicated on my "medical chart" had ended, and I should have reported to my unit—if I had known where to go. Amid the general retreat, it would have been difficult to find my company. One of my ailing comrades suggested that this

---

[118] Small town south of Danzig, called Pruszcz Gdanski in today's Poland.

would be a good time to just take off. We were all convinced that the war would end soon, and none of us wanted to die just before the war did. It wasn't our war but a German-Russian war. Yet we saw no viable options. We couldn't appear on the roads, since the gendarmes would summarily shoot or hang us. Could we hide in the forests? There were no forests around Danzig, only clumps of bushes. Should we wait for the Red army? They wouldn't welcome us either since we had been fighting against them. We needed to get to Danzig and board a ship for Kurzeme. This plan sounded best, but we quickly realized it would be impossible without the necessary papers. We deliberated to little purpose; no one felt able to take the decisive step to the north or the south.

Leaving the barn, we were joined by four Latvian boys from the 15th division. Now we were ten Latvians and three of unknown nationality (with whom we spoke German). For everyone, the medical clearance slips were no longer in force, though we continued to wear them on our uniforms to provide a preliminary justification for being away from our units. The solution to our dilemma, like everything in the war, came quickly and unexpectedly. On the first of March, with the snow already melted and nature ready for its annual awakening and only we left awaiting our bad fate, we ran into several vehicles from the housekeeping unit of our battalion.

We learned that, during the retreat battles a few days ago, our company had been nearly wiped out; the remaining men were entrenched two kilometers away. Any thoughts of slipping away were gone now. We were counted and registered and driven in a food truck back toward the front, where we joined our remaining comrades at arms. Before we had finished linking our trenches, a major Red Army attack began.

Our fortifications were solid enough but our ammunition very low. We hoped that the direction of the attack would be along the highway toward Danzig, whereas we were dug in two or three kilometers west of this road. Not to be. A large Russian force was advancing toward us over the fields and through the woods. The morning was sunny and bright and the visibility excellent. From our trenches, we observed the usual Russian tactics: tanks first, followed by foot soldiers (some riding on the tanks as well). At first, the roar of the tanks drowned out all sounds, then we could hear the calls as well: "*Za Staļina! Za roģinu!*[119] *Urraah!*"

We had been ordered to let the Russians get as close as possible. Unfortunately, our trenches were no longer manned by a disciplined, elite force but a patched-up accumulation. Someone lost his nerve and began to fire early, thus giving away his position and drawing deadly counterfire on himself and his fellows. But the Russians apparently had not expected to meet resistance here either. Their infantry losses held up the attack, except for the tanks, which rolled over our positions and pushed ahead, while the foot soldiers took cover and began firing. In the meantime, they had pulled up their mortars and *Katjushas*.[120] Then the heavens and the earth started boiling. Their aim was to seed our hill with explosives so densely that nothing would be left of our defenses, and they could safely move ahead. Their usual tactics did not include any particular concern for their foot soldiers, whom they drove into the enemy's fire without reckoning the cost. The Germans, even at the war's end, did not permit a senseless slaughter of their troops.

Crouching in our trenches, we had few options. We couldn't retreat, since the rear was under close and constant bombardment. It made no sense to attack either; we would only become easy targets for the Russians on the open field between us. We stayed in place and waited, leaving it up to the mortars and rockets to blow us to bits or, failing that, for the Russian foot soldiers to advance and pick us off one by one. No help came on either flank from the thinned-out German forces, and the rear held only the tattered remains of forces no longer willing to fight. The desire to stay alive was all that was left.

I felt hemmed in by the explosions around me and near me. My ears stopped up from the noise, my face smeared with mud, I found myself in a half trance. Then I felt a blow to my right leg below the knee but no pain. When my trouser leg began to turn red, I understood I had been wounded. There was no time to think about that, as the explosions continued, and I kept diving down to the bottom of the trench. We had to keep watch for the Russian infantry also. For now only the tanks crawled back and forth over our lines, convinced we couldn't stop them. But one of our men managed to get off a successful shot. There was a huge explosion and a tower of smoke, and a tank ground

---

[119] "For Stalin! For the fatherland!"

[120] Truck-mounted rockets.

to a halt. The sight gave us a little encouragement, and a machine gun began firing to our right, met with answering fire from the enemy.

A boy next to me slumped to the side and slid down to the trench bottom. Not seeing the wound, I asked him how I could help but heard only moans in reply. I tried to raise the boy to a sitting position. At that moment, my neighbor on the other side passed along a command: at the end of the exchange of fire, a smoke screen would be laid down, during which we had to get back to the second line of trenches behind us. I bent over the wounded boy and told him I would try to haul him along on my pup tent if he couldn't move on his own. No reply from the boy, who stayed sitting in the trench bottom without moving. His eyes were open now, no longer seeing anything. I listened for breath, felt his pulse—nothing. The war had ended for my comrade.

I crouched next to him, not knowing what to do. Even today I reproach myself that I did not pull him out of the trench and take him to the rear. But it didn't seem possible then. The smoke screen was not dense enough to permit standing straight, and my wounded leg drew off some of my strength. The Russian bullets whistled all around me as I ran bent over as fast as I could, feeling that my heart would stop any moment. My boot was soaked with blood, but I still felt no pain. I ran and fell and ran again and fell. Later, I saw the new bullet holes in my camouflage suit that had just missed my body.

The smoke was blowing away quickly, and we stayed only briefly in the second line of trenches. Some additional German units appeared after all, sent to strengthen the lines. Later, we learned that the Russians had stayed in our first trenches instead of pursuing us, perhaps because of the gathering darkness. We crawled to the rear under the cover of night. When we reached the edge of the forest, we saw that our company had arrived last. The Germans had left before us and used us as cover for their own withdrawal.

The wounded were gathered in one place; the combat-ready, such as they were, stayed at the forest edge. We were all so tired that we didn't think about eating, just getting something to drink. Where to find water in the dark of the forest? We ate snow. Though I began to feel pain in my leg, I couldn't pull off my boot, which was encrusted with blood. Almost everyone had been wounded, some heavily. Fortunately, the medical orderly was with us and helped as much as he could. There was no possibility of getting a doctor in the present situation. We had to draw back farther before dawn came, since the Russian attack would continue. The skies were clear, and we navigated by the stars and a compass.

But we were wrong in our assumptions about the enemy, who did not press their advantage. The route would have been much shorter in daylight than the meandering path we traced, carrying two heavily wounded men and assisting the more lightly wounded. We didn't know either how many of the fallen had been left lying on the battlefield, how many had just disappeared. Our exhaustion had turned us all into automatons plodding along on a journey that seemed to have no end. Next day, we took up positions at the edge of another hill, not sure whether these were the second lines of defense or not. By our reckoning, the Russians would be appearing no later than mid-day. We were wrong again. No attack materialized, and we never did figure out why the enemy had changed his tactics. We sat all day in our trenches, hearing the battle sounds to the left near the highway, but no tanks or airplanes came directly toward us.

After our rest, we moved out again next evening in the direction of Danzig. We were still hopeful of reaching the port there and boarding a ship. The city was like a vast fishing net, trapping thousands of soldiers and civilians, all desperate to save themselves. On the way, we ran into a field infirmary unit waiting for transportation to evacuate the area. I finally gained access to a doctor. Pulling my boot off hurt more than the wound itself, which looked clean. The doctor said the piece of shrapnel in the leg should be removed, but he didn't have time for minor procedures; he had to get to the seriously wounded. He dressed the foot, the wound healed up well, and I no longer felt it after a few weeks.

Meanwhile, we were assembled into a new fighting unit without a name, something unusual for the pedantic Germans. The unit had become even more international in character, including Germans, French, Norwegians, Latvians, Spanish, Italians, Yugoslavs, and who knows who else. We called all the Latvians together, gathering about 20 men. We elected a squad leader ourselves, with no objections from the Germans as fed up with the war now as ourselves. The whole group came to about 100 men of questionable fighting caliber. The German *Hauptmann* (captain) commanding the unit was ordered to position us in Praust, south of Danzig, as a last line of defense for the city. This would allow evacuation by sea of the wounded—and the generals, the Party notables, and the other big shots.

It seemed that the Russians had decided that Danzig was not going anywhere and that they would capture it sooner or later and, for that matter, with fewer casualties if later. Instead, they were pushing straight west to the Baltic coast to cut off Danzig from the rest of the front. But first, there was a lull in the fighting as the Red army paused to consolidate its forces. In our company, the Fritzes themselves devised a story for the gendarmes: we were traveling to Praust to link up with some German battalion. The cover story allowed us to march along calmly to the north. Right by the roadside, we saw a large barn, also serving as a hangar, where we decided to stop and rest. The *Volkssturm* guard toting his ancient rifle repeatedly told us that opening the hangar was strictly forbidden. The ban was meaningless to our boys and the old man no barrier, until he threatened to phone headquarters. Then we threatened him in turn: We would tie him up and leave him tied for the Russians unless he held his tongue. This was enough to make him back off.

Opening the doors, we beheld an unbelievable sight: the whole barn was piled full with bags of raw sugar. We stuffed ourselves to the gills with the fine brown powder and filled our bread sacks, kettles, and even pockets. We regretted having thrown away our backpacks and gas mask satchels that could have held a few kilos more. Our overindulgence quickly turned to thirst, and it's a good thing we were able to find water along the way. Soon enough, we also shook out the extra sugar we were carrying to lighten the burdens of the march. By then we had also realized that sugar without bread is no meal either. We were at least careful to open only two sacks of the powder and to close the doors after we left. (Some ten days later, passing by on a return trip, we beheld a very different scene: The doors were wide open, hundreds of sugar sacks were strewn around the yard, the bags shot and stabbed through and torn, and the sugar scattered and trod into the ground. But these were already different times and different people.)

We were stopped by gendarmes several times, but our *Hauptmann* knew how to talk to them, and we were allowed to walk on until we reached the small, bleak village of Praust. Just as we drew near the first buildings, we were attacked from the air and found ourselves dodging a whole barrage of bombs. A fuel depot was hit, igniting a nearby store of highly flammable materials, which spread a stinking cloud of dark gray smoke over the village, driving us into the surrounding brush. The smoke and the explosions had little effect on the refugee flow on the highway. The road remained crowded with civilians obeying Hitler's orders to leave their homes ahead of the advancing Russians, whom they also feared.

The next day, we reached our designated positions outside Praust. We were joined by a unit sent from Danzig. These were relatively well-supplied reservists, whom our *Hauptmann* convinced to share their bounty with us. We finally took in a little warm food, and their trucks took some of our more seriously wounded back to Danzig. We never knew whether these men were able to leave the port on a ship or if they had fallen captive to the Russians. At the time, the rest of us envied these wounded men and would have sacrificed a hand or a foot to join them and get away.

The late March weather had been holding warm and springlike for a week now. The first buds and the new grass were emerging, and nature competed with men—one striving to destroy everything, the other to bring it back to life.

The lull in the front near Praust did not last long. As the Russians advanced, the battle noises grew, and the consternation on the roads increased. Artillery rounds began to fall within our defensive sector. Many of us followed the practice of jumping into the holes created by exploding shells, believing that a second round would not fall in the same place. (I happened to see instances, however, in which several artillery shells fell into the same hole, carrying away the believers in the myths taught in our training.)

The artillery barrages told us that soon we could expect our "visitors." The *Hauptmann* dropped by our squad to instruct us on the positions we needed to defend, where his command post would be, who would serve as runners—covering everything by the book. Our Latvian group had to defend the forest edge against attacks from the south. The other units would be to our right in a line right up to Praust. Our left flank would be covered by the presence of a marsh, from which no attack could be expected. Satisfied that his instructions were well understood, our commander left us—for good as it turned out.

Near our positions in the forest, the *Volkssturm* groups have built a fairly decent bunker, not sufficient to withstand the heaviest bombardments but enough for lighter calibers of shells. We post sentries in the evening. My watch is till midnight, during which time there is little action except for occasional artillery rounds that fall in the forest behind us. The action is heavier to our right flank, where we hear the sound of *Katjushas* and machine-gun fire. An occasional stray bullet thwacks through the branches. A bullet strikes my left arm. Again, I feel no pain, just some moisture seeping through my sleeve. I press the arm into the mud. After I'm relieved, I feel my way in the dark toward our bunker. More bullets overhead. Have they discovered our positions? With pounding heart but without further incident, I reach the bunker.

By the candlelight, I check my arm, which has a small hole in front above the elbow and a slightly larger hole in back. The bone has not been hit. My comrades help me dress the wound. If I had been hit in the right arm, I wouldn't have been able to shoot; but with this wound, there's no reason to leave the unit. We are all in the same predicament and need to hold together .This would be a time to catch some winks, but sleep does not come. I listen to the shots and judge their distance from our positions. It seems that the action has quieted down in the sector toward Praust, and the rounds are not falling on our sector either. An unusual quiet has settled around us.

The springlike morning of March 24 dawns slowly. The first rays of the sun glisten in the treetops, and a bird begins its song. To hear birdsong in the midst of war is a wonder of its own, one of many on this ordinary spring morning. I leave the bunker. It looks to be a calm, warm, beautiful day. Does the silence mean that the Russians have been held up or even driven back? Not likely. From where would the forces for a successful counterattack come amid the current chaos of the German army? Our own men are so widely separated, and it's unlikely that the force concentration would be any greater in other sectors.

Since we left our positions at the end of the bridge in Marienburg a month ago, we have been constantly retreating, day and night, with and without fighting, but always under tension and in fear of death. Our constant companions have been the Russian reconnaissance planes, rockets, bullets, *Katjusha* salvos, bomb explosions, and the sharp reports of anti-tank and anti-aircraft weapons. And how many men were left along the way? How many of us are still left—a few dozen exhausted men who had never really wanted to be soldiers. Here we are, the collected remains, still ten kilometers from Danzig, farther from the sea. Last night, the Germans had promised to spell us in the morning, bring warm food. We'd like to believe them.

I listen to a silence filled only with birdsongs. To the east, I note moving shadows as the sun rises. So the Fritzes have come to spell us after all..... I crawl back into the bunker to wake my sleeping comrades. The six of us gather our belongings and what's left of the ammunition. We crawl out of the bunker. The Germans seem to have come closer, though they're difficult to see against the rising sun. We call for the password but get no reply. Instead, bullets whistle overhead, and we hit the ground. Aren't these Fritzes after all? We raise our weapons and wait. We hear indecipherable calls and more shots. They shoot and yell out but not in German! They're Russians!

We whisper to each other that we need to stay low and try to crawl back into the forest behind us. We move back, but shots and yells meet us from behind as well. As we move to the left, we can see the forms clearly against the sun now. It's the Russians. We're surrounded on three, maybe on all four, sides. The Russians are shooting into the air to avoid hitting each other, and they're closing in from both sides. Each Russian feels duty-bound to empty the magazine of his automatic and yell at the top of his voice, *"Ruki verh!"*[121] More automatic bursts and more *Ruki verhs*.

"We have to give up," calls out Antons, the only Russian speaker in our group, "or they'll mow us down. We can't get away." He pulls out a not-quite-white handkerchief, sticks it to the end of his rifle barrel, and raises it as high as he can. A new salvo of bullets rips through his surrender signal. The Russians sense that we are not many and shoot less frequently but yell more often. Now we are only some 40 paces from each other, and we can see that they are at least five times our number. Then we see four of our boys with raised hands marched up from their guard positions on the flanks. We are completely surrounded.

The Germans have betrayed us. They have withdrawn toward Danzig during the night, leaving us to cover their retreat. The Russians have quietly circled our positions and scoured the forest behind us, while the front has shifted somewhere to the north.

---

[121] "Hands up!"

In Enemy Hands

We raise our hands as the Red soldiers cautiously approach, their automatics pointed at our chests, fingers on the trigger. They look strange in their padded green jackets and felt boots (some displaying fancy footwear, probably taken from the Germans). Some wear the shallow-dish helmets, others the boat-shaped summer hats, but all carry automatics. We're not able to decipher their service insignia but note that everyone's chest is hung with medals. They yell at us to drop our weapons and to also discard our belts with their cartridge bags and other attached items. Now they're on top of us, and we are pushed together, some dozen of us milling in one place.

There's no more shooting or yelling, "*Ruki verh,*" since all of us stand with raised hands. Seeing that we are not resisting, the Russians turn more personal. We hear the first words directed specifically at each of us: "*Urr jesk?*" Every Red soldier hastens to select his personal prisoner, but since they are many more than us, every Lett's chest is targeted by two or three rifle barrels while the calls continue: "*Urr jesk? Urr jesk?*" The calls are meaningless to us, and we wait for Antons's translation. Before he can speak, the mystery is solved. A Red soldier grabs Antons's left hand and in the same motion pulls off his wristwatch. So the Reds have learned the German word *Uhr* (watch), added the Russian *jesk* (is), and found the combination sufficient to enlarge their watch collections.

We all have watches—wrist or pocket types. In a few minutes, all the timepieces find new owners. We part from them without regret, even gladly. Let them take everything, just let us live. We face each other no longer as enemies intent on filling the opponent's chest with lead. A new relationship is forming. The Russians compete with one another to collect the most watches. Gone are the most basic concerns for security, even for appointing someone to hold the prisoners under close watch.

When all the watches have been collected, reality sets in again. If one of us starts to lower his hands, he gets whacked with a rifle butt, and the hands shoot up again. A more thorough search begins. All our pockets are turned inside out and the contents scattered. Our documents, *Soldbuchs*, money, letters, and photos hold no interest for these boys. They crumple any paper and stuff it back in our pockets or throw it on the ground. But if they find an item they lack—a pocket knife, a razor, or a pencil—it's gone in a moment. We have no food or drink, our changes of clothing and socks have been discarded on the road long ago, and our dirty, torn, and mud-covered uniforms are just so many rags to them.

A third expropriation round is focused on our boots. They like our hobnailed boots but find the fit elusive. I get to keep mine, which are too large for them, but some of our fellows have to part from theirs. The Reds have gotten choosy—rejecting the common laced boots, for example—since they have such a large selection to choose from. Their backpacks have grown full with the belongings of the Fritzes surrendering every day. Even the fallen must give up their belongings— till the day that the rifler of bodies himself becomes a body.

The first wave of shock and fright passes as we realize that the Russians are not preparing to liquidate us. We've given up our watches and some of our boots (all these in "exchange" for Russian boots, unlike the practice of the Germans in Russia three to four years before), and we note that the Red soldiers have hung themselves with every conceivable kind of timepiece. Every trench warrior wears a dozen watches on each arm, from palm to elbow, and his pockets are full of wrist and pocket watches, some with the torn wristbands still attached. Some wear their plundered watches around their necks like medals. I wonder if watches are really such a rarity east of the Zilupe River.[122]

With Antons's help, we found the means to communicate with our captors. The Russians became aware that we were not Germans, though they continued to call us Fritzes. We displayed the Latvian flag shields on our sleeves and told them we were *Latishi*, not *Nemci*.[123]One of the Red soldiers repeated, "*Latishi, Latishi*," and then remembered,

---

[122]   The border river with Russia.

[123]   "Latvians, not Germans."

"Hlopci, Latishi ze nashi, sovetskije."[124] To our surprise, many of the faces took on friendly smiles. We were "theirs," Soviet people, not the hated Germans. When they learned that we had been left here by the Fritzes to guard the forest edge while they took off, the atmosphere of benevolence grew. The soldiers took us with them, still under guard, to a Red Army field kitchen on the road; stood us in a row; and poured a good portion of thick soup into each of our field kettles.

We had not eaten anything like this for months, maybe not at all since the war started. It was a genuine meat stew, rich and aromatic. After the past weeks of terror and hunger, it was wonderful to fill our bellies again. And that was not all; we each received a hunk of bread broken from the loaf. And what a loaf! This was not the German pressed-sawdust concoction of uncertain origin but real rye bread. You could grow dizzy from the aroma of this bread. We didn't know how well they had fed the Red soldiers earlier, but here in March 1945 in Poland and Germany, they ate their fill. The supply of food was greater than at any time in the Soviet era. Every day, they slaughtered prize livestock and broke open dozens of warehouses filled with grain. The stingy Germans had fed their army with *ersatz* (substitute) stuff—margarine, artificial honey and mustard, and pigweed[125]—while the warehouses were filled with high-quality food held for some never-realized opportunity. (Even in 1945, the German high command harbored hopes of the war turning their way.) The Russians found all these storehouses, broke them open, and plundered them in as wasteful a way as possible. They didn't worry about tomorrow, so in the last few months of the war, their army gorged itself. And the Russians were not stingy; they willingly shared their booty with everyone, except the Germans, of course.

When we prisoners had finished our portions of soup and bread, we lay back in the meadow feeling a great burden lifted from us. The world had turned 180 degrees in the past few hours. This morning, having reached our limits, we waited for the fated moment of our violent expulsion from this world. Only moments later, we sat by a steaming pot of soup, relishing an indescribably powerful feeling of release. It seemed that the horror stories about the Reds' atrocities were myths. These simple, naïve Red soldiers were so humane, so generous.

---

[124] "Boys, Latvians are ours—Soviet."

[125] A weed of the goosefoot family that includes spinach.

What more could a prisoner of war wish when he was well fed and even called "ours"?

We asked Antons to find out what would happen with us now. Antons talked to an older man, a sergeant with a drooping mustache and many decorations on his chest, who said it was a real shame the Germans had forced us to fight against our own people but that he and his comrades were still our people and would not abandon us to destruction. They were a frontline unit and would be moving ahead any moment, bent on beating the Fritzes to rags and taking Berlin, confident that "Gitler kaput,"[126] and Berlin would surrender within two weeks. But for us, the war was over now. We would soon be going home. His words rang in our ears like bells from heaven. Could we believe them that we were free now and would be allowed to go home?

It was hard to absorb so drastic a change—from the darkness of hell to bright sunlight—but we were young and wanted to believe the old battle-wolf's promises. Where was home for us? The Russians motioned toward the east. We saw that the Red forces were moving toward the north. We agreed among ourselves we would go south, later swing east, and so get on the road to Latvia. We understood the way would be long and far, but we would deal with that later. For now, it was important to get as far away from the front as we could—away from the blood and the death and destruction. For us, the war had ended.

When the Red soldiers rose to continue their advance, we stayed in place, undisturbed by anyone. A few passing soldiers cursed us out as "damned Fritzes" but took no further action. Everything had already been taken, and no one asked for our watches, knowing that they had been appropriated by the first-line units. After a while, our numbers swelled with the addition of other prisoners, apparently Germans. We nine Latvians decided we would not stay with the Germans and found an alternate route to the rear. The Red soldiers were paying little attention to prisoners now. They were driving forward not only on the orders of their commanders but also to be the first to grab the watches of the prisoners they would round up. Bullets were less of a threat to them than the fear of being outdone in seizing and displaying loot taken from the enemy.

---

[126] "Hitler is finished."

Parting from the Germans, we took refuge in a nearby barn to remove ourselves from sight and talk over our next steps. After the initial enthusiasm about the war's end, we quickly realized that we wouldn't get far with only the sergeant's spoken permission for us to go home. After all, we were dressed in the enemy's uniforms. We decided to tear off all our insignia except for the Latvian flag shields on our sleeves. In a corner of the barn, we buried our *Soldbuchs* and all our other documents. I left my journal there, along with Mother's and Velta's last letters. I still don't understand how I was able to carry these papers across so many Prussian fields and forests that winter and spring. I had been diving into water-filled ditches to escape the Red planes, soaking in the melting snow in foxholes. The papers had to be completely washed out and unreadable, though in the rush to shed our identification items, I had no time to confirm this. I hadn't done much writing anyway during our months of "straightening and improving" our lines at the front. Now I also had no belt to hang anything on. I hand-carried my bread sack filled with essentials, such as a mess kit, water flask, and spoon, items that would be most useful in the coming years. Having rid ourselves of the testimonies of the past, we felt safer.

We also wanted to find some civilian clothes and discard our dirty, shot-through, bloody camouflage suits. I changed the bandage on my arm, not having had time for this in the past day's rush of events. The wound only hurt when I changed dressings, a few more of which I found in the discarded bags of my comrades. The problem now was to find civilian clothes. There were all sorts of abandoned items in the German and Polish houses, but we saw no inhabited areas nearby. We decided to move along the side of the road toward a church tower looming in the distance. There had to be a village there. No one took notice of us along the way. The road was filled with tanks and other war machinery, carving deep ruts in the mud. The sun was high, and it was warm as May.

We hadn't gone 300 meters before we heard an approaching tank column. The hulking monsters were crawling straight toward us over the fields and ditches. We sat down to let the column pass, but the first tank stopped right before us, spewing smoke and gas fumes in all directions. The turret opened, and a small dark fellow crawled out of the tank's innards and after him another even darker guy. Both hopped down and walked over to us. "Hey, you, Fritz, come here!" said one of them pointing at me. I didn't understand what the man wanted and hesitated. The tank driver pulled out a pistol and pointed it at me. I went up to him. Smiling and laughing, both tankists pointed at my boots, motioning that I should take them off. After I did, the smaller man pushed his rag-covered foot into my giant boot as though stepping into a boat. He laughed and stepped back into his own footwear, but his fellow pulled off his slightly scorched felt boots, wrapped an extra rag around each foot, and pushed them into my prized boots. "*Horosh, horosh!*" (Good, good) he said happily. Though my boots were too large for him as well, they were of good leather with a hobnailed sole and would serve well in the spring melt. "*Na, voz'mi na pamyat'!*"[127] And the tankist tossed me his old felt boots and hopped back into his machine. His fellow meanwhile searched for a fitting pair among the other prisoners. Not finding anything suitable, he let out a string of curses (which we understood well enough from the 1940-41 year) and clanged the turret cover shut behind him. With the footwear exchange completed, the tank column resumed its drive northward.

I tried to fit my feet into the tank driver's old boots but in vain. No matter how wide they'd been stretched, they were just too short. Our bayonets and knives had been taken away, but I managed to gouge holes in the toes and push my feet inside. At first, I was waddling in these boots like a bear, but I got used to them in time, and they actually served me a long time. Though I found other better-fitting boots later, I didn't part from these, and they kept my feet from freezing next winter. They were also so worn and ugly looking that they tempted no one. I parted from them only in the summer of the following year, after they had been worn to shreds.

The loss of my boots didn't take away the feelings of relief. Walking was more difficult, but so what? We were on the way home, and I would have been willing to do that on all fours. We were nearing the village, and the day was sliding toward evening. Our first day of.... Then everything changed.

A box-shaped Russian truck was tearing down a country road. Seeing us, the driver squealed to a stop, and two Red soldiers leaped down. They were wearing blue-red caps, green blouses, blue riding breeches, and khaki-colored canvas boots. Sharply etched in my memory is the Russian truck: it was not one of the Studebakers[128] liberally supplied to

---

[127] "Take these as a keepsake."

[128] The US6 2.5-ton trucks supplied through Lend-Lease.

the Red Army by the United States but the square-shaped green box of
the kind we had seen in Latvia in 1940–41, especially on the morning of
June 14.[129] These Russians were not the naive, well-meaning soldiers in
their padded coats and faded hats, hung not only with automatics and
magazines but also with watches and chains. These were lightly clad
politruks (political officers), their pistol handles protruding from leather
holsters at their belts. These Chekists[130] ordered us out of the ditch
and into the cargo area of the truck. Several other prisoners greeted us
there. A Red soldier with a weapon sat on the roof of the driver's cabin.

A short drive later, we pulled into the courtyard of a country estate
whose principal buildings lay in ruins, the main girders charred and
still smoking, while the housekeeping buildings had been spared. We
were ordered into the barn, which was full of previously rounded-up
prisoners. Our guard decided that there was no room here and sent
us Latvians, along with some Germans, to the basement of one of the
main buildings. We were still wearing our uniforms, while the barn
seemed to be filled mostly with civilians (or those who had changed
into civilian clothes). A dim light shone through the small basement
window. Later in the evening, stars appeared in the clear spring
heavens, but we were not in a romantic mood, thinking only of what
would happen to us now.

The booming noises of the front sounded from outside, likely
the last hours for the Danzig defenders. An acrid burning smell
filled our nostrils. Everyone tried as best he could to deal with his
exhaustion. Some dozed sitting, some standing, others stretched out
on the basement shelves. Around midnight, perhaps later (given that
our watches were gone), the door opened, and someone called in bad
German for two men to come out. The Germans were nearest the door,
and two of them were taken away, not to return, to our midst at least.
After a while, two more were summoned, and so it went. The tension
grew in the basement, and conversation died out. The darkness of night
added to the feeling of dread.

---

[129] The day of the deportations from the Baltic states in 1941. The victims were
taken from their homes in trucks to railroad stations and loaded onto freight
cars.

[130] Members of the Soviet security service, the Cheka, which went through a series
of reorganizations and name changes, e.g., GPU, MVD, NKVD, KGB. The
term Chekist remained in wide use despite the name changes.

After the Germans, it was the Latvians' turn to endure the torments of the passing moment. Well toward morning, they called out Antons and me, leaving only a few others behind. Antons and I had been keeping together the previous day. He had offered to help me change the dressing on my arm, and I had lent him my water flask. He was from the border area near Russia, had a Russian last name, had attended a Latvian grade school, and spoke Russian and Latvian equally well. The guard motioned us with his automatic to another basement room, perhaps a former beer bar. We could see only two tables, two chairs, and two kerosene lamps shedding a flickering light on the room. At the back of the room at a table opposite the door sat an officer, his legs stretched out, his red-and-blue hat pulled low on his forehead, leaving his eyes in the shadow. His lamp's shade had been replaced with a shiny piece of veneer angled to direct all the light toward the door, leaving him in the shadows. His table was crowded with papers, an empty glass, and a pistol. He wrote with an indelible pencil, occasionally pausing to sharpen it clumsily with a pocketknife.

At the smaller table, also covered with papers, sat the bad-German speaker who had called us out of the holding area of the basement, a Polish translator. Whatever he had been doing during the German occupation, now he wanted to help the victors with his Russian language skills, showing us no sympathy. The guard pushed us forward with the barrel of his automatic, then disappeared behind the closed door. The Pole told Antons to step up to the officer's desk and me to keep a few meters to the side and behind, leaving us both in the glare of the light. He rattled off a series of well-rehearsed questions—What? How? Where?—rolling them out quickly after a night's repetition. Then he sat down at his desk and looked at the officer. This man was about our age, with a European face and a piercing voice. His brash, aggressive manner indicated he had been drinking liberally as everyone did in those days, from foot soldiers to generals. He began the interrogation, with the Pole trying to translate every word but struggling. It's hard to say what the Pole's Russian language skills were, perhaps no better than his German. Seeing that the translator was searching for the right words and knowing that he could speak better in Russian than German, Antons began to answer the officer in Russian, giving his name, father's name, birth date, birthplace.

When the Chekist heard that Antons had a Russian name and had been born in Russia, his sullen, bored face turned red, and glaring at the prisoner before him, he let loose a barrage of violent curses. The Pole shrank back and stared at the officer with open mouth. In the heat of the exchange, I understood only that the officer wanted Antons to admit that he was a Vlasovist and a member of the ROA.[131] Since Antons had had nothing to do with Vlasov, he categorically denied the accusation, driving the officer beyond patience. (After this incident, I understood better why many in the Soviet Union were afraid to admit they knew a foreign language; this could be taken to suggest contact with spies and betrayal of the fatherland.) To every denial of Antons, the Chekist bellowed ever louder, "*Svoloch!*"[132] and called Antons a traitor to his country, leaping to his feet. I stood unable to move and understanding little of what I heard, awaiting my turn.

Whether Antons said something impertinent to the interrogator or whether the Chekist had lost all control in his alcohol haze, I would never figure out, then or later. Bellowing something, the officer suddenly grabbed his pistol and fired. Antons fell heavily toward me. Instinctively, I tried to hold him up but failed, and he fell to the floor. The Chekist continued to scream his curses as though nothing had happened. Then he called on the guard to remove the body, telling me to stay where I was. The soldier grabbed Antons under the arms and pulled him out the door. Two other soldiers ran in, but the officer sent them out of the room, slamming the door. In the shock of the event, I couldn't grasp whether Antons was dead or wounded. My mind at that moment was not working at all, and I stood unable to speak.

After a while, the Pole grabbed my arm and asked if I was deaf or just pretending, and if the latter, then I would get a bullet in the ribs as well. Today it all seems unreal, but this was a time and place where human life had little value. I saw many men killed and wounded at the front, and much more of what I saw has faded from memory, but the terrible cries of the Chekist at that moment and the unexpected, lightning-fast shot have haunted me in nightmares for many years since. After that spasm of madness in a basement on the outskirts of

---

[131] Andrei Vlasov was a Red Army general who collaborated with the Nazis during the German invasion and founded a Russian Liberation Army (ROA) in hopes of overthrowing Stalin.

[132] "Villain" or "blackguard."

Praust on the night of March 25, 1945, I never saw Antons again, alive or dead. No one could tell me what had happened to him. Likely, the official report stated that another betrayer of the fatherland had been liquidated.

After recovering my senses, I told the Pole that I was so and so, born in Riga on such and such a date, my parents working people and nonparticipants in counterrevolutionary activities who owned no properties and employed no workers, that I had attended such and such schools and worked such and such jobs, was drafted into the German army from school and so ended up in Prussia, and was never a member of the Communist or any other party, etc., until I had answered all the standard questions put to me. The Chekist, somewhat calmed down, posed the questions in a monotone voice; the Pole ineptly translated them into German; I answered in even more inept German; and the translator tried to repeat my replies in Russian. Who knows what ended up on the official record the Chekist pushed up for me to sign. No one read out what I was signing, and even today I don't know what the archive contains. Such documents were being filled out for thousands in those days. I was mildly surprised that I was still alive, since the Pole had tried his best to get me to admit that I voluntarily joined the German army. The Poles had suffered so much in the war that they hated the Germans beyond anything else. This Pole was no exception. Likely, the uniform I wore filled him with revulsion and more so the fact that I had worn it fighting for the Germans in his country.

Learning that I was a Latvian, the Chekist spat out his standard charge, "*Predäķeļ roģini!*"[133] and the Pole added that not only the Germans but also the Latvians should all be shot, for the betterment of the world. But the Chekist had expended his anger, having claimed his fill of victims for this night. He kept cursing but didn't reach for his gun again. Perhaps the alcohol's effects were wearing off. The guard led me out of the basement in the gray light of dawn, keeping his automatic trained on my back. I found myself under a roof, probably in a horse stable, the doors locked behind me. Growing used to the darkness, I could make out that I was with my Latvian comrades again and that Antons was not among them.

---

[133] "Betrayer of the fatherland!"

It was warm there, but we were very hungry, not having eaten since our captors fed us with their rich soup 24 hours before. About mid-day, they brought in a little bread and a pail of water, which made us almost feel like people again. We could hear the courtyard filling with new prisoners speaking various languages other than Latvian. We dozed all day among the piles of horse manure. Toward evening, they led us out of the stable and into the back of a truck, joining some other prisoners in a group of about twenty. On the way, we heard shooting and saw rocket trails overhead. Had Danzig withstood the assault, or had it fallen, and the fighting was by Gotenhafen? In any case, the front had moved a considerable distance.

We disembarked in a small new-growth pine forest. They brought us ten spades from a nearby *Vilītis*,[134] and the Chekist who had rounded us up from the roadside yesterday measured and staked out a space of about 2×10 meters. The ground had already thawed, and it wasn't hard to dig in this sandy soil and to cut the small pine roots with the spade. We took turns digging, so it wasn't hard labor, but it was hard work in another sense. We spoke little among ourselves, but we all understood this was a grave we were digging. Was it meant for us? The guards with their automatics stood nearby, and though it was growing dark, escape seemed impossible. A few bursts from the automatics would cut us all down in one round. The guards yelled for us to hurry before darkness set in. When it was my turn to dig, I had to toss the sand high over my head. Then I recalled the whispers of our neighbors in Riga a few years before: The Jews had dug these kinds of pits and then remained in them at the end. There was little open discussion of these things for fear of the Germans, but many knew about them. "Brutes, animals, butchers!" said Mother in the privacy of our family.

When we parted at the railroad station in Riga, Mother asked me to promise her: "Don't shoot at anyone. If you have to shoot, then shoot in the air, but never aim at a person. Your enemy is also some mother's son. Do this, and God will protect you." I promised her and kept my promise. I never aimed and fired at anyone, but I have fired often in the enemy's direction, mostly to reassure my comrades. Maybe some of my bullets found their unintended mark and men died, but I never deliberately tried to take a life. But now I was before the judgment of

---

[134] The Willys MB four-wheel-drive U.S. Army jeep. About 50,000 were sent to the USSR during Lend-Lease.

God. Would Mother find out someday that here was my bed of sand, fashioned by my own hand? I tried to remember the things in my life I would most regret to lose, but my mind would not obey. I hefted and lowered the spade mechanically.

"*Davai, viļezai!*"[135] called the guard. The pit was now two meters deep. Was this when they line us up beside it? We looked at each other, searching for support. Would we really let them kill us without resistance? We had to at least try to escape. It had grown fairly dark, and if we could get beyond the nearest pines, then maybe . . . *I wouldn't get very far with my new old boots*, I thought and considered taking them off once I had climbed out of the pit. Why was I feeling so weak? Why did I lack courage?

But they did not line us up at the edge of the pit. We were ordered to gather the spades and take them to the jeep. Then we were herded back into the truck, the guards took their posts, the motor fired up, and we were driving away!

The horse stall was filled with other prisoners now. *Let them stay*, we thought. It's also good in the fresh air. Give us a hundred nights in the fresh air, in the dark forest, anywhere. We wanted one thing above all— to live. And that was the second night after the war had ended for us.

Next morning, we woke to explosions from the direction of Danzig. Over the treetops to the northwest, a red glow signaled that the city was burning. Had it fallen? We no longer had a Russian speaker among us, the Germans knew nothing, the Poles ignored us. We felt like sheep in a pen. A kettle of soup was rolled into the courtyard, and the war was forgotten amid cries of "*Loeffel!*" and "*Kochgeschirr!*"[136] The iron discipline of the Germans had not been entirely lost among the prisoners, and though we were very hungry, we lined up in an orderly row without trying to jump ahead of each other. Later, I witnessed the degradation of the German *ordnung*. It was the habitual Russian disorder that infected the Germans and all the rest of us. Before too long, there was no more order and no more lines, just the strongest or the quickest grabbing all they could, while the weakest and clumsiest went away empty. In the Russian view, this kind of injustice was no more than the reality of life, survival of the fittest.

---

[135] "Enough, get out!"

[136] "Spoon!" and "Mess tin!"

We received a rich soup with a thick film of fat on top because we were being fed by the regular army, not the NKVD.[137] These were two different organizations: one fighting and dying for Stalin, plundering and letting others plunder, helpful and happy that *"Gitler kaput."* The other followed in the rear, rounded up soldiers and civilians, and judged them on their own authority, as well as keeping an eye on the regular troops, pistols at the ready. They did not rejoice in the war's course but spewed their hate in cries of "Fascist!" Their authority was already in force a half-kilometer behind the front lines. We learned only later how far this authority really extended.

In March 1945, on the German side of the front, civilians carried food ration cards, and the army was served with subsistence rations, precisely delivered all the way to the first trenches. It was too little to sustain life and a bit too much for starvation. The Russian side of the West Prussian front was a banquet table. The Russian soldier had never in his life enjoyed, or even seen, so much food and other abundance. Unsure that they would still be alive next day, Red soldiers of all ranks lived only for the moment and as wastefully as possible. Food had been scarce in Russia, a bit more plentiful in Poland (though the Poles tried to hide their goods from the one and then the other occupier), but in Germany, everything was available, since it didn't have to be conserved. All the Russians thought of was revenge for the atrocities in their villages, for the ruined cities, for the slaughtered partisans. Primitive instincts were unleashed, food was consumed to the point of surfeit, any leftovers were smashed and scattered. They'd be able to tell their wives at home—oh, how they had lived on the way *"Na Berļin!"*

The guards rounded up our crew of twenty from yesterday and drove us back to the grave we had dug. Now our orders were to gather up the bodies of those killed here in the last three days of fighting. The sun had been shining the past few days, and the smell of decaying bodies already hung in the air. There weren't enough stretchers, and some of us had to carry the bodies, stiffened into various positions, by the feet and shoulders. This was no easy or pleasant duty but one to be carried out without any show of emotion. We had to lay all the bodies at the edge of the pit, without distinction of sides. The truck driver

---

[137]   The Soviet security service operated in peacetime but also during the war in a "supporting" role to the regular army. Some of their wartime activities included the murder of 22,000 Polish officers in the Katyn massacre in April and May 1940.

returned with another group of prisoners, who set to work digging a second pit nearby. When it was ready, we were told to separate the bodies by uniform for separate burial in the two pits.

The bodies had to be looked for over a large area of fields, ditches, and clumps of bushes. It wasn't possible for the prisoners, as well as the guards watching them, to locate all the bodies. The gathering process was left less than complete because the guards were more concerned with watching the prisoners than finding all the bodies. There were frequent prisoner counts. In the evening, back in the truck, we were counted once more by our guard, who informed the Chekist that all were accounted for. The latter yelled back, "*Za ļuģei otveķiš golovoi!*"[138] And so some of the bodies stayed in the bushes or the trench bottoms.

The German bodies roused the interest of the Chekists in two primary ways. First of all, did they have good boots or other valuable items? Usually, nothing worthwhile was left, having been cleaned out by the first-line troops. If the boots were still on, these had to be removed by a prisoner, while the Chekist went through the pockets. All items of value had to be put aside for counting. For officers, their documents, maps, and pistols were to be placed in another pile. These items were to be sent to headquarters. When the search was completed, the Germans were heaved into burial pits, left as they fell and without counting. (Some number of bodies would later be made up at headquarters.)

By the burial pits of the Red soldiers, an officer recorded any details about each body from the available documents. These bodies were stripped only of their weapons and field packs, leaving the uniforms in place. The bodies were not thrown into the pit but carefully laid out with the heads all in one direction. When the bodies were buried, they shoveled more earth on top to form a raised upper layer on which they fixed a memorial sign in the shape of a pyramid with a red star at the tip. (A large quantity of these signs had been prepared beforehand.) For the present, the markers recorded only the number of bodies and the number of the unit. Later, they would adjust the markers to give the full list of names—most of which remained "unknown," however. There were no ceremonies over burials.

No pains were taken with the German bodies and any other soldiers in German uniforms, including our Latvian Legion boys. The pit was filled hastily, the earth left uneven and not shaped into a gravesite.

---

[138] "The guard is responsible for every prisoner."

The numbers buried were left unknown, much less any thought given to drawing up a list of names. No one cared to know who and how many of these human leavings had been here and were here no longer. Likely, we will never know how many soldiers and soldiers' graves lie between Moscow and Berlin. The grave we dug yesterday will also be overgrown by forest, or maybe there's a Polish village there now or a highway. The mothers have long ago cried out their tears, and it's best they didn't know their sons' final moments.

A "Pilgrimage to Mecca"

They count us and order us into the trucks. Back in "our" courtyard after the burial duty, we receive our hard-earned soup and bread. The cook doesn't stint on extra helpings. After supper, we fall asleep on the spot and sleep like the dead we have been handling, till the call rings out in the pre-dawn: "*Vstavai, Fric, vstavai!*"[139]

Now there are lists with our names on them. The numbers of people have grown, and we are a mix of military and civilian prisoners. The guards try to bring some order to the proceedings, but order does not come, and the noise increases. This might be the moment (again) to look for a chance to escape. But which way? We've had our fill of the front; Danzig is burning. The other direction? It's a long way to our homes, unreachably long. The Chekists would catch us next day or the days after that. We can't expect the Poles to hide us, we don't speak Russian, and passing for civilians won't work without documents or food or footwear and with a festering wound visible (the arm is not healing for want of a clean dressing). Despite the hopeless prospects, one of our group has decided to escape. Will he succeed?

On the fourth day of our captivity, our long journey to "Mecca" begins. The kitchen arrives in the morning, and they dish out a meat soup and a quarter loaf of bread. It's a generous feeding, but as we learn later, this was the last time we would be able to eat as much as we wanted. We had naively assumed, or hoped, we would eat like this in the future as well. We should have saved the bread.

---

[139] "Get up, Fritz, get up!"

They call us out according to the list and form us into a column four abreast (the eight of us Latvians manage to keep together). Our column is about 100 men, to which they join another hundred German prisoners. Then we stand on the road for hours while they round up and add a large group of civilians. The German soldiers are to march in front, our group to follow, then the civilians. It takes the Russians two hours to check everybody and reform the column four abreast. The Germans would have done it in fifteen minutes. So it goes with Russian attempts to create order. No one can figure out who is in command, who's subordinate, and who below that. Everybody is swearing at the prisoners and the guards at the same time; everyone considers himself best qualified to decide. The Russian word for this kind of disorder is *bardak* (mess), in which everyone operates according to his own sense of how things should be done.

Finally, a command sounded, "*Šagom marš!*" (Forward march!), and we began to move. This command has a different meaning for the Russians than the Germans. German and Latvian soldiers are accustomed to marching in step, which makes it easier to go as a group. This column moved in fits and starts. The Germans in front kept their own order and marched in step; by the middle of the column, there was no more unison, and the tail dragged well behind . . . till it had to run to catch up. The road was wide enough to allow guards with automatics on both sides, though the guards in their gait looked clumsier than the prisoners.

In the first days of the march, the military prisoners, at least, retained something of the upright bearing drilled into them by German discipline. But with every succeeding day, the prisoners' strength faded and with it the discipline. The guards did not allow anyone to leave the column, and if they saw someone squatting in a ditch, they shot in the air and yelled, "*Auf, auf!*" (Up, up!) The guards learned three or four words in German and didn't need more; the rest was handled through cursing, which was very expressive and soon became understandable to us.

Prisoner columns, spring 1945

We learned we were going to the Prussian town of Stargard,[140] about 40 kilometers as the crow flies. But we were not going by the main roads, which were reserved for the Red army. Over these roads, headed northwest, flowed ever new Soviet troop units and war machinery. In the opposite direction streamed the mountains of war

---

[140] Today part of Poland and called Stargard Szczeciński.

booty, the walking and riding wounded, and, most numerous of all, the hordes of prisoners. The American Willys and Studebakers raced in both directions, not sparing the fuel, which was plentiful. Sometimes the Red army traffic appeared on the side roads as well, and then the prisoners had to clear the way. These occasions created difficulties for the guards, and they took out their anger on us. We spent the first night of the journey by the roadside out in the open, surrounded by a circle of guards. It was forbidden to go outside the circle, and for violating this rule, two prisoners lost their lives the first night. During the day, the guards fired warning shots in the air if someone strayed, but at night, they shot directly at a prisoner without warning. The dead prisoners were left lying in the field as a warning for the next columns.

All the roads in Prussia were filled with war prisoners, detained civilians, and herds of cattle (especially the German black-and-white cows). The victors were not prepared for this mass movement and hadn't made any provisions for feeding either people or animals or for watering and milking the cows. The main imperative was to take everything they could from the Germans; how to make practical use of the loot had not been thought out. The prisoners began to feel hunger and thirst. It hadn't rained in a week, and the roads were dry. Here and there, a rare puddle remained, from which you could scoop a handful of dirty water. Water still stood in the lower places of the surrounding fields, but the guards did not allow anyone to cross the roadside ditches. The springtime sun shone brightly, thirst increased, and fatigue pulled everyone down. The column commanders gave no thought to the well-being of the marchers. Their orders were to deliver the prisoners to a defined location. If a hundred of the two hundred made it, fine. If the number was less, just as fine. As demonstrated so many times, human life had little value here on the eastern front in the war.

We also had to answer the calls of nature within the perimeter of the surrounding guards. It was very uncomfortable at first; later, we got used to it. In our common exhaustion, we learned not to stare, to look past the visible, and to ignore the smells. We also learned to take our toilet breaks before the eyes of women, since they had added old German men and various women, from girls to grandmothers, to our column. Any civilians seen on the road, in the fields, or in hiding were immediately driven into our midst. Many of the civilians found themselves in a worse predicament than we soldiers were; they had not been given a chance to grab any clothes or food, and they weren't used to going for days without eating and to sleeping for weeks in the same clothes out in the fields.

And those calls of nature . . . The women could squat, with their skirts covering any bare flesh, but the men had no such advantage. While I struggled with my own inhibitions at first, others only laughed. The roadsides were lined with piles of manure, to which we added our own as did those who came after us. Starting the war, the Germans could not have imagined that their country would be fertilized by the wastes of people from Europe, Asia, and other continents.

On the third day of our march, a barrel of water passed alongside the column. What an event! Not everyone was able to reach the barrel, of course, and they had to slake their thirst in the roadside ditches if there happened to be water there during a pause in the march and if the guards were feeling generous. But you could poison yourself with this roadside water, since human and animal bodies still lay by the road. The dirty ditchwater had another unpleasant and dangerous consequence. Diarrhea afflicted many marchers already weakened by exhaustion.

New gangs of prisoners, primarily German civilians, joined our column in Stargard. The farther south and farther away from the front, the more German civilians were joined to our pilgrimage. Our course now led through Marienwerder.[141] The column had stretched to more than a half kilometer and grew ever longer with each stop. No one knew how many thousands of prisoners were slowly moving to the southeast, since no one was counting the civilians. They separated the men from the women (for later reunification, they said). Then they added horse-drawn wagons about every three hundred meters within the column for the sick and the incapable. The horses were real hacks, since the best horses had been commanded by the Germans during their retreat, the rest by the Soviets, leaving only seriously emaciated, near-invalid horses for the task at hand. If the horse wasn't lame, then the cart had only three wheels and a harness from Biblical times. Understandably, such wagons could handle no more than ten of the disabled at a time. In the first week, there had still been hopes of finding a place on the wagons, but these hopes faded as the journey stretched out and the numbers of the weakened grew.

---

[141] An administrative district in West Prussia, as well as the district capital; today the town is called Kwidzyn, in northern Poland, southeast of Gdansk.

Those who couldn't go on remained in the road or by the side of the ditch. Those who strayed outside the defined boundaries were "written off" one way or another. The older Germans, unused to hardship and unable to fight their way to a sip of water, fell by the wayside first. Some died a natural death; others were helped to their end by the guards. Their bodies were pulled over the ditches and left in the fields as a warning to the following columns and a treat for the flies. The caravan slowly and inexorably moved on. At the rear of the column rolled two trucks filled with Red soldiers. During the days, the number of walking guards was minimal for our greatly lengthened column. From a hilltop, we could see the column snaking along the dusty road. Our Latvian group marched among the German soldiers near the front of the procession.

For the first three days, no food was distributed. You fared somewhat better than others if you had brought some rations of your own. Few of us had the foresight to do that. We were in the habit of carrying as little as possible in our movements at the front. Moreover, in the last few days, no one had thought about stocking up on food, when all our energies had been focused on just staying alive. Almost all the prisoners were thinly dressed and empty-handed. On the other hand, the guards ate well and three times a day. Having eaten their fill, they often threw a crust of bread into a crowd of prisoners for the enjoyment of seeing the resulting scramble. Fights among the starving were frequent.

On the fourth day of our journey, the guards killed several cows, found a few wilted potatoes, and brewed a soup. The entire stretched-out column caught its breath in hopes of finally getting something warm to eat. The Germans would have first calculated how much soup there was for each prisoner, but the Russians had no interest in such reckoning. The soup kettle was surrounded by the most agile and resourceful prisoners, and they took away the best part of the brew. Later, the soup was "stretched" with water; but even then, only half of the prisoners, at most, got something lukewarm into their stomachs. Many got nothing. Farther along in the march, the cooks tried to divide the food more evenly. Still, these soups were nothing like the front-line soup we had tasted a week before on the day of our capture. We were lucky if we got a half liter (about a pint) of warm water with a few potato skins and a sliver of meat floating in it. There was no bread.

I remember our passage through Marienwerder in connection with this struggle for food. I was marching between two Latvian boys when a German in the row ahead of me asked a passing guard for bread: "*Bitte, Hleb; bitte, ein bisschen Hleb.*"[142] Usually, the guards didn't respond to these kinds of pleas or, if they did, answered with curses. This time, the Russian took pity on the man, fumbled in his jacket pocket, and pulled out a piece of bread with a burned crust. He threw it into the midst of the prisoners. Unexpectedly, the bread landed in the dust three steps in front of me. If I had been more nimble and quickly bent over and grabbed the bread, I would have gained something that was worth gold then. But I've never been nimble. While my system was gearing up to the realization that I must leap on the bread and then defend it against at least ten other grasping hands, someone else had grabbed the prize. He was an elderly German immediately set on by other starving prisoners, all trying to wrest the bread from his hands. Howling in full voice, the man pressed the bread against his body, but two younger, stronger Germans grabbed him, broke his hands apart, and tore away the bread.

Now the struggle over the undivided piece of bread continued between the victors. One of the combatants belted the other in the temple, grabbed the bread, and plowed ahead into the next rows. The loser fell to the ground and stayed there unmoving. The guard shot in the air and yelled at the prisoners to keep the procession going. He ordered that the fallen man be pulled to the side of the road and then ignored him completely, yelling at the prisoners to keep moving. "*Strełak budu!*" (I'll shoot!), he threatened, to get everyone back in line. The death of a prisoner meant nothing to him, but keeping the column moving was his assigned responsibility.

And what was our destination? It was Graudenz[143] as we later learned. We had covered some hundred kilometers, leaving the sick and the dead by the roadside but growing in numbers every day. The Russian offensive in March had been rapid, and with the way to the west cut off, the German civilians found themselves trapped. Now the Chekists combed the occupied districts and pushed all the inhabitants into prison camps.

---

[142] "Please, some bread; please, a piece of bread."

[143] Today's Grudziądz, in northern Poland, on the Vistula River.

On the evening of April 1 on the east bank of the Vistula River, our hungry and exhausted column beheld a large medieval fortress with three- to four-meter thick, high walls with serrated battlements and large round towers at the four corners. One of the walls rose out of a riverside cliff. The fortress had not suffered much in the recent fighting, but the city behind it had been largely destroyed. We crossed the Vistula by a temporary bridge and stood before the gates in a staging area. We were not interested in the fortress or the city or even in something to eat any longer. We wanted to drop down and sleep. If we had to move on from here, half of our numbers would stay where they were, completely exhausted. After the posting of the guards, peace finally settled in. I took off my boots, propped them under my head, and instantly fell asleep.

In Graudenz Prison

Next day, they moved part of the prisoner horde into the fortress, another part to the city prison, and the rest to barracks on the edge of town. Along with the other Latvian boys, I ended up in the Graudenz prison inside the fortress. The fortress and the prison were the largest structures in the city, and they had suffered least during the fighting. They stuffed more than 2000 prisoners into this prison. I don't know where they put the rest of the 5000 who had been brought here or what happened to them.

Before the war, Graudenz might have been about the size of our Jelgava.[144] About half of Graudenz had been destroyed in the war, and only a tenth of the Polish inhabitants were left as we learned later. We saw nothing of the city because our cell windows opened on the prison courtyard. When we were later led on work details, always down the same street, we couldn't get an overall perspective on the condition of the city. We did see apartment buildings in ruins, half-destroyed Catholic churches, and streets filled with rubble. Meanwhile, we got to know our prison very well, more than we wished to know it.

I spent five months in the Graudenz prison, from April to September. Why were we there, since we hadn't been tried yet? It seems they simply used the prison as a holding area for the huge number of prisoners, who had to be put somewhere while they examined them individually and assessed their degrees of guilt. Probably, it also provided a large free labor force for the victors without drawing off troops from their march to the west.

---

[144] A pre-war population of about 40,000.

There were various rumors about the situation at the front. Some guessed that the Russians were already in Berlin, others that they had been beaten back, and the Germans would soon launch a major counterattack with superweapons. It was all the same to the prisoners, since no one believed in a German victory anymore. We wanted to eat, not to march or fight. Our thoughts about home lingered in visions of fog-wrapped faraway places. But we were too worn-down then to go anywhere, even if they had let us go.

Assembled in the prison courtyard, we were handed a piece of bread and a slosh of coffee (actually, a lukewarm brownish liquid without aroma). Maybe it was some of the German *ersatz* coffee remaining in the warehouse, but it was so diluted that it had even lost its coffee color. Still, we were satisfied to finally get some bread and some boiled water in place of the dirty ditchwater of our journey. After a week spent on the road, we consumed the bread in one sitting, satisfying our hunger only briefly.

Then a Chekist appeared in the courtyard with the list compiled back in Praust. They called out thirty men, and a guard marched them off to a designated cell. Then another thirty were sent to another cell and so forth, until all the prisoners had been accounted for. Those who didn't answer were simply crossed off the list. How simple. We had had chances in the past week to disappear into the bushes, but we had not acted on them. Still, the remaining men of our squad of Latvians managed to stay together again, going to the same cell. In April, there were about one hundred Latvians in Graudenz prison, but as conditions worsened, no more than fifty were left in September.

The guard led our group of thirty to the third floor, unlocked the last door at the end of the corridor, and motioned us inside. The heavy door clanged shut, and the key turned in the lock. Now I was really in prison, which was a new experience for me. I could compare this place with the prison cells I had seen in movies and read about in novels. There's a big difference. Today I can also think of it as enriching my life's experiences. At the time, it mattered little whether the place of captivity was a prison, a fortress, a barracks, or the open field. The important thing was to stay alive.

The prison consisted of four buildings that together formed a closed courtyard. The largest building, which stood parallel to the street, had four stories, the rest three. The structures were fashioned with thick walls and had been built at the beginning of the century. A hallway ran down the middle of each story, with cells on either side. The cells were of different sizes; ours was one of the largest—six by six meters (387.5 square feet), with two windows and a corner door next to the end wall of the hallway. The cell was empty except for a barrel (about 2.5 feet high, 1.5 feet across) with a cover and handles for carrying. This was to be our toilet. The glass in the windows had been blown out in the recent fighting and lay in shards on the floor. Our first job was to gather all the shards and throw them into the barrel and then, once the guard brought a broom, to sweep out the cell. We set to work—some of us, that is. In our group were eight Russians who had been sitting in prison for some time already and were savvy about prison ways. They were the first to occupy places by the far wall, away from the door and the toilet barrel. As we came to learn later, these were the best places in the cell.

These experienced prisoners knew when to come forward, when to stay back, when to raise their voices, when to remain silent. In this case, they let us know that picking up glass was not their responsibility and let us newcomers do it. When the broken glass was in the barrel, the guard designated two of the men standing near him to carry it away. One of the men was me.

When we returned to the cell, all the places had been taken except for a small space by the door right next to the barrel. Thus, my first day in prison provided a valuable lesson. Through the glassless windows and under the door, a strong draft blew constantly, while at the Russian end of the cell, the air was calm. To survive sleeping day and night in such a draft was possible only for boys like us, toughened by drill and frontline fighting. In some ways, it was worse to be also placed near the toilet barrel as I was; at times, the stench was so strong I grew nauseous though I was holding my nose with a sleeve. A third problem was that there was no rest at night; those who came to sit on the barrel clambered over me and my neighbor, often stepping right on us. Meanwhile, the Russians complained that we had purposely lain down in front of the barrel to get in their way.

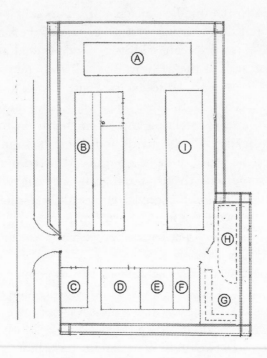

Graudenz prison layout. A. Women's blockhouse; B. Men's blockhouse with author's cell at top; C. Guardhouse; D. Kitchen; E. Warehouse; F. Sauna; G. Toilet area; H. Burial pits; I. Men's blockhouse.

We were a motley group. The thirty of us in the allotted space meant no personal comforts were possible, but we were able to stretch out at full length on the floor, with about 80 centimeters (2.5 feet) of space side to side. We slept in four rows of about eight men each—the two middle rows head to head, feet toward the feet of those lying by the walls. There were no nails or hooks in those walls for hanging clothes or other belongings; we rolled up our belongings in our blankets, if we had any, or in our greatcoats. The rolls served as cushions during the day and, unrolled, as bedding at night. The spring weather was warm enough, if it hadn't been for the constant draft. It was futile to think (as we did) about glazing the windows. Likely, not a single unbroken window was left in Graudenz, not only in the prison but in the whole city. If they did find some glass, no one would use it for fixing *our* windows. The prison commanders and guards were content to close their windows with veneer or cardboard. The Germans on the front lines had glazed the windows of their bunkers at a time when the

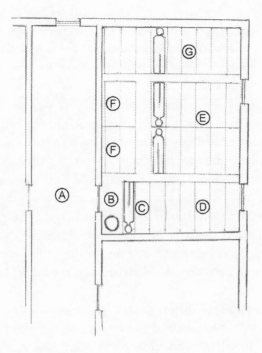

Author's prison cell in Graudenz. A. Third floor hallway;
B. Toilet barrel; C. Author's place first three months; D.
Latvians; E. Germans; F. Poles; G. Russians.

bullets were whistling overhead, but the Russians, even several years
after the war, did not think to replace their veneer windowpanes with
glass.

The bright side of having empty windows was that we could see and
hear everything that happened in the courtyard below. You only had
to climb on the windowsill and pull yourself up by the bars. This sort
of climbing was forbidden, but we quickly learned to evade the guards'
scrutiny. When we heard the guard walking away down the corridor,
one of us stood by the door, blocking the view of the window, through
which others were surveying the courtyard. In the beginning, while we
were not allowed outside our cell, the windows were our only contact
with the outside world.

Our Latvian group occupied eight spaces from the door and the
toilet barrel to the window. Each of us had his quirks, but on the whole,
we got along well and helped one another. It was important also that we
could talk in our own language. We knew little Russian at first but added

words each day till we were conversant in the essentials. Meanwhile, German was no longer in fashion. There were fourteen Germans in the two middle rows, some wearing civilian clothes, though these were probably also soldiers. The Germans also kept together and talked in half voices, looking uneasy.

The Russian group lay by the back wall, though we weren't sure if there were any actual Russians in their midst. They talked to each other and to everyone else at high volume and only in Russian. (At the time, I wasn't yet able to distinguish Russian from Belarusian or Ukrainian speech.) They were more self-confident and held themselves as more knowledgeable than the rest of us. They were always in front around the food deliveries, avoided emptying the toilet barrel. Things were always cheerful and loud at the Russian end; they recounted all sorts of likely and unlikely experiences, and they forecast the future confidently. So it was interesting to mix with the Russians—if they didn't get aggressive or brutal, that is.

Each Russian was different, but the one who stood out most sharply was a stocky red-haired fellow with a face like a broken brick. He took on himself the position of ranking member of the cell. I noticed him already on the third day of our captivity back in Praust, where he acquired the nickname *Rizhik*. There, he talked to us in accented but passable German. No longer now. Though he listened in on German conversations, he answered only in Russian. He had a great command of Russian swear words and of prison jargon, and though we didn't understand half of them, we could only marvel at his inventive combinations of crude words.

We all detested Rizhik because he sucked up to the guards and tattled on his cellmates to gain advantages for himself. He had an opinion about everything, and his opinion was always final and admitted no challenges. He blamed others for his own misdeed and always managed to avoid punishment. It was unrealistic to think of challenging him physically. He was strong and aggressive and gave way only to a guard carrying a weapon. His threats to kill any opponent had to be taken seriously. It's possible he had lived near the German border, been taken prisoner early in the war, been sent to Germany, and served in Vlasov's army.[145] He never talked about his experiences, but he was

---

[145] Vlasov's Russian Liberation Army was formed in Germany and from German-
       held areas.

dressed in civilian clothes collected in Germany or Poland and likely was hiding under an assumed name. We were sure he had reasons to fear punishment. Just as he had cursed the Russians back in Praust, so he now flung Russian curses at the Germans, as well as us Latvians in our German uniforms. His piercing, lowering gaze and powerful fists ensured his role as overseer of our cell. Though we chafed at this presumption, it was convenient to the guards and satisfying to Rizhik.

Settled into the far corner of the cell was an older and much more likable Russian named Osip. He was said to have sat in many prisons and seemed to know prison protocol in great detail. He saved his strength and avoided unnecessary movement. He didn't smoke, even when cigarettes became available later, never cursed but gladly explained things and tutored those who asked. His most impressive feat was to raise and lower the lid of the toilet barrel with his foot to avoid soiling his hands. He spent every free moment hunting for lice in his shirt and, when he found one, squashed it with a distinct crack that no one else could achieve. If Rizhik had been a butcher in peacetime, as he boasted, then Osip might have been a schoolteacher. His refined manner suggested he had not done physical labor, and he could give exhaustive lectures about medical and hygienic matters. Encouraged to reminisce, he willingly recounted experiences in various cities, prisons, and prison camps. But he never disclosed the substance of his past and how he had come to be locked up here.

In the months we lived together, a variety of interesting Russian types and characters showed themselves. Till now, we Latvians had had little contact with Russians or other nationalities in the great Soviet melting pot. The first Russian year (1940–41) simply meant a change in personnel for us at the Teachers Institute. We remembered the comic aspects but did not quite grasp the tragedies all around us.

Our days settled into an unvarying routine in an unchanging environment. Two masonry walls enclosed the prison, a thick outer wall about four meters high (a bit over thirteen feet) and a lower inner wall swaddled in barbed wire. Likely, the wire had been electrified during the German occupation, but there was no current in the city now. In the cells, names were scratched into the walls in various languages: Polish, Czech, French. Had the Russians freed these prisoners, or were the Germans able to transport them west as they retreated? Perhaps they had just slaughtered them. The Fritzes were also specialists in prison matters.

At 7 a.m., a duty guard in the courtyard swung a steel bar against a piece of rail hanging from a chain. The ringing could be heard not only by all 5000 prisoners but also by inhabitants beyond the prison walls. After the morning bell—let's call it that—the guards began to clamber up the metal stairs to the hallways and to pound their key bundles against the cell doors. Once the doors were unlocked, our first job was to carry out the toilet barrel. In a corner of the prison courtyard, a gate led to a second fenced courtyard featuring two pits designed to receive our human wastes—one for the emptying of the toilet barrels, the other for direct deposit by prisoners during exercise periods. The arrangement for the latter was as basic as could be: a round pole resting on crossed stakes at either end of the pit. When the pit was full, the prisoners would throw dirt over it and dig a new one next to it. It was quite a sight: clouds of flies swarming over a reeking pit. Fortunately, we couldn't see these pits from our cell windows, but when the wind blew from that direction, the stench from our toilet barrel was doubly reinforced.

It would have been nice to wash up in the mornings, but the city water main was broken (and would stay broken all summer). The citizens of Graudenz used the Vistula River for their bathing, but we prisoners had to manage without this luxury. At eight, the guards led us down to breakfast .First, there was the count by our cell door, then the trip down to the courtyard where we lined up for another count, and finally the walk to the kitchen window. We always looked forward to this part of the routine; the walk was a welcome break from the hours spent lying on a cement floor. The prisoner column wound over the whole courtyard attended by the clanging of mess kits. A large army kettle stood by the kitchen window, and a cook's helper used a ladle with a long handle to pour a cup of so-called coffee into our mess kits or, if these had been lost, into a tin can.

At the next window, we got a piece of bread, an eighth part of the loaf, with the best parts—the end pieces—going to the four lucky ones.[146] It was good Polish bread, baked from rye flour with only a little sawdust mixed in. In time, the quality of the bread declined; but good or bad, it was never enough for us. We felt we could eat the whole loaf by ourselves but felt thankful for what we got. We also learned of the

---

[146] The loaf (20 × 10 × 10 cm.) would be cut in half, then into quarters, and then cut again lengthwise to create eight pieces. The end pieces, with more crust on them, were preferred to other parts of the loaf.

buying and selling and looting of bread. It began in the bread-cutting room, and the pieces went through various hands, until a piece reached a prisoner. Some prisoners put that piece into their pocket and, along with their watered coffee, carried it up to the cell to consume in peace. But they couldn't be sure the plan would succeed, since anyone stronger than they were could take the bread away, either right in the courtyard, or in the hallway, or the cell. No one would help either, and they would have to wait for the next feeding. The smarter ones ate their piece of bread on the spot, ensuring they would actually have their breakfast.

The breakfast line winds back toward the building doors and then up the stairs to the cells. The whole procedure takes several hours. Lying back on our bedding, we feel our hunger only beginning to wake. But it's seven hours till the evening meal. About four in the afternoon, we go for a second walk and then to dinner, which consists of a cup of soup. The soup is always the same; it's called a meat soup, though there's no meat in it, a tendon or sinew at most. Still, from the little specks of fat floating in the water, we know there had been meat there and that it had found another table. On occasion, our cup of soup might include a chunk of unpeeled potato, a shred of cabbage leaf, a few grains of barley. It was a far cry from the soup we had enjoyed a few weeks ago at the front, but compared to what we ate six months later, it was splendid stuff.

If they had also made us work, these rations would have quickly led us to a breakdown, but we were just lying day and night on the cell floor with no expenditure of energy. After the first few weeks, we looked for ways to supplement these norms; we might find a piece of bread or a cigarette end discarded by a guard and trade the butt for bread or soup. It was also possible to trade for bread with a decent piece of clothing or some other possession that had stuck to one's fingers during the walks in the courtyard. (This kind of trading was a rare event, however, since the amount of possessions among the prisoners had been reduced to a minimum.) You could also volunteer for digging the toilet pits. You could even get picked for the "refined" jobs in the kitchen or for splitting firewood, but for these jobs, there was a price—something truly valuable, such as a good pair of boots. Among the best commodities for barter was newsprint. For a small piece of a newspaper, which is the best material for rolling a pinch of *mahorka*,[147] the smokers gladly gave up their daily bread ration. If they didn't have *mahorka*, they made do with dried leaves, or grass, or anything else that would create smoke. (I was fortunately a nonsmoker, thanks to my father's influence and example.) To get to the newsprint, you had to bribe a guard, since they were not very receptive to beggars. In our search for new ways to access food, the opportunities expanded, especially after the war's end, when the prison regimen loosened up, and we were able to work outside the walls. But even then, we were always hungry, and we stayed hungry for two years.

In an exercise walk in the courtyard, one of our guys noticed some cartons labeled *Knäckebrot*[148] behind the bars of a second-floor window of the warehouse. This was a commodity familiar to us. But how to get to it? It would be nothing to crawl up to the window, were it not for the armed guards in the corner towers. There was also the guard who had led us down from our cell. We talked it over and formed a plan of operation: some of us would hurl rocks through the glassless window to break open the cartons, hoping that some of the *knäckebrot* would fall to the ground. Meanwhile, others would simulate a fight to draw the guards' attention away from our bombardment. In vain. The rocks penetrated the carton, but the bread crisps did not fall out.

Later, we learned that the breads were also stored on the first floor of the warehouse. You could jump and pull yourself up by the window bars, stick an arm inside, feel for the bread packets, and throw these down to your comrades. The risk of getting a bullet in the back remained, but we were hungry enough to take it on. Gradually, we learned how to fish out the *knäckebrot* packets and fed on these for a good while, so long as we could still find any within arm's length of the window bars. Our operation was spoiled when other prisoners noticed what we were doing, gathered at the warehouse window, and drew the guards' attention. Shots in the air cooled off the general excitement. They boarded up the window the same day.

We met other Latvians in the courtyard. A glimpse of a Latvian flag on a sleeve or overhearing a Latvian phrase in passing provided an opportunity to make contact with countrymen and learn the latest news. In time, we came to know all the Latvians dispersed among the prison buildings. There were even a few Latvian women in one of the

---

[147]   Cheap tobacco issued in the Soviet army.

[148]   Bread crisps issued in the German army.

buildings. Both of these middle-aged women had accompanied their Legionnaire husbands from Liepāja to Danzig. The husbands had been assigned to Sofienwald,[149] but the wives had headed south from Danzig, where food and shelter were scarce, and so ended up in the region of Stargard in Prussia. The rapid Russian advance had cut them off from Danzig, and the Chekists had rounded them up and forced them to join our pilgrimage to Graudenz. We did not meet a second time. Perhaps they had been sent to a different camp or, less likely, set free.

The prison guards and administrators exploited the younger and prettier women sexually, particularly the German women. By the end of August, many of the women prisoners were walking around with swollen bellies. They might have been raped, or they might have agreed to the encounters in exchange for some American canned meat or other desirable food. They may also have hoped to speed up their release this way. Certainly, when we were relocated to another prison in the fall, the pregnant women were set free. The exploitation of these women was another tragic event in the German nation's history. Today their Russian-German babies conceived in the spring of 1945 are approaching seventy. Their lives cannot have been easy.

In the courtyard, I met my Teachers Institute colleague Pēteris Vīksne (Class of 1941), who was interned in another building. He was suffering from diarrhea and had become so weak it was hard to look at him. I gave him a couple of *knäckebrot* packets, thinking his days were numbered anyway. But he survived. We met again in the 1960s in Riga and shared memories.

No one in the prison slept on the night of May 8, 1945. Firing from every available gun barrel mixed with shouts of *"Urrah!"* and fireworks lit up our cell walls like the brightest sunshine. We understood that the war had ended that day. We had imagined all sorts of endings to the war, but we couldn't foresee that we would be spending the first day of peacetime in a prison cell. We understood the Russians' joy at their victory, hard earned after four years of war. We felt our own joy that the war was finally over, that we had remained alive, that now we would have a better chance of getting back home. But the joy did not drive out the pain we felt for our country, for its scattered population, for all the lives destroyed and those left unlived. And we had been defeated.

---

[149] A village in today's Czech Republic.

Next day, even the prisoners were granted a royal feast: an American canned meat tin for every three men. This was something unprecedented for us. It turned out that the prison warehouse was filled with American canned food. The Americans had sent the food to Allied prisoners through the Red Cross, but the Germans had kept it and saved it for harder times. Their withdrawal had been so rushed that the food had been abandoned to the enemy. Whatever the true course of events, on Victory Day, we opened a Yankee tin with the help of a nail and celebrated along with the whole world.

From our first day in Graudenz to our last, as well as later in other prisons and on the way to them, inspections and searches were a constant factor of our lives. Inspections followed one another but at irregular intervals, sometimes several in one day or night, sometimes every two or three weeks. The inspections and searches were both open and secret. If on returning from our afternoon walk we found our belongings scattered and some of them missing, we called that a secret search. The official motive for these searches was to remove prohibited items such as knives, needles, matches, belts, and bootlaces; the practical reason was, just as much, to remove some previously undiscovered desirable object. And something always turned up.

In the open inspections, prisoners were called one by one to the hallway with all their belongings. These were inspected and sorted into two piles: items to be taken away to the right, those to be kept to the left. The owner would then take his "left" items to another empty cell and wait there until the cell filled up with his mates. When all cell inhabitants had been checked and moved to a nearby cell, their own empty cell was carefully inspected. These inspections might turn up small but useful items, such as pencil tips, pieces of chalk, a mirror fragment, a shaving blade; these might be hidden in the toilet barrel or in a crack in the wall or the floor. A rare and valuable find was a gold wedding band, since rings and watches had been taken away in the first inspections.

No matter how thorough the searches were, the prisoners learned how to keep some of their things hidden. Perfecting this skill not only relieved the monotony of prison life but became a kind of sport. It was a form of entertainment to hear stories about fooling the guards during inspections. We were all united in opposition to the guards, and we all enjoyed these stories of small victories retold in our darkened cell late at night. Anyone who gave up his possessions without trying to hide them was a *durak* (sap); a *geroi* (hero) was someone who after an inspection could show his fellows a prohibited item not confiscated.

Besides the official inspections, all cells were also subject to "self-inspections," in which the stronger, more aggressive prisoners simply took from the weaker prisoners their bread rations or cigarette butts, doing so without the slightest compunction in front of everyone else. A second variety of confiscations involved the small, wily thieves who robbed the big and strong as they slept. We quickly understood that we truly possessed something only when it was in our stomachs. At night, we slept on top of our possessions, which did not provide complete security but improved the odds that we wouldn't wake in the morning as naked as church mice.

Our soldiers' possessions seemed to melt away with each inspection. On Victory Day, my belongings consisted of a *laiviņa*,[150] a shredded camouflage suit, a blue-gray jacket and pants, dirty underclothes, dirty foot-wrapping rags, and my felt boots with the gouged-out toes. There were also my bread sack, mess kit, and spoon. That was all, though I turned my pockets inside out dozens of times. Later, I became more well-to-do. I found a pair of lace-up boots that had been abandoned because they were large, unsightly, and full of holes. I also found a thin, frayed blanket and a worn pair of socks. The boots (without the laces, which were prohibited) and the blanket proved very useful, not only in prison but later in the north. I don't know how my pants stayed on without a belt or suspenders, but they did. The lesson I took away from these circumstances was that tough times reversed the order of preference for possessions. It was best to avoid the good and attractive things and be satisfied with the humble things that would not tempt others. You ended up with more by striving for less.

The war had ended, but prison life got worse. The Chekists were in a frenzy to nab civilians and continued to round them up even after the Germans had laid down their arms. Every day, the prison gates opened and let in new streams of people. Every cell now held more civilians than prisoners of war. Our building filled up as did the women's building, and our cell held twice as many prisoners as in the beginning. Now every occupant had only about 40 centimeters (just under 1 foot, 4 inches) of lateral space to sleep in; sitting or standing was more comfortable during the days. The space was not enough for

---

[150] The boat-shaped soldier's hat.

sleeping on our backs, so we lay on our sides at night; on command (issued by Rizhik, according to his own waking-sleeping rhythms), the whole cell turned over to the other side. The toilet cover rattled all night, and all night, someone was stepping on my feet. Sleep was intermittent, and the toilet stench made it difficult to breathe. Thanks to the broken windows, however, there was enough air for everyone. We lived the reality of the old saying "Like sardines in a can"; except for a brief walk in the yard, we were pressed against one another day and night. And no one had bathed or changed clothing for several months.

During our "crush" stage, sleeping next to me was *Saimnieks*,[151] which was our name for him and whose real name I don't remember. He was my height but wider in the shoulders and stockier, aged about forty. His civilian clothes were too small, but they emphasized his athletic build. He had owned a farm near Ērgļi parish (in Vidzeme), and his broad speech marked him as coming from Piebalga (farther north in Vidzeme). He had been a strongman and won contests of strength in his district. Our poor diet was not helping him stay in shape, but he did not give in to pessimism and encouraged the other Latvians through his tales of overcoming obstacles. He found Russian difficult and pronounced the few Russian words he knew with an accent that left the Russians scratching their heads. His best characteristic was a sense of fairness, and he always defended the weaker prisoners against the bullies and thieves. Even our "overseer," the recidivist[152] Rizhik, left him alone. The Latvian boys kept near Saimnieks and felt safer in his presence. I have only the best memories of him.

On my other side slept Mārtiņš, whom we called Mārcs—a slight skinny boy of sixteen or so, youngest in our cell, who had been captured in the last months of the war as a member of the Luftwaffe helper battalions,[153] sent to the prison in Danzig and later to Graudenz. Mārcs was a quiet, good-hearted, even naive boy in an ill-fitting uniform, who attached himself to me. He was ashamed to cry before the others but

---

[151] Latvian word roughly translatable as "boss" or "head of household."

[152] In this context, someone who habitually relapses into criminal activities or behavior.

[153] The *Luftwaffenhelfer* companies were formed late in the war from classes of schoolboys aged 16 to 17, including about 3100 boys from Latvia. Their duties included helping to maintain and operate anti-aircraft batteries and searchlights. A 16-year-old inductee from Bavaria named Joseph Ratzinger became, in 2005, Pope Benedict XVI.

at times pressed against my chest, cried soundlessly. At his arrival in
our cell, my own situation improved to the extent that Mārčs now slept
in the space right next to the toilet barrel; I was next, then Saimnieks,
and, toward the windows, the rest of the Latvians. The best places were
still claimed by the Russians, including their new arrivals. The new
arrivals also included the older *Volkssturm* Germans, who joined their
countrymen already in the cell.

The overpopulation in the cells could not be sustained. Indeed,
a solution to the problem arrived, though not the kind we had been
waiting for. In the second half of May, the lice attacked, then typhus,
and then death. The lice had appeared already in the second week of
our captivity, and they were easy to fight off then. But in Graudenz
prison, they began to increase in geometric progression. Within a
month, we were so lice-ridden there was no escape. Between meals
and inspections, our only activity was trying to delouse ourselves in
the most primitive ways—shirts off and squashing the bugs that no
longer had to be searched for since they were crawling under our
fingernails already. Undoubtedly, the sight was the same in all the cells
in June—emaciated, half-naked prisoners fighting over their shrinking
spaces, cursing or encouraging each other, grimly pursuing their tiny
tormentors.

The lice were unwelcome guests, but you could get used to them.
Typhus, the spotted fever kind, was unstoppable. The lice carried the
infection throughout the prison, despite the presence of a doctor, a
number of orderlies, even a hospital. But the epidemic spread so fast
that the orderlies could only manage to deal with the needs of the
prison staff. No one gave a thought to the prisoners or to organizing
an eradication campaign. There was no water or soap or disinfectants.
The open toilet pits attracted millions of flies, which also hovered near
the kitchen kettles. And every day, the prison gates admitted new bands
of worn-out prisoners to our unsanitary, overfilled abode. It's a wonder
the disease didn't spread over the whole city and its surroundings.

The prison administration was unprepared to combat the epidemic.
A deadly harvest began. The first to die were the older Germans,
who were numerous in the cells next to ours. Each morning, the cell
"overseer" had to take a count and announce the number of the sick
and the dead. The survivors had to carry the dead down to the second
courtyard. Every day, the prisoners dug new pits two to three meters
deep next to the toilet pits. I also carried down bodies, which was

nothing new for me or for other veterans of the war. The old Germans were not heavy. Living on our rations for a month and one-half, they had shrunk to just bones and skin. Having slept and died in various positions and partly stiffened into them, they looked horrible on the stretchers. It was just as horrible to see them rolled into the pits just by raising one side of a stretcher, to land however they fell—lying, sitting up, sprawled on top of other bodies. Fearing infection, no one tried to take anything from these corpses. From time to time, the guards shook a layer of quicklime into the pit to combat the flies and reduce the smell. The next assortment of bodies was thrown on top, then more quicklime until the pit was full, then covered, and another one dug. The numbers of the dead did not decrease. Without any official count, we estimated later that, in the month of June in Graudenz prison, fifteen hundred prisoners had died of typhus, most of them German civilians.

During the epidemic, our cell lost eleven prisoners. Among the first to go was Mārčs. One night, he huddled against me, complaining of the cold, though he had a high temperature. I pulled out my old blanket from beneath and wrapped the boy inside. I felt that my own turn would come someday, since there was no way to protect against the lice and their diseases. We informed the guards of Mārčs's condition, but there was no help; they stayed even farther away, fearing for their own safety. Only those who made it down to the kitchen were fed. You could bring up some of the "coffee" for the sick if you wished. I offered my chunk of bread to Mārčs, but he ate nothing and didn't even ask for a drink. He raved for three days and nights, sliding in and out of consciousness. On the fourth morning, I no longer heard his breath. The boy's organism had given up the fight without a prolonged struggle that would have been hopeless anyway.

Mārčs's hand was cold already, so he must have died in the early part of the night. *Somewhere in Latvia*, I thought, *a mother was reassuring herself, "Now that the war is over, my son will soon be home."* I didn't have the strength to carry Mārčs down the stairs, and the guard chose someone else in my place. I was glad I wouldn't have to see the boy tossed into the burial pit. In the past months, I had worked to suppress my emotions; but this time, I was shaking all over my body. I caught myself thinking that I must close my mouth when my last moments came. I was seeing the bodies with their eyes and mouths open as if they were glaring at me and yelling. I didn't want to see Mārčs that way and made sure to close his eyes. That was my leave taking of him.

The next to go was my new neighbor to the right, Saimnieks having found a better place a week before. The neighbor grew delirious and mumbled in a strange language, occasionally throwing in some German words. The deadly pattern repeated itself: a high temperature, tossing and turning, nightmares. I brought him some of our tepid soup. I had swallowed my bread ration already in the courtyard. All his strength gone, my neighbor slept quietly with eyes closed. A week later, this space next to me was also free, along with other spaces in our cell. Both my neighbors had died, but I was left fighting the lice.

Now death began to visit the administrative corps and the guards. Then the prison heads woke up. They were determined that after their victory in the war, they would not stay behind in the damned German (really Polish) lands. Perhaps the delayed decision to act came from the Germans, not the Russians. More likely the Germans.

On a day when we carried the tenth body from our cell, the guard called out, "Get all your things ready. You're going for disinfection. Take the sick with you. The cell will be scrubbed out." This was unprecedented, and it fanned a spark of hope among us. Later, we learned that one of the military prisoners, a German doctor named Wolf, had offered to rescue the prison from the typhus epidemic on condition that the warden allow him to work without restriction and organize a meaningful disinfection campaign throughout the prison. The warden understood that Wolf was his last hope and allowed the hated German a free hand.

And Dr. Wolf fulfilled his promise. Working with three assistant doctors, he quickly turned from a prisoner into a commander. He visited all the administrative offices, the kitchen, the warehouses, and all the cells and then organized the rescue campaign. Russian officers hung with medals followed Wolf around and carried out his directives, snapping orders to their own subordinates before the translator had even finished restating the directives in Russian. The Russians understood that they couldn't do the job without Wolf and that otherwise the same fate awaited them as the 5000 prisoners. On Wolf's requests, they provided white lab coats for the medical staff, suitable spaces for installing disinfection ovens, as well as the disinfectants themselves. Once it had been launched, the process unfolded as planned.

On first entering our cell, Dr. Wolf said the space had not been properly cleaned and would have to be scrubbed again. Then he used a cane with a piece of chalk on the end to draw a circle around the toilet barrel so that no one would have to sleep closer to it than two meters. My distancing from the barrel was given a boost. Thereafter, all the cell inhabitants were led to a space in the basement once a week to use the sauna and the delousing chamber. While we were in the basement, our cell was disinfected with a reeking liquid whose smell lingered in the air long afterward. In the delousing chamber, all our belongings were thrown on top of metal screens, the doors were sealed, and our stuff was baked nearly to roasting.

In the anteroom of the sauna, we had all our body hair shaved off with hair clippers so dull it felt like skin was being shaved off along with hair. The haircuts came out almost comically grotesque, even though we had really forgotten how to laugh. After the "barber" was done, another sanitary worker dipped a rag wrapped on a stick into a bucket of pungent dark brown liquid, anointed our armpits and crotches, and smeared our heads, leaving a brown halo in place of our hair. Thus tattooed, ten men at a time were admitted to the sauna.

In the warmish basement space, a fire kept a large black kettle of water simmering. Devils in hell might use a similar apparatus, it seemed. The washing procedure started with a half pail of the warm water emptied on each head and a lump of green soap dropped into each palm. Then as quickly as monkeys, we had to soap up and get in line for another half pail of the warm water. Rarely did anyone manage to wash off the soap. We wiped most of the soap off when we got to our heated clothes a few hours later. We had been turning blue waiting for the clothes but quickly warmed up hunting for our own clothes in the pile thrown out into the courtyard. Some of the clothing had been singed and parts burned through, but we were overwhelmingly happy that the lice had been killed off.

Many days passed while they cleaned out all the cells and deloused the thousands of prisoners. During this time, the sick continued to die, and the burial pits continued to fill, but our hopes had been kindled. I believe I was saved by the fact that disinfection on our floor started from our corner cell, and we were among the first to be treated. I didn't get sick, and I avoided diarrhea by chewing on the coals I found in an ash pile in front of the sauna. Using coals this way was suggested by some of our Russians, who had spent time in prison before. When the lice began to increase again, we were disinfected a second and a third time. The amount of water for each prisoner had increased already with the second round. Apart from this process, I had been living without washing for the past six months. Nevertheless, both of my wounds had healed up, leaving no lingering effects. (Even today, a small piece of shrapnel nestles harmlessly inside my leg; we get along well.)

Dr. Wolf set up a hospital in the first floor of the women's building, and all the sick prisoners were sent there. I don't know how many of them recovered, but they were so gaunt and weakened that death would have been welcome to many of them. Dr. Wolf was everywhere during June in his white smock and white hat, walking around without guards. Once, as I stood by the coffee kettle, I saw the German doctors go into the kitchen to fill their cups from the guards' kettle. They were doing well now, and they had earned it by saving thousands of lives. It's frightening to imagine our fate if someone like Dr. Wolf had not been there.

One morning in early June, a guard opened our cell door and called out, "*Na rabotu!*"[154] We thought this meant cleanup work in the corridors or courtyard or digging pits for the toilets or the dead. We were in a feeble condition but went gladly for the chance to find a cabbage leaf, a potato peel, or a bread crust. This time, the guard chose mostly big men, such as Saimnieks, a few other Latvians, as well as me. He picked from other cells too, and we formed a group of twenty men. He led us to the prison gates and to a truck with a canvass covering over the back. We climbed on board, guards with rifles at the corners. The gates were opened. And we drove out of the prison. Stunned, we gazed out the back at the city ruins sliding by, then at the road bordered by grass, then bushes, then trees. We hadn't seen so much green in a long time. In the area around the prison, all the leaves had been torn off and the grass pulled up, and trees didn't grow there. We couldn't get enough of the summer greenery and the nearly forgotten beauty of nature.

After a half-hour's drive, the truck stops on a forest path next to a pile of felled trees. We're ordered out of the truck and shown the borders of our working territory. Guards take up positions at the four corners, and we are handed a number of two-man saws. We are to prepare firewood for the prison, a tough job the first day at least. We're not used to pulling a saw, and we are dizzy from the forest air and the effects of our prolonged idleness and lack of food. But the guards are tolerant and do not hurry us unduly. We spend more time sitting against tree trunks than pulling saws. The hardest worker is Saimnieks,

---

[154] "Let's go to work!"

whom one of the guards singles out for praise: "*Mologec, Fric, mologec!*"[155] Working with another Latvian, Saimnieks piles the logs into the truck, with only slight assistance from the rest of us in our weakened state. But this trip to the forest has been a wonderful experience after so many unchanging days, dragging out from the toilet barrel in the morning to the toilet barrel at night.

Next morning, they call out Saimnieks and tell him to assemble a team for more work in the forest. Despite his poor Russian, Saimnieks deciphers the commands. He picks all the Latvians from our cell and as many more from the neighboring cell. Rizhik does not object, since physical labor is not to his taste. We are happy to be all by ourselves for the first time. A beautiful sunny summer day awaits us. We drive back to the same spot in the forest to saw the felled trees into logs. We have kettles and spoons along, since we'll be in the forest till late at night. There are only two guards this time, both familiar to us from yesterday. For lunch, we've been given some American canned goods, to which we have to add a soup that we prepare ourselves. Saimnieks designates one of the weaker men to be our cook and sends him to hunt up some wood sorrel and other grasses for the soup. The truck driver lends us a pail, the guards some matches; the cook finds some water and collects dry wood. We have all we need.

After working a while, we loosen up and try to talk to the guards. They're reasonably well-disposed toward us, if for no other reason than because we are not Germans. Gradually, we get into discussions about the war, home, wives, and kids. When words are inadequate, we add gestures and mime. The guards learn that we are not only "Fascists" but also people. We get to know the guards better as well. They want to go home to their families too, and they're tired of guarding prisoners who are not really criminals. After four months, we hear again the promises of simple soldiers—words that enter a prisoner's soul like a balm: "You Latvians will soon be going home. Very soon!" Later, we heard the words "*Skoro, skoro!*" (Soon, soon!) quite often. Logic said the words were empty promises, but in our illogical hearts, we wanted very much to believe.

We have won the trust of the guards. Every morning, they call only our group, headed by Saimnieks, to provide the firewood. With every day, we're able to do more, thanks to the improved food, the fresh air

---

[155] "Way to go, Fritz, way to go!"

and sunshine, the chance to move around. We chew on pine needles, new shoots of fir, bark from oak trees (good against diarrhea). The forest is our fountain of health.

In the prison, typhus has been arrested, at least in our building. After four trips to the disinfection station, all the lice should have been wiped out. We sleep better at night, on a warmer floor and away from the toilet barrel. The summer continues warm and dry. We have been to the forest ten times already with these guards we have come to know. They're decent guys. The older man, Bakka, is quite convivial. At times, he calls us *hlopci* (boys) as though we were his sons, not prisoners. There's plenty of firewood in the forest, and we have learned how to collect it efficiently. We work hard in the morning, then brew our soup at mid-day, and take it easy in the afternoons. How wonderful to lie back in the moss, gaze up at the treetops, and listen to the birdsongs. At those times, the war, captivity, and prison all seem like a bad dream that's behind us. The guards sit against their own trees, weapons in their laps or even on the grass beside them. They chat, smoke, and occasionally share their smokes with us. There's almost a friendly feeling between us.

One day, we see a Pole, a forest ranger, coming down the trail with a *Berdanka*[156] on his shoulder and a long-stemmed pipe in his teeth. He looks at us "Fascists" with reserve but begins a conversation with the guards. He speaks in Polish and Bakka in half Russian, half Ukrainian, but they understand each other well enough. He says his house is nearby, and the younger guard agrees to go with him to get some onions for the soup. They leave, deep in conversation. Now we are thirteen prisoners and one guard. It wouldn't be hard to overpower the old guy, tie him up and gag him, and disappear into the woods before the other guard returns. The truck won't be coming for the logs for another few hours, and in that time, we could be far away. Another chance like this might not come. Is it likely they would keep sending only our group to gather the firewood? They could very well send a group from another cell next, and then our days of freedom would be at an end.

We sit in a cluster and try to decide: do we flee or stay put? Some think we will really be set free anyway. What sense is there in feeding

---

[156] Russian hunting rifle, originally invented by American Hiram Berdan in the nineteenth century.

thousands of nonworkers when there's such a demand for workers after the war? If they let us go, they'll give us a document to board a train going toward Latvia. It would be foolish to risk all that before being released and ruin everything. Others point out that we are not strong enough to get far enough away to escape from the area. The Poles are likely to deny us shelter, looking as we do, and send us back to prison. There's also Bakka, dozing peacefully under his tree; how could we attack someone like that? We could get his rifle, but we would have to split up anyway to avoid detection. Hide in the forest? Maybe, but for how long? At least now we can count on a daily piece of bread that a fugitive couldn't.

But what if the experienced old Russians in our cell are right? They're predicting we will all be sent to Siberia. Whom to believe, and what to do? It feels like our brains are in a fog, and our feet are hobbled. We remain sitting until the other guard returns with a bunch of onions in his hand. The opportune moment is past, and we have to rely on fate to give us another chance at another time, if ever. This is the third time in our captivity that we have let the opportunity to escape slip by.

At the beginning of August, they organized a number of prisoner gangs for work outside the gates. Our main task was to dismantle German factories and send their contents to the USSR. The results of this campaign were pitiful. Neither the guards nor the prisoners took any pains in breaking down and packaging the machines. We knocked together some rough crates, threw the machine parts into them, nailed up the crates, and loaded them on to open railroad cars. Half of the cargo sent out got scattered at the other end or rusted for months in some uncovered Russian storage facility exposed to the rain and the snow. The Soviets gained little value from these dismantled German factories.

A more productive work assignment was the clearing of ruins. Our first targets were the main streets and roads, chosen to improve the routes for military traffic. For this kind of work, there was no need for intelligence or precision; our directions consisted of *"Davai, davai!"* (Come on, let's go!), and that was enough. The prisoners fashioned their own wheelbarrows, chipping tools, and crowbars and day after day moved the stones and bricks and everything else left over from the destroyed buildings. Our unofficial orders were to take it easy and at the right moments steal something to eat from the Poles. The guards sat on the brick piles, rolled their *mahorka* cigarettes, and now and then broke into song. How the prisoners worked and how much they accomplished didn't interest them. On the other hand, the Polish foremen were genuine slave drivers, who tried to drive us to exhaustion and cursed us out as damned dogs. We were used to such curses and didn't take them to heart.

There were accidents too. On several occasions, unsteady walls collapsed and buried prisoners. They were left under the rubble without particular notice. In the evening, the convoy leaders gave the prison guards the numbers of those killed, and these were crossed off the roster. Life had little value after the war too.

There were other kinds of work assignments, but our favorite job was still collecting firewood in the forest, where we felt almost like free men. The less closely we were guarded, the richer grew our mid-day soup and the less we wanted to take the risk of fleeing. We had not had enough to eat from March to August; now we could pick berries in the forest and filch a few potatoes or onions for the soup. Once, we caught a stray chicken belonging to the forest ranger; this was a world-class event. The guards generally supported our foraging activities. Sometimes in the evening, we had to wake a guard and tell him it was time to head back to the prison. By now we had become so spoiled that we wanted not only to eat and sleep but also to look good. We used the pieces of glass we found as razors. At first, we walked around with slashed faces but in time learned to trim our stubble with decent results.

The inspections in the cells came less frequently now, since most of the useful stuff had been taken already and our oak tree bark did not interest the guards. Any food we managed to find outside the prison walls we made sure to consume on the spot so as to not tempt the guards or Rizhik. In the forest, we were warmed by the sun; on the cell floor, we were warmed by talk of going home soon, in our dreams, we were already free. Thus, we were not too surprised on the morning of September 1, when we were told to gather our possessions and prepare to go down to the courtyard. At last, the first leg of our trip home. We had spent exactly five months in the Graudenz prison, and we parted from it without regrets. Except for the past several weeks, it had not been an easy time. But it was past, and the future was going to be brighter. And we too would be able to put a period to the Second World War.

IN THE STALAG AT TORUŃ

We marched south toward Toruń.[157] Our long and ragged column had shrunk considerably from the one that dragged into Graudenz in April. Not even half of us were left. Many were lying in the mass graves of the prison, the German women had been sent home, another part remained in the cells facing an uncertain future. The NKVD screening process ground slowly and thoroughly. We were told that Toruń was a distribution point where prisoners would be sorted, and each national group would be sent by rail back to its homeland. Naturally, no one thought about escaping any longer.

The march took two days. Since the weakest prisoners had already died, the column moved faster and more smoothly than in spring. But an observer from the side would also say we looked pitiful in our frayed and disintegrating clothes rescued from the delousing chamber, with our unshaven faces and gaunt frames. We got no sympathy from the Poles, who threw rocks and cursed us for our German uniforms. We met very few civilians, however. A strange postwar quiet had settled over the Polish fields.

Toruń, where we arrived before sundown, was the first large city we saw after the war. It was heavily damaged but full of civilian life—movie ads, music in the parks, people on the dance platforms, small shops open for business. The streets were filled with bicycles, strange covered wagons drawn by emaciated horses, even a few autos. We gazed at these sights like visitors from another planet.

---

[157] Polish city on the Vistula River, south of Graudenz. During the war, Toruń was the site of a major prisoner-of-war camp known as Stalag XX-A, which housed as many as 20,000 prisoners at its peak. Today's Toruń has a population of over 200,000.

Our prisoner column wound through the streets and stopped before a large set of gates with a sign reading *"Arbeit Macht Frei."*[158] So this was a German prisoner-of-war camp for Russians, Poles, and other inferior peoples. For themselves, the Germans had built solid barracks enclosed with strong fences. The large central field of the camp was occupied by a precise row of identical wooden barracks, with paths between the barracks and flower beds lined with white stones. However neat and orderly it had all been before capitulation, it was wild and unkempt now. The fields had been trampled, the barracks windows dirty, many of the glass panes broken and replaced by cardboard, the doors off their hinges, and paper blowing everywhere (a boon to the smokers at least).

We were divided among the barracks, which were already partly occupied, and our Graudenz social network was disrupted. We lost old comrades and gained new ones. There were actually more Latvians here in camp than in the prison. The number of barracks was impressive too—almost a whole town's worth. My barracks number was 66. At one end were the Vlasov soldiers, at the other we Legionnaires. A delightful company.

Compared to our life in the prison, the Toruń camp had both pluses and minuses. We no longer slept on a cement floor but in plank bunk beds and were able to undress at night since each of us received a thin German army blanket. The kitchen operated from morning to night, and each barracks had its appointed feeding time. The exercise field, enclosed with barbed wire, was much larger than the prison courtyard. No one was sent to work outside the camp, and we loitered near the barracks all day like gypsies. The barracks were not locked, and you could wander around the whole camp, but if you came too close to the barbed wire, you heard a warning from the guard, followed by a shot in the air if you didn't immediately move away. We all appreciated this highly relative degree of laxity.

There were unpleasant aspects as well. The interrogations began on the first night already. These were not inspections as in the prison but real NKVD interrogations like those we went through in the first days of captivity. In the middle of the night, a Chekist and a guard came into the barracks, called out names from a list, and led the men to a distant barracks with barred windows and locked doors. There in the

---

[158] "Work Will Set You Free." The same promise was inscribed in a sign above the gates of the Auschwitz concentration camp.

middle of a large room stood a table with a stool three meters before it for the prisoner. Behind the table were two lamps with bright bulbs and reflectors. (The camp had electricity in all the barracks, lights on the fields and along the outer wire, and strong projectors in the corner guard towers. The electrical and lighting system built by the Germans had not been damaged in the war perhaps or might have been repaired during the summer.)

In the interrogation room, the lights were turned toward the prisoner, while the interrogator sat behind the table in half shadow, and a guard stood by the locked door. We were questioned frequently, at least three or four times each. When I first sat on the stool in the bright lights, I remembered the first interrogation back in Praust, the killing of Antons, and everything else from that night. There was no pistol on the table this time and no translator. The interrogator, a Russian Jewish officer, took out a clean sheet of paper, posed the questions in a monotone voice and in broken German, and then wrote down the answers and his comments in Russian. The questions were similar to those asked in Praust and were repeated during the several interrogations. Likely, they wanted to compare the answers and try to uncover inconsistencies. Unlike some of my comrades, I was not badgered repeatedly about a particular issue, nor was I threatened with being shot.

Yet the night interrogations were very unpleasant. One of the prisoners from our barracks did not return one night, and the word was that men had disappeared from other barracks as well. These men were placed behind bars in another barracks. In the morning, a guard came for the belongings of the imprisoned but did not respond to any questions.

Another unsatisfactory thing at Toruń was the food. Though we were not working, we still wanted to eat. But the food here seemed even worse than in Graudenz prison. We had been spoiled by our feasts in the forest.

And then there were the lice. Our "friends" from the prison had returned and embraced us from all sides. The good doctor Wolf had been sent home, but the Toruń doctor, if he was even a doctor, paid no attention to such trivialities. This doctor was campaigning against dysentery, and lice were not in his locus of attention. Those afflicted with dysentery were moved to a separate barracks and treated there.

God was with the rest of us too, and the typhus did not break out here in September. We resolved to live with the lice, since we had to.

Idleness may be preferable to crushing physical work, but idleness is agonizing if you see no end to it. All the days in the camp at Toruń were equally monotonous and gray. The sameness was not altered if someone died, hanged himself, or escaped. We had lived through events of a larger scale in our six months of captivity. Talk of going home resumed. The camp rumors circulated with the speed of the telegraph. Every rumor spreader added his personal twist to the news and next day got it back in completely new packaging. Believe, or don't believe—your choice.

A month went by, and autumn was approaching, marked by rain in early October. We languished in our bunks all day and night. The barracks were not heated, and dankness seeped in through all the cracks. The thin and tasteless soup was cold already when served. We were sick of it all. We should have taken off that time back in the forest....

On the morning of October 4, with a light rain falling, ten men from our barracks were called out for work. I volunteered. Our workforce from the various barracks came to fifty men. They drove us through the camp gates, counting us several times along the way, and took us to the freight cars parked in the railroad yard on the edge of the city. Hundreds of red cars stood on the tracks. We were given different assignments. One group had to clean the animal wastes from the wagons, which had been used for transporting pigs and cattle. Others had to repair the floors, doors, and walls of the wagons. Still others had to install bars on the windows. Our materials were brought up in army trucks and dumped in the yard.

We also had to install a precast trough in each wagon and bore holes in the roof and floor for the cast-iron stove's flue. These projects proved to us that the rumors circulating in the camp were well-founded. We just didn't know who would be sent away, where to, and when. The Russians remained convinced that all of us would be going to Siberia. The Germans thought they would be sent to Berlin for distribution to other camps. We Latvians were the most naive, since we could only see one destination for us—Riga.

Our work in the railroad yard went on for four days. The guards, worried that someone would try to escape, repeatedly told us that we would be sent home. Did we think it strange that this same train was going to send home a Russian from the Urals, a Ukrainian from Kiev, an Italian from Sicily, as well as the Norwegian, the Spaniard, and everyone else working there? Did we believe it? Yes and no. Obviously, not everyone would be sent home. The train wouldn't stop in Poland, where there was not enough to eat, or in Germany, where there was less. It was clear that the train was being prepared for prisoners like us. It was easy to imagine our homecoming, and we embraced this hope, throwing logic to the wind.

Cattle wagon for transporting prisoners to the Gulag

It was still possible to escape from the train yard, but we held back for the same reasons as before: The Poles would give us up, and then we would never see home again. If we had known that till now we had been only in the antechamber of hell and that hell itself was yet to come, then we certainly would have tried to disappear. A day later, it was already too late.

TAKEN EAST

On October 9, 1945, about 1000 prisoners from the Toruń camp were driven to the station and loaded into the red freight cars 40 at a time. The remaining thousands might have been allocated to other trains for shipment soon afterward. Before *loading* (the precise word in this case), each man was individually searched, and any items recently acquired were taken away, including knives, mirrors, pencils, paper, etc., as well as the Toruń camp blankets, if these had somehow ended up among one's possessions. Almost no one had good clothes anymore, and if he did, they got smeared and torn by the owner to decrease their appeal. We knew well by now what would be taken away and what wouldn't.

After the fortieth prisoner had climbed into a wagon, the guards rolled the doors shut, locked them, and then wedged a rough-hewn pole across the doors. Now the shipment was secure. All twenty-five wagons were loaded in this way. At the head of the train, right behind the locomotive, they hooked on two wagons for the train commanders and the guards. Another guard wagon rode at the end of the train, and somewhere in the middle were the kitchen and the food stores. Everything pointed to a long trip in the offing.

Once underway, whenever the train stopped, guards toting automatics ran around their assigned cars on both sides, crawled underneath to check the floorboards, and ran on top of the cars from one end of the train to the other, rattling the roofs. These guards were not the lovable old guys from the Graudenz forest details, with whom we had shared soup and cigarette butts. The railroad guards were forged from different metal. They yelled and cursed at every violation of their rules, shot into the air in long bursts of automatic fire to intimidate the prisoners. Though it was early fall, the guards were already dressed in sheepskin coats and winter headgear. Their fleshy red faces testified to their ample diet as did their energy and speed in running past the wagons on the gravel embankment of the railroad. At their waists, they carried vodka in German army canteens, and we could see them treating each other at idle moments on their rounds.

In the middle of the day, the wagon's interior stayed in twilight, the rest of the time in darkness, since the four small windows had been nailed shut with metal slats, allowing little light inside. We had no sense of the direction in which we were traveling. On the first day, over the course of several hours, the train started, rolled a while, stopped, reversed direction, stopped again, moved forward, and stopped again. That was the pattern. A steady movement began only at night. We squatted in silence on the wagon floor, jammed against each other, frightened, cowed by the aggressiveness of the guards, not yet adapted to a new situation. The clatter of the wheels at rail crossings, the piercing whistle of the locomotive, the jarring side-to-side motion of the wagon all left a depressing effect on us. I remembered the night of June 14, 1941, when similar convoys of red freight cars crossed the Latvian border going east. Back then, the deported had been able to bring along more possessions; our edge was in experience, in knowing more of what to expect. We were alike too; neither of us knew where we were being taken and how long our trials would last.

Next morning, someone saw a sign reading Posen[159] through a window slot. We saw nothing of the city as the train backed and filled in the rail yards. New freight cars were hooked on, others were removed, then the train stood again. After a while, our wagon doors opened halfway, and two men in padded coats hoisted a milk can filled with soup inside and threw four loaves of bread after it for division among us. The soup was divisible using the cover of an army field kettle, but the bread was hard to divide without a knife, and half of the railcar occupants went without bread as a result. Later, they doled out bread already cut into pieces, but the pieces were uneven, and fights broke out in all the cars over the larger pieces. Good manners are the first to disappear among hungry people as we had learned some time ago. The longer we went hungry, the greedier some of the prisoners became and the more envious the others. Usually, the quarrels were settled through

---

[159]   German term for Poznan, a large city in west-central Poland.

sheer brute strength. Having delivered the food, the guards had no further interest in its consumption. While the train was still in Poland, the soups were good compared to those in camp, and the bread was tasty as well, but the portions seemed very, very small. In the evening, we received a can of water. It was windy and cold rolling along, and rather than drink the water, we used it to wash our faces and hands.

We were not allowed outside while the train stood in Posen. When the train began moving next day, we couldn't determine which of the wagons had been left and which added, but we could tell from the direction of the sun that we were going east. The train picked up speed and moved without stopping all the way to Warsaw. In the evening, those of us who got near the windows saw the destroyed city from a distance. I had never seen worse devastation. Here and there, life stirred amid the ruins, however.

We rode through the city and stopped at a station in a less devastated section on the outskirts. A passenger train hauling German cars filled with Red army soldiers stood on a sidetrack. At an open window directly opposite our sealed wagon stood a Russian lieutenant, carefully observing our "red box." He was attentive to our calls to other Latvians in the next car while the guards were away. Listening a while, the lieutenant raised his eyes to our barred window and to our surprise asked us, in Latvian but with a Yiddish accent, "Who are you? Why are you prisoners?" We were happy at this chance meeting and explained to the lieutenant that we were Legion soldiers who had been in a prison camp at the end of the war and now were being taken to an unknown destination. Perhaps he could tell us what they were planning to do with us.

"Well, if you're still alive, they won't shoot you now," he answered. "You'll have to go to work for a while, but then you'll be sent home. As to where you will have to work, the Soviet Union is huge. They will find a place for you somewhere."

The lieutenant added that he was in his third year of army service and was going to Berlin on assignment directly from Moscow. After the war's end, he had also been in Riga. Now our questions intensified, tripping over each other. How does Latvia look now? Is the city destroyed? What is going on there? Are Latvians being sent to Siberia as the Germans had once predicted? And so on and on.

The officer was quite gracious and answered our questions readily, though less fully than we wished. His willingness to engage in conversation with enemy prisoners ("Fascists,""Jew killers," etc.) was a very forthcoming gesture. In the Red army, you were not supposed to talk with such people if you wanted to stay out of difficulties. Fortunately, the guard was lingering by another wagon, and we learned quite a lot in those few minutes. In the lieutenant's opinion, after the victory, the bad times for Latvia were over. Those who had sided with the enemy had been forgiven, and now the people were building a new and beautiful life. We would be able to share in this beautiful life too, once we had worked off our share of the responsibility for the destruction. At that, he motioned toward Warsaw. That seemed to mean that we had turned the city into ruins and would have to build it up again.

A sudden command, *"Po vagonam!"*[160] and the passenger train to Berlin began moving. The lieutenant waved a hand, and the departing train disappeared. I was glad that, just that morning, I happened to be standing by the barred window and was able not only to hear but see a little too. After this unexpected encounter in a Warsaw station, my zest for life had returned. Riga was not destroyed. Latvians were living in Latvia. Then our relatives and friends were still alive, and we might meet again someday. It turned out too that Latvians (or at least Latvian speakers) had also served on the other side of the front. So the war had torn apart our nation as it had so many other nations and people. After his assignment in Berlin, the lieutenant was going to demobilize and return to Riga. Maybe we would get home even sooner than he.

The trip settles into an irregular routine. We ride for a time and then stop on a sidetrack to let other trains go by. Demobilized soldiers are going back east; other soldiers—the "guardians of Europe"—are being sent west to the borders of the Soviet zone in Germany. We wait on very long trains filled with the plunder of war—machinery, worktables, everything that can be disassembled and transported— and on very long trains carrying cows, horses, hogs, sheep. Why did the Fritzes scrimp on food so much during the war when they had so much livestock? Hour after hour, the wagons zip by with their live and inanimate cargo. Where will it all end up, and who will make use of it?

With the rails finally cleared, we resume our ride east till we pass Grodno[161] and the last Polish signs. Then we're in Soviet territory. Our

---

[160]   "Back in the wagons!"

[161]   City on the Polish-Belarusian border.

ride slows again, we are shunted onto a sidetrack, and we stay in place all next day and night. What we can see of the surroundings is bare and monotonous, with few civilians about. Our measure of passing time extends from the soup and bread in the morning to the water can in the evening and then to the next day's soup. For now, there's just enough to eat to ward off starvation. Our wagon holds six Latvians, three Poles, eleven Russians, and twenty Germans. The Germans are all civilians, older people, rounded up in Prussia in February, March, and April. The Latvians are all soldiers. The backgrounds of the Poles and Russians are not clear, though they're all wearing civilian clothes. It's quite a mixed company, and I'm relieved that it doesn't include the self-serving, coat-turning Rizhik.

For the elderly Germans, the favorite and nearly exclusive topic of conversation is food. Subdued voices rise from their corner of the wagon, providing exhaustive guidance in the culinary arts—how to prepare one dish or another, how to present it on the table, where the best food deals could be found, how they had eaten and drunk before Hitler, how after him, and so on, without end or limit.

"*Ein bisschen Salz, ein bisschen Pfeffer, dann mache ich . . .*"

"*Nein, nein, ich mache das ganz anders.*"[162]

You can almost smell the lard, see the cookies and sweetbreads. When will they stop? Someone should tell them to stop torturing the rest of us, but how can we take away their only remaining pleasure? They do not swear and holler across the wagon like the Russians at their end. But these old Germans will never enjoy something delicious again. Only their memories will stay with them for the rest of their days.

At the Russian end, they're also talking about eating but without the niceties. They have no pleasant memories of the old days, but they do talk about the war years, especially the last one spent in the enemy's territory. What operations they had conducted—slaughtering German hogs and Polish cows, breaking into basement storehouses filled with food but, above all, the vodka, the wines, the liquors. It's amazing what riches these damned capitalists had amassed. Germany has been a real Cockaigne[163] for these Russians, and it's a shame they've had to part from it so soon. They discuss who is to blame for cutting their happy

---

[162] "A bit of salt and pepper, then I mix . . ." "No, no, I do that completely differently."

[163] An imaginary land of luxurious and idle living.

days short. "*Sam ja bil durak vovremja nesprjatalsja.*"[164] These Russians along with the Germans understand that their game is played out, that only memories remain. Neither will escape the clutches of the NKVD.

The Poles are always together, hatching some sort of plans, which never materialize. They stay away from the Germans and show their contempt by never replying to them, though they know German. The Poles lean toward the Russians. They're polite but reserved toward us.

The quietest are the Latvian boys. Our mood changes with each stage of the route: despair in the beginning, a surge of hope after meeting the lieutenant in the Warsaw station, gloom again at the desolate sight near the Soviet border. But now the train heads north, toward Latvia, and our spirits lift.

Next day, we are in Vilnius and getting closer to home. We're headed for Daugavpils, for Latvia. In the city, they will surely take the Latvians (and maybe the Poles) off the train and send them on to Riga. The rest will likely go on to Russia. How else? The Germans are the enemy; they're headed for Siberia. These Russians fought against their own army or surrendered to the Germans at the wrong time and place. They are enemies of their people, traitors, and they are also headed for Siberia. When the peace agreement is signed between Germany and Russia, the Fritzes will be able to return to their *Vaterland*. But we will soon be home again. How will they receive us there? Will they set us free right away, or will we have to clear ruins while we wait for the necessary papers? Whatever happens, we'll be home.

We cross the Latvian border at night and in darkness. We're received without fanfare in Daugavpils, where we stand several hours with wagon doors closed, hearing only Russian on the platform outside, no Latvian or the Latgalian dialect.[165] All the Latvian boys are by the wagon windows, peering into the darkness but gaining no recognition or understanding of the situation. The train jerks forward and back, cars are hooked on and others unhooked. "To be expected," we tell one another. We'll be brought together and put on the detached wagons and sent to Riga. It's all according to the script in our heads.

Finally, the train starts up, the guards yell out their usual warnings, and we are rolling again. In our excitement and joy, sleep is impossible, though we can see nothing outside. I reckon it might be October 30,

---

[164] "I was the idiot myself that I didn't hide in time."

[165] Spoken in Latgale, the easternmost province of Latvia.

but what does it matter what day we arrive back in Riga? With daybreak, we look for familiar landmarks in the landscape but find nothing other than woods, clumps of bushes, half-harvested fields. The autumn rain casts a grayish tinge over everything. It looks just like Poland . . . or Lithuania. We ride on. Shouldn't we be coming up on Krustpils?[166] It's raining without letup. We stand somewhere for a long while and then ride again. The Germans and Russians are dozing resignedly, waiting for the next soup allowance. But the Latvians are on tenterhooks, waiting for glimpses of the landscape of home, snatches of the familiar language.

The wagon doors open at a station, and the soup and bread are loaded on. Our car is distant from the station building, and the guard does not tell us the station's name. This soup is worse than in Poland, with almost no fat content. The wheels resume their drone, the crossing switches clatter, the wagon swings from side to side on the uneven rails. "*Polotsk!*"[167] yells one of the Russians by a window. Polotsk? But that's in Russia! The word drives all six of us into a dark hole, into hopeless despair. It's clear now that we will not be seeing Latvia.

We ride on east. The next station is Vitebsk,[168] where I'm reminded of Father's stories about serving in the local hospital during the First World War. Anything I manage to see through the window slats is so rundown and depressing that I stop looking, wrap myself in my frayed blanket, and lie down in a corner. The dream of reaching our homeland is dead. Our destination is Siberia as the Russians had predicted. I feel myself sinking into apathy. After nearly a month of enforced idleness and unvarying, non-nourishing food, our depression grows in force.

We undergo further delays on the route to Smolensk, including standing in place for two days and nights. Finally, we pick up speed and reach the suburbs of Moscow. We can't see the city, but there's a glow in the darkness now. This is the heart of Russia, a city of millions, almost reachable from our train. A new rumor sweeps the train, rising from an unknown source as always. At the distribution point in Moscow, they will separate us by nationality and by degree of guilt and then send each group in a different direction. Latvians and Estonians will go back to

---

[166] Latvian town 100 kilometers west of Daugavpils (i.e., on the way to Riga).

[167] The Belarusian town of Polatsk, about 175 kilometers east of Daugavpils and the Latvian border.

[168] Another 100 kilometers east from Polatsk.

the Baltic region, the Poles back to Poland, and just the Germans will remain to help build the Soviet Palaces of the People over the ruins of the churches. A new hope stirs in the Latvians. After the Russian victory in the war, Moscow is now almost a center for all Europe. They will judge, differentiate, and distribute us; and here, we will finally gain justice (so went our logic). As reinforcement for the rumor, we are let out of the freight cars in small groups and led to a nearby pond to wash up. The guards hold their weapons in readiness and yell their heads off if anyone tries to go into the bushes to relieve himself. Next to the rails, there's a pump where we line up to get some fresh drinking water drawn from a well. It tastes delicious. The air is cool, but we are invigorated at being able to wash and move around and feel new energy in our bones after a month of wasting away in the wagons.

But our joys are brief. The number of railcars is great and the number of prisoners forty times greater. The older, weaker prisoners have yet to reach the water when the guards call out, *"Po vagonam! Davai, davai!"*[169] I manage to pump some water into my field kettle and dash back to the wagon. It's a wonder we can still run. Then the inspection, the body count; then the doors close, and the pole slams across. Now there's a totally different feeling in the wagon. We speculate intensely and long: there must be a camp nearby, and tomorrow they'll begin the sorting, and then our ride to the east will be over.

It's November 7, 1945.[170] I remember this date well because, that morning, our train began to approach Moscow itself. Through the car windows, we caught glimpses of holiday finery. Buildings were hung with flags, people dressed up, apparently heading toward the city center. The route of our pleasure excursion, however, did not include the Red Square with its military processions and the living, breathing Father, Teacher, and Humanity's Best Friend[171] standing on the roof of the Mausoleum. Our train took a circuitous route around the city center that lasted two days. Of course, no one would be dealing with our affairs during the holiday. Not that we were in such a hurry now.

---

[169] "Back in the wagons! Hurry up!"

[170] The twenty-eighth anniversary of the Bolshevik Revolution, which took place on October 25, 1917, by the Julian calendar then used in Russia, or November 7 by the Gregorian calendar adopted in January 1918.

[171] Stalin, as characterized in Party propaganda. He and other notables stood in review atop the Lenin mausoleum.

On Victory Day, May 9,[172] all of us in the Graudenz prison had been treated with American canned goods. On the 28th anniversary of the Soviets' October Revolution, the prisoners received the same rations as always. Now the celebrations were only for the people outside the prisons; the rest of us would have to spend a little time "waiting by the wagons." I was fortunate in receiving my first *gorbushka* (end piece of bread with extra crust) on this day, a small prize but welcome. Yet I was far more interested in identifying the distribution point and estimating the time of our release from the freight cars.

Standing in a suburban station, we noticed barrels being loaded on to a large gray freight car. ("Herring," said the Russians.) The gray car was added to our train, right after the two locomotives[173] at the front. Our train moved out and soon picked up speed, rolling along without interruption. The last buildings and garden districts on the outskirts of Moscow disappeared from view. We entered the region of forests and the broad fields of the kolkhozes (collective farms), unharvested and carelessly tended in places. We had lingered three days and four nights in Moscow. It was time to quit enjoying the comforts of the capital; we were being called to the "sunlit distances" of the land. The barometer of our morale fell below zero once again, along with any hopes of redirection toward home. All of us finally understood: There would be no return path. We were going to Siberia.

We put Vladimir behind us, then Gorky,[174] catching sight of both cities only partially and from a distance. Farther on, we entered a vast forest region, with only trees flashing by on both sides for hours. The track became more uneven, and the wagons jerked from side to side. We had had lots of experience with all this. We had become insensitive to the clatter of the wheels, the smell of our own wastes, even to the unremitting draft that accompanied us the whole way. But now our spirits had been gravely wounded, and the future looked uniformly bleak. Conversations died out, and everyone drew into himself, sinking into indifference.

---

[172] While the rest of the Allies celebrate Victory in Europe (V-E Day) on May 8, the Russians celebrate their victory a day later as a way of emphasizing Russia's sacrifice and major role in defeating the Germans.

[173] A second locomotive had been added at the Soviet border.

[174] Vladimir is 187 kilometers east of Moscow; Gorky (today named Nizhny) is on the Volga River, 400 kilometers east of Moscow.

We were a week en route from Gorky to Kirov,[175] though this is normally a six-hour trip. The farther northeast we traveled, the slower our progress. At some small station, we were shunted onto a sidetrack, where we stood a long time. As unpleasant as our travel had been, this idling in place was worse. We were forty unwashed people crammed together and unable to stretch our legs. Though we all shared the same fate, we found it increasingly difficult to stand one another in these circumstances. Intolerance and unkindness spread their tentacles among us.

Winter had already begun in Kirov (where it might have been November 20 or so).Though there was little snow as yet, the cold was setting in.We were on a side track again.I wondered if the June 14 victims traveled north as slowly too.Beyond Kirov, in a thick forest setting, our train stood again for a long time, moved ahead a while, stood again, and so on, till the beginning of December. These wagons had been our home now for two months. We were let outside a few times when they needed firewood for the cast-iron stoves. We did not see the wood gatherers, but it was our task to bring the firewood inside. We felt dizzy in the fresh air outside, staggering around like drunks. The hopes of warming ourselves by the stove gave us the energy to crawl outside and bring back a few armfuls of kindling. Overcome by apathy toward everything and everyone, however, the old Germans did not stir from their corner. The guards left them alone since there were plenty of others who wanted to move around a bit.

The landscape became more mountainous beyond Kirov and the thick beautiful forests more sparse. Leaf trees were replaced by conifers. There were a few civilians still to be seen in the Kirov district, but the farther north we went, the fewer the people, not counting the railroad guards and the service staff in the railroad stations. The countryside was increasingly bare and impoverished. But we could stand this bleakness better than the hunger, and the stretch between Kirov and Kotlas[176] claimed many lives. Our old companions, the lice, stayed with us the whole way, though we had almost learned to ignore them. Maybe an infectious illness took over the wagon; maybe it was

---

[175] Kirov, formerly Vyatka, is a city on the Vyatka River, about 790 kilometers northeast of Moscow.

[176] Town 970 kilometers northeast of Moscow.

weakness from hunger. No one was looking for reasons then; no one was interested in our well-being. There were no doctors or medicines.

In the last analysis, no one outside cared what happened inside our freight cars. The guards watched to make sure the prisoners did not escape; others made sure the prisoners were fed once a day with "warm food" (if a tasteless, watery, and completely cold soup could be called food). Others made sure the train moved or stood in place when so ordered. Nobody was told to make sure the prisoners arrived at their destination alive. It seemed to us after a while that there really was no endpoint to this journey and that we would keep traveling as long as anyone was still alive in the wagons. Perhaps that was too dire a projection, but it was clear that no one would be held responsible if a sizable portion of the prisoners did not reach the final destination. Plenty of forced labor was becoming available in 1945, and if the number of new arrivals was less than projected, it only meant fewer mouths to feed.

The first to die were the older Germans. In the region of Kotlas in December, the trackside became the final resting place for many Germans and those of other nationalities as well. As we entered the taiga[177] region, disposal of the dead fell under a new order of procedure and new rules. It would be overstating things to talk of cemeteries or even graves. When the train stopped, the guards walked around the wagons and checked the roof, the floor, the walls, and the doors. Then they opened the door a few inches and yelled, "*Vse?*" (Everybody there?). Our part was to tell them the numbers of the dead (not bothering with the numbers of the sick). If no one was dead, the doors were rolled shut with a mighty clang, to be opened again at the next delivery of the soup can.

When there were dead prisoners to report, the guard climbed into the freight car and checked each body to confirm fatality. Usually, confirmation was achieved by a swift kick between the legs. When the guard had made sure that a prisoner was indeed dead, he ordered removal of his boots and any outer clothing in passable condition. Then the body was dragged to the doors and pushed outside onto the embankment. If the train was standing in a forest away from the railroad station, then "burial" ended when the guard had pushed the emaciated, light body into the railside ditch with his foot. If the train

---

[177] Boreal forest, largely of conifers, such as spruce, pine, and larch.

stood in a station area, two of the stronger prisoners had to carry the body by the hands and feet to the nearest pit or cluster of bushes hidden from the station's sight. The whole length of the trip, I never saw anyone buried. Who would have done that anyway? The guards were not going to get their hands dirty, and the prisoners were too weak to dig up frozen ground without shovels or pickaxes. The only tools available were the weapons of the guards.

It seemed that the Germans no longer cared what would happen to them after death. They had already prepared themselves for death, listening to the clatter of the wagon wheels for months during sleepless nights, relying only on God. Ten of the twenty Germans in our car died during December, along with two old Russians. The Poles and Latvians were still holding on, though everyone was worn to the bone. The wagon slowly emptied, and sleeping became easier. But the cold increased. When the firewood was consumed, the stove died out, and the wind blew through all the cracks. Our clothing could not keep us warm. It had been roasted in the delousing chamber in Graudenz and worn threadbare.

For a while, we tried the tactic of not informing the guards that someone had died. This ensured a larger share of bread for the rest of us. We pushed the dead body into the coldest corner of the wagon, where it stiffened in place and then froze. It rattled like a bag of sticks when thrown from the train. We were afraid to hide these bodies any longer than a few days for fear of discovery. The penalty might be to withdraw the bread ration altogether, which would be a death sentence for us within a short time.

Our Germans were not the only ones to die. There were deaths in the other cars too. All were "buried" the same way. If there were prisoner trains that came on this route after us, they passed through a region as densely littered with bodies as the battlefields of Europe, though the front had never reached this far. The war's end did not end this dance of death. It found its victims long afterward and sought to finish what had been left undone in the war.

I did little of this kind of philosophizing in the wagon then but fantasized about eating like everyone else. I stopped worrying about the growing distance from Latvia and stopped thinking about how to get back to my loved ones. I simply wanted to eat, simply to survive.

We rode by Ukhta.[178] Here and there in the taiga, we passed the prison camps. They were all built according to a standard model: a quadrangular field fenced in by three-meter high (9ft 10in) pointed stakes, with a second barbed-wire fence inside and four guard towers at the corners. Inside the second fence stood the prisoners' log barracks with small windows at the sides and a door with a porch at one end. A strong gate with a guard hut framed the camp entrance, and several barracks nearby housed the camp commanders and guards. A narrow grubby road led to the railroad station or the rail spur, where a single bulb atop a lamp post shed a weak light on a loading-unloading ramp.

That was the model. One camp might be larger, another smaller, but all were uniformly bleak and gray. Ten kilometers farther were another clearing and another camp much like the others. Then the rails started their clamor again, the forest slid by, till it faded into tundra farther north. There only stunted birches remained amid the scattered firs, dried to a bluish-green and gray color and covered with lichen.

Around Christmas, we stopped in Pechora,[179] where it appeared that our long train had lost a number of its wagons, but we continued north at a snail's pace, till we stopped and started and stopped again. How much longer?

My dark days began soon after Pechora. Till then, I had withstood hunger and cold without getting sick. To guard against diarrhea, I continued to chew on my remaining strips of oak bark and on the coals left in the cast-iron stove. My place was in a corner of the wagon, which had been a good location during the warm weather between Poland and Gorky. Then the cold set in, magnified by a sharp wind that blew through the window slats and the cracks. My German uniform blouse, shirt, and pants—unchanged for months and roasted thin in the delousing ovens—no longer kept the cold out. My worn blanket was of little help as I shivered in the cold. I felt my temperature rising. An hour later, I was shivering like an aspen leaf, and my fever intensified. I shrank into my corner half conscious, craving something to drink. Friends heated the remaining water on the stove, but this did not slake my thirst. Someone mentioned that it must be Christmas Eve.

I was tossing in a fever delirium. Sometime that night, I found myself crawling to the car doors to scrape the frost off the metal door

---

[178]   Industrial town 1,250 kilometers northeast of Moscow, at latitude 63.56 north.

[179]   Town 1,500 kilometers northeast of Moscow, at latitude 65.1 north.

mountings. The frost melted in my palms, and I smeared them over my cracked lips, imagining I was relieving my thirst. When the train stopped for a while again, I heard the Russians talking (having learned enough of the language by now to understand). They were saying that the tall guy in the corner would have to be tossed out at the next stop. They were predicting my imminent demise. Maybe this gave a spur to my stubbornness and boosted my strength enough to stand up to the fever. I did not "lay down my spoon"[180] that Christmas Eve.

Next day, the first day of Christmas, when the soup can arrived, I did not even look in that direction, but friends forced me to swallow a few mouthfuls. I slept like a dead man for two days and nights after that. About them, I remember nothing.

I can't explain how and why my temperature gradually went down. I don't recall sweating. (I do recall a similar crisis during the retreat battles in Prussia, and I can only say I withstood what I had to.) On the third day, my appetite began to return, and I gathered my strength enough to move closer to the stove. The Russians, who had been occupying the warmest places near the stove, usually did not let soldiers displace them but made room this time to let me warm up for a while. Maybe I impressed them with my ghastly appearance. Somewhat warmed up, I felt better and concluded that I was not going to die. At least not then.

The train resumed its northward route. Both days and nights stayed dark. We were nearing the Arctic Circle. After we passed Inta, the Russians said we were headed for Vorkuta.[181] Riding in uninterrupted darkness, it was easy to lose track of times and places. We had to orient ourselves during the feeding times, when the doors were briefly open. Reckoning by these moments, one of our guys scratched a row of lines with the end of his spoon into the wagon wall. That was how we counted the days from Moscow to the end of our journey and to Christmas. That was our calendar for the year 1945.

---

[180]   Latvian expression similar to "give up the ghost."

[181]   Inta is 1,845 kilometers northeast of Moscow, at 66.1 north latitude. The Arctic Circle is at 66.3 north latitude. Vorkuta is 1,887 kilometers northeast of Moscow, at 67.5 north latitude. Both cities are sites of Soviet-era forced-labor camps.

IN THE GULAG: LAGPUNKT NO. 2

On the last night of the year, our prisoner train stopped on the tracks with a clash of freight car couplings. A long whistle sounded from the locomotive, some of the wagons were uncoupled, another whistle rose in the night, and the train departed . . . without us. Five cars had been pushed onto a sidetrack a good distance from the station, whose name we never saw. The station was about halfway between the towns of Inta and Vorkuta. A kilometer away stood the established labor camp *Peresilk II*.[182] Somewhere to the northwest lay the Arctic Ocean and Novaya Zemlya[183] but to the southeast the Ural Mountains. A hundred kilometers north was the nearest and only town in the area, Vorkuta, along with its coal mines. There was a single rail line—Ukhta-Pechora-Vorkuta—and no roads for auto traffic. But there were a lot of forced-labor camps. Only Beria[184] knew how many.

At that moment, I knew nothing of all this geography or politics and had no wish to know. I was just recovering from my illness and felt very weak. My only interest at the time was in gaining some warmth and some food. Commands rang out outside, but we paid no attention and dozed on. Repeated stoppages and standing in place during an 80-day trip north had become familiar events. Things proceeded differently this time: the pole across the doors was yanked off, the doors were thrown open, and a guard yelled at us to get outside with all

---

[182] Russian term loosely translatable as "Transfer Point II."

[183] Archipelago in the Arctic Ocean north of the Russian landmass.

[184] Lavrenti Beria, head of the NKVD under Stalin during the war years, architect of the vast expansion of the Gulag system after the war, executed by his Politburo rivals after Stalin's death in June 1953.

our belongings. We saw that we had arrived in the middle of a forest; the tracks ended twenty meters ahead, beyond them only underbrush and then mature trees.

Climbing down or, more precisely, falling out from the wagon, we found ourselves in meter-high snow. The sky was clear and cold and filled with stars. The prisoners from all five wagons were herded together into one spot, so a guard perimeter could be set up. It was deemed necessary to guard ailing, weakened prisoners standing in waist-high snow in the middle of a forest above the Arctic Circle. Where would we have fled to when we could barely walk?

Our zone of detention was marked at the four corners by the campfires of the guards, some dozen of them, who remained clustered around the fires for warmth. We were to spend the night in place right here. The Russian prisoners taught the rest of us to dig down into the dry, powdery snow, or we would freeze like cockroaches by morning. We paired up, scooped out holes in the snow, and crawled inside, squatting back to back and pulling as much snow as possible over our heads. So we spent the first night drifting in and out of sleep. It helped that there was no wind. In fact, it was even warmer than in the freight cars. Our stomachs were empty, but this was in the range of our experience and so tolerable. The silence of the Arctic night was broken only by the guards calling to each other from their campfires. The prisoners were silent as though having lost the power of speech. It was New Year's Eve.

Next morning, still in the dark, we were roused by the guards and lined up to march. (Daylight arrived for only an hour or two around mid-day here; illumination came from the snow, the moon, and the stars at other times.) My belongings were on my back, with the blanket around my shoulders, my spare boots under one arm. I was still wearing the felt boots ceded to me by the tank driver last fall because they had kept my feet warmer than any others I could find. Now in the deep snow, they were unmatched, even with holes in the toes. A few prisoners were somewhat better outfitted, but no one really had anything worthwhile left. We had gone through repeated "inspections" in the past months.

The guard commander led our procession into the forest, followed by four of the guards, then the column of prisoners, and finally the remaining guards. After an hour's slow advance, held back by the weakest prisoners who needed assistance, we came to a half clearing.

There, just like Peter I, who pointed to the place he wanted to build his new capital,[185] so our guard commander declared, "Here, we will build our camp." Work assignments were given out. Some men were sent to gather and prepare firewood from the ample supply of dry branches on the ground. Others built the campfires; still others melted snow for our meal. A worn-out little horse appeared, all his ribs showing, more of a pony than a horse. He was drawing a sleigh every bit as run-down as he was, and the sleigh was carrying our food, drawing every prisoner's eyes to the boxes on the sleigh.

That was our beginning. Perhaps that was how our ancestors in the Iron Age began their lives too, building encampments in the wilderness. Yet it was not too terrible. They provided for us after all. Every day, we received a skimpy but, at least theoretically, warm meal. They passed out saws and axes, not fearing that we Fascists might kill all the guards and escape to the moon. On the first day, we felled a few dozen large fir trees and cut off the branches. (Leaf trees did not grow here, if you didn't count the occasional clumps of stunted, twisted birches.) From the fir branches, we fashioned huts with sloping roofs and covered the roofs and walls with thick layers of snow. We lived in these huts till we had finished building log barracks according to the standard Gulag design. We built three barracks—two for the prisoners, one for the guards. While the camp fence had not been put up yet, prisoners and guards lived in one "friendly" community, almost as equals.

That is one of the paradoxes of the far north—that under the force of necessity imposed by life's realities, the boundaries between the established rules and the actual choices made often fall away. We knew that, in time, we would be pent up behind a fence, that we might even remain there for life. Yet we willingly built our prison, hoping for a larger piece of bread now and a warmer place in the barracks the next day. On a given day, we and the guards alongside us hoisted the same logs so that, the next day, they could point their weapons at us and yell out the familiar warnings, "One step to the right or one to the left is an escape attempt! I'll shoot without warning!" We were happy—if that was the word—that our arduous journey in a closed freight car had ended, that we had stayed alive, and that now, working in the forest, we would be fed twice a day—once in the morning before going out

---

[185] St. Petersburg, which Peter the Great founded in 1703 at the head of the Gulf of Finland and to which he moved his capital in 1712.

to work, and again in the evening after returning. So little is needed for people to feel better off than before.

Many of the prisoners sent to the north in the postwar period were placed into established labor camps. We started from scratch in the middle of the forest, our snow-covered huts made from fir branches were replaced by log barracks, and the camp of only a few barracks grew into the much larger settlement called *Lagpunkt*[186] *No. 2.* New *zeks* (prisoners) arrived, and we built four more barracks, a stronger fence, a guardhouse, and gates. Then we built a kitchen, a storehouse, a bread-cutting room, a sauna, and an isolation chamber. We all took part in these construction activities, which were led by the many specialists in our midst: the builders, carpenters, and other masters of their trades brought here from all over. There was no lack of lumber, moss was available to fill the cracks, and we found ways to make up for the lack of materials, such as window glass and nails and other basic items. Using wooden pegs to hold the logs together, our carpenters built all the barracks without nails, to my amazement.

Our food rations, tools, and clothing were supplied from the main work camp near the railroad station. The only means of transport for this purpose was the minihorse we had seen on our first morning in the forest. Several more of these little animals came to our *lager* in time. They were quite hardy, though they were fed only dried birch branches. We couldn't understand where they found the strength to pull their considerable loads through the snowdrifts.

Model of a Gulag barracks

---

[186]   A smaller-scale labor camp in the Gulag system.

In the beginning, we were a camp of 200 prisoners with a certain level of organization and few conflicts. When another thousand *zeks* arrived over the next few months, a typical Russian disorder emerged, with various self-proclaimed bosses and various privileged types jockeying for precedence; all these loafers lived off the efforts of the rank-and-file prisoners. The camp commander and the guards reacted arbitrarily to these dislocations, and the hardened criminals exploited and brutalized the political prisoners, ruling the barracks to suit their own desires.

So as the newspapers might report, we had worked harmoniously to build our little *Lagpunkt No. 2*. That was one side of the coin. To describe the other side, I would need the pen of Solzhenitsyn.[187] Though I feel incapable of the entire task, I will sketch out some episodes, a small part of all we experienced and lived through.

At six in the morning, a guard hammers on a section of rail hung by the camp gates. In each barracks, the head man yells, *"Padjom!"* (Get up!) If a prisoner is slow to hop out of bed, he gets a whack or two from a stick on the soles of his feet; if he's still in bed, the head man unleashes a volley of three-story-tall curses in his ear and shakes him up and down. If, after all that, the prisoner stays in bed, it's clear that he is sick (and is sent to the infirmary), or he's dead (and is carried outside so he's not underfoot). Working in the forest, a few of the prisoners have been killed by falling trees; but in the camp, the criminal types also kill other criminals, though more often their victims are the political prisoners.[188] The most common cause of death is starvation. So death is available in many forms, and one does not have to look far to find it.

The dead man's clothes are removed, and a wood chip marked with his name or number is tied to his foot. The body lies at the edge of the camp overnight and is then taken outside the fence and laid down under a layer of snow. This is largely symbolic, since by the next night, the wolves have done their work. In the summer, after the ground has thawed, the prisoners dig a meter-deep pit for the bodies, but the

---

[187]   Author of *The Gulag Archipelago* and *One Day in the Life of Ivan Denisovich*, accounts drawing on his own experiences in the Gulag (1945–53).

[188]   Political prisoners were those sentenced for ideological reasons, such as membership in a social class or a profession or ethnicity (e.g., Kulaks, Poles, Jews, Balts, Jewish doctors, project managers, airplane designers), or for a long list of other offenses that varied according to the perceptions and suspicions of the Soviet leaders.

animals manage to pull these bodies out as well. The wolves do not attack people during the day, but at night, they operate by their own laws. Listening to the chorus of wolf howls, we understand that they are frequent visitors in large numbers in our *lager* territory. In the forest, they keep their distance, likely intimidated by our fires and the sound of axes and saws. There are brown bears too and many smaller animals. Life above the Arctic Circle is abundant.

A day in the barracks opens with an important objective—to wrap one's feet thoroughly in any and all available rags, traded for or stolen. Dried moss is also used, but paper is scarce and newsprint even scarcer. The January–February temperature holds in the range of minus 20 to minus 40 degrees Celsius (minus 4 to minus 40 Fahrenheit). Frostbite is a constant threat to hands, noses, and other uncovered parts of the body; but the most frequent area affected is the toes of the feet. (Here, my felt boots from the tank driver have served me well, much better than would the common leather work boots.)

Once dressed, our work group hustles to the kitchen window, carrying a little board listing our names, and jealously monitors the distribution of the food. There are few incidents in the mornings, since all the portions are the same—a cup of soup and 300 grams of bread (10.6 ounces). We tote this food back to the barracks, where we don't have much time to enjoy the breakfast experience. Everyone wolfs down his portion. The soup—a *balanda*[189]—is composed of a half liter of water (about one pint), in which float some ringlets of fat, shreds of cabbage, an occasional pea-sized potato (the only kind that grows locally), and a fish head or bone. If our group is first to be fed, we get some warmth into our stomachs; if we're last, the soup is cold. So we try to be among the first every morning, but so do the other groups, and some must be satisfied with a watery soup without warmth.

The bread is baked in brick-shaped sheet metal forms smeared with fish grease or, more often, with a tasteless, odorless concoction we call "axle grease" that comes in barrels from the storehouse. When we receive our bread ration, we try to get an end piece with crust, which tastes better and is more nutritious than the soft middle pieces. When breakfast is wolfed down, we hustle to stand with our work groups by the gate in a column four abreast. Each group leader is responsible for his ten men and the *prorab* (foreman) for all the groups together. The

---

[189]   Drawn from plants of the goosefoot family, including spinach and beets.

prorab's status is somewhere between that of a free camp leader and a prisoner. In fact, the *prorab* is a prisoner but one with many years of camp experience who has "earned" his way into the work leader position and enjoys certain privileges. Only the camp commander and the guards have authority over the *prorab*.

Each work team at the gate counts its own members and informs the team leader, who recounts and informs the *prorab*. Once the *prorab* informs the guard commander of the total number assembled, the guards begin their own count, not relying on the received information. Two guards walk down the column on either side and tap each man standing on the outside with a stick and count in a loud voice, "*Raz, dva, tri...*" (One, two, three ...) If they lose track in the middle, they pause to relieve their frustration with a stream of curses and begin again, until both guards arrive at the same number. It's a process much like Ķencis counting the Čangališi in the Slātava Tavern.[190]

The counting process would be laughable if it weren't tragic. Standing for an hour in minus 40 degree temperatures meant frostbitten fingers and toes for many prisoners. I remember an occasion when the gate guard was already moving to open the gate, but the guard commander felt that the count was still not right. Or maybe he just wanted to demonstrate his authority. "Everybody, ten paces back!" he shouted. While the guards drove the prisoners away from the gate, the commander went back into the guard hut to warm up. He was wearing a thick lambskin coat with a high collar, a winter cap with earflaps, lambskin mittens, and new high-top felt boots; dressed like that, he could have gone to the North Pole in comfort. Having warmed up sufficiently, he came out of the guard hut, counted the first row, sent it three paces forward, counted the second row, sent it three paces forward, and so forth. If his count hadn't agreed with those of the guards, the whole process would have started from the beginning. In this case, the numbers matched up and the command was given to open the gate.

When the gates finally swung open, the march outside seemed a true salvation. Now the joints could move again, and the blood could resume circulating. Ten hours of hard labor lay ahead, but everyone

---

[190] Ķencis is a comic character in the classic Latvian novel *Mērnieku Laiki* (1879) by Reinis and Matīss Kaudzītis. A count of those present in the tavern is taken in order to divide the bill for a common meal. The count varies from one person to the next, particularly when the counter does not include himself in the total.

focused on the possibility of fulfilling and even exceeding the work norms and, for that, receiving a larger portion of bread in the evening. For that larger piece of bread, every prisoner was ready to work to the last ounce of his strength. A hellish system.

Accompanied by its guards, every group trudged toward its designated work location. With every month spent in camp, the work sites had moved farther away in the effort to find the right-sized straight trees that met the required standard. By spring, the distance from camp to the work sites had grown to a kilometer or more. The greater distances reduced our work output and thus our food rations.

We were felling trees, lopping off the branches, and heaving the logs into piles by diameter. At the end of the day, the group measured the amount of logs piled up and informed the leader. Using the minihorses and their wagons, a special work group transported the logs to the railroad station and loaded them into the freight wagons. The logs were shipped to the mines at Vorkuta and used in construction and for support in mine shafts. Compared to work in the coal mines, our forest duties were greatly preferable for the fresh air and the ability to move around. The downside was that we didn't have the right clothes for this forest work nor the right tools or transport for the logs. Our axes and saws were primitive and worn-down, but the main deficiency was that our food rations did not provide anywhere near the number of calories needed for heavy physical work. Our productivity suffered.

But over the decades, this system of work rewards had been polished to such an extent that all the prisoners strove to the utmost, even beyond their powers, and no one tried to "stretch the rubber."[191] The norm for one man had been set at three cubic meters per day.[192] For fulfilling the norm, the man received 600 grams of bread per day (about 1lb 5oz). For exceeding the norm, he might receive 700 or 800 grams, and for results beyond that, additional rewards in the form of fish, sugar, or tobacco. The prisoners kept an eye on each other to make sure no one was living off the others' labor. Because the work output was measured by a group's totals, the lazy and the incapable were reeducated and motivated by the work group members themselves. If these efforts

---

[191]   Latvian expression meaning to mark time or goldbrick.

[192]   About 106 cubic feet, thus, for example, a pile of 7-ft logs 4 ft high and 3.86 ft wide.

fell short the groups tried to rid themselves of the freeloaders by any available means, including inhuman ones.

Someone who couldn't or wouldn't fulfill the norm received only the 300 grams of bread in the morning and nothing at night. If the norm wasn't filled the next day either, the man faced the threat of being sent to the isolation cell in the bunker, where he would get water the first night and only plain soup after that. This made it difficult for the prisoner to regain enough strength to fulfill even half the work norm. Shed by their work groups, these laggards were forced to stay in camp to support other workers and to get by on the minimum rations. Those who remained in camp had only two choices: to get to a kitchen job to supplement their rations or to slowly and irreversibly waste away.

The Germans who hadn't died in Graudenz, in Torun, or on our journey north died of starvation here. Some sat down in the snow to rest, froze, and so found their eternal rest. By regulation, we had to carry the dead back to camp. We felt it as an added burden to carry these bodies in the evening through the deep snow so they could be carried again beyond the camp fence that night.

We worked ten-hour days, six days a week and often worked on the seventh as well because the plan for the camp had to be overfulfilled. The extent to which we met or exceeded the plan determined the camp commandant's pay and bonuses. It was all connected, and we were completely in the commandant's power. He could grant a day of rest on Sunday or take it away. No control over matters was exerted from the center,[193] and if unbeknownst to us it was, it ended in the commandant's quarters by his vodka bottle. Theoretically, we should have received suitable work clothes and rations; in practice, the guards sold the clothing to those being released and kept half the rations for themselves. Toward spring, a few of the older Russians with prior gulag experience registered a protest. They were immediately assigned to the hardest tasks for which they were unable to fulfill the norms. In response, their bread allowance was decreased, and they were thrown into the bunker to live, as long as they could, on plain soup and water.

During the winter months, our working days seemed longer than ten hours because daylight was limited to the hours between 11 a.m. and 2 p.m. On clear days, we could see the red wheel of the sun appear low in the sky and disappear below the horizon a few hours later. We

---

[193]   That is, from NKVD headquarters, which operated the Gulag system.

marched to work in the dark, worked in darkness, and returned again in the dark. The return was a somewhat happier event; we looked forward to the warmth of the stove in the barracks, to the *balanda* (soup), and the *gorbushka* (end crust). How often this legendary *gorbushka* appeared in our waking and nocturnal dreams. Bread was our only real sustenance, since the soup had almost no food value.[194]

We were obsessed with the formulas governing the relationship between work accomplished and food received. The basic formula 1-1 provided 600 grams of bread and one liter of soup to a prisoner who met the quota of three cubic meters of logs per day. The formula 1-2 provided 700 grams of bread for 3.5 cubic meters, 1-3 meant 800 grams of bread for four cubic meters, and so on. At five cubic meters of logs, the formula doubled the volume of soup to two liters, and the pinnacle of the reward pyramid was the 3-3 formula, granting 800 grams of bread, two liters of soup, as well as some herring or a soy pudding called *zapekanka.* Today, I would be hard pressed to consume a 3-3 portion, but back then I and my comrades were so hungry we could have eaten twice as much.

Our prisoner society had its gradations as well. The elite consisted of the work leader (*prorab*), the cook, the bread cutter (*hleborez*), the storehouse manager (*zavskladom*), and the medical orderly (who was honored with the title *doktor*). Our chances of survival depended to a great extent on these five people. They were all uneducated, crude, physically strong fellows (having eaten well on others' account). They had won their privileged positions by buying off the camp commanders. All five were long-term prisoners for criminal, rather than political, offenses. Their experience in different camps had taught them all they needed to know in their respective "professions."

The rest of the prisoners envied the elite and dreamed of replacing them. The reins were in firm hands, however. The camp commanders found the current elite useful in maintaining discipline within and outside the camp. The most powerful of the five was the *prorab*, who could assign you to the warming task of burning branches in minus 30 degree weather (minus 22 Fahrenheit) or just as readily to pull a dull

---

[194]   The high-quality rye bread baked at the *Lācis* bakery in Riga today has a calorie value of 774 for 300 grams, and 1548 for 600 grams. Even if the *lagpunkt* bread were of comparable quality, the prisoners were receiving less than half the calories needed (3,288) to maintain themselves given the hard physical labor they were performing.

saw or roll logs in the snowdrifts. The *prorab* could assign your work group to a tract of forest where even the strongest would be unable to gather three cubic meters, or he could assign the group to work a stand of good straight trees near the road for easier hauling. There were many ways to increase or lighten someone's workload.

Such decisions depended also on the resourcefulness of the work groups themselves. The details of the next workday were decided in the evening and depended on contributions (extra bead, newsprint, a pencil, etc.) left under the *prorab's* pillow. (Yes, the *prorab* had not only a pillow but also several blankets and a cabinet by his bed, just like the guards.) The elite lived at one end of the barracks, behind a partition that did not have a door, making their quarters accessible only from the outside through the door at the barrack's end. The separated area had a special stove kept burning by one of the sick prisoners confined to camp. Our *prorab* was a man of privilege and power.

The other four were lesser lords but sometimes even more powerful. Take the medical orderly. He could classify a healthy prisoner as sick, pull him out of the work group, and sign him up for *usiļennij pajok* (supplemental rations). At the same time, he could declare a sick man a dissembler and send him to the bunker on a water and soup diet. The orderly could release someone from heavy work and even assign him to the kitchen, which was the best of all assignments for its potential to snare a little extra for one's stomach. Thus, the orderly was also a man of privilege and power, and you had to learn how to get along with him.

The bread cutter was just as powerful. His domain was a corner of the storehouse, where he plied his art. The bread was baked at the main camp near the railroad station in brick form and transported to *Lagpunkt No. 2* by sled under heavy guard. The task of the *hleborez* was to weigh the bread according to the magic formulas, that is, into 300 gram breakfast portions and also, depending on work results, into 300, 400, and 500 gram sizes for the evening meal. It was quite an art. From morning till night, the sick prisoners whittled splints into match-sized pieces, which the *hleborez* used to pin additional chunks of bread to portions that hadn't been cut precisely. Often, two or three or more smaller pieces would be pinned to a main portion. This created visual assurance that the weighing had been scrupulously done. The effect on the prisoners also worked psychologically: the more the added pieces, it seemed, the more bread overall.

Bread weighing took place behind a locked door, and prisoners were forbidden to enter this sanctum. I don't think the bread cutter bothered much with the scales. So many prisoners and only one man to weigh the bread. Who could expect all the portions to be equally divided? The important thing was to create the appearance of fairness. We had no way of checking the weight of our portions anyway. If someone did protest, the result was a foregone conclusion: the bread cutter was always right. But excessive pilfering of bread by the *hleborez* was somewhat limited by his fear of retribution. It was a small thing for the criminal types—who were at least a fourth of the population—to smother someone in his sleep or dispatch him in any number of other ways. The bread cutter knew from experience which work groups could be dealt short rations and which ones had to be served correctly.

Inside the camp, bread was the same thing as money on the outside. In a regimen of low rations, it had an even greater value; it could settle the existential question, to be or not to be? The prisoners' dreams were filled with images of bread pieces pinned to larger pieces. These were really like hallucinations that lingered in the mind during the workday as much as lying in a bunk at night. These images were the fuel devised to force the prisoners to their utmost efforts and beyond.

After the work in the forest and the slogging through snowdrifts on the way back to camp, after freezing by the gate while the guards did their count again, and after we were back inside the camp, we were all consumed by a fever of expectation: it was almost supper time. Then the line by the kitchen window seemed to move so slowly, ever so slowly. But once the bread and soup were in your hands, once the disputes within your work group over uneven distribution of the food had been settled, once the fear that someone could grab your portion had been allayed, then the blissful moment of the combined lunch and supper was at hand. Some consumed their meal quickly; others ate the bread first and then the soup. Others reversed the order. Some, wishing to prolong their enjoyment, heated their cooled soup on the stove and crumbled their bread into it, simmering and stirring, trying to convince themselves that their supper had been substantial.

We found other ways to supplement our meals. Trees in the north grow very slowly because the period of active vegetation is only a few months in the summer. The growth rings on a felled tree are so dense you can hardly distinguish them. The hardy trunks and branches are covered with light-gray films of lichen, which we gathered and dried at a campfire or on the stove in the barracks and then crumpled into a powder. Then we melted snow in a kettle, poured in the lichen powder, and made a soup. Without salt, the taste was not very appealing, but if we came across a few herring bones or even a head, we had a feast.

We never tasted meat in those days. The guards did do some hunting, but they had their own kitchen outside the camp, in which we had no role and from which we gained no benefit. Likewise, we had forgotten what milk and butter tasted like. Neither cows nor goats were kept here in the north. The kitchen workers got to taste a little sunflower seed oil, but this was also not meant for the working prisoners. If you don't count the bits of herring, which were indeed highly larded, we were not getting any fatty component in our diet. The non-nourishing, monotonous rations we received further weakened our already weakened population. Gums were bleeding, and teeth began to loosen. You could pull the teeth out and push them back into the gums without pain. In that six-month period, many prisoners lost their teeth altogether.

We fought against scurvy[195] by chewing and sucking on fir needles and by eating the new shoots of fir and spruce. In late summer, we were able to find berries in the forest, and our dental condition improved. A remaining affliction was the result of too much water in our diet. We brewed fir needle teas and bread soups to increase the volume of the food, but the constant liquefaction left an impact on the heart. Feet swelled up, then faces and other parts of the body. A finger pushed into the flesh would leave a lingering impression.

Meanwhile, the heavy physical work and the meager rations knocked men out of the working ranks. With the medical orderly's blessing, they could stay in camp, but not everyone could get into the kitchen to recuperate. After cleaning up the barracks and providing firewood for the stoves, the prisoners loitered along the camp fence, hoping to find a fish head or a cigarette butt discarded by the guards. But there was little there to share among so many weakened men. To amuse themselves, the guards sometimes threw a fish head in the space between the two fences, where it was forbidden for a prisoner to go and where he could be shot. The starving prisoners gazed at the prize, yearning to reach for it but stayed back frozen with fear. When

---

[195]   A disease related to Vitamin C deficiency, characterized by weakness, anemia, and spongy gums.

the last of their strength ebbed away, they no longer climbed out of their bunks in the morning but lay unmoving with eyes open till they finally moved no more.

Yet thanks perhaps to the clean air of the northern forest, we contracted no infectious diseases in *Lagpunkt No. 2*. Nobody complained about pains of the head, stomach, or lungs. The only one to suffer from a stomach ulcer was the cook, though this affliction might have been carried over from his previous life. If not for the constant hunger, you could look on our camp as a sanatorium. And we stayed free of the lice. Not to let us off too easily though, in the summer we were beset by bedbugs. Fortunately, these revolting creatures did not convey any diseases to us. The only "patients" in the camp were those worn-down from malnutrition and those suffering from work accidents involving axes, saws, trauma, and frostbite.

Evenings were special. After supper, the prisoners hung their foot wrappings on lines near the stove, crawled into their bunks, and, in the moments before sleep, felt almost like human beings. Now they could talk about their experiences, recall the faces of loved ones, remember former times. But their thoughts were so lazy and one-dimensional they didn't stray far from the soup kettle and the spoon. Be that as it may, the stomach had been filled, and a night's rest lay ahead. Let's hope the wrappings dry out by morning…. Then came deliverance—sleep.

There was no mail in *Lagpunkt No. 2*. In the main camp (*Peresilk II*), we learned there was a mailbox and much more, including a loudspeaker on a post that broadcast radio programs. It began each morning with a rousing rendition of "Vast is my motherland."[196] (We found the last lines especially tuneful: "I know of no other country/ Where a man can be so free.") In our own camp, there was no writing paper either, but there were prisoners who wanted to write letters. This proved advantageous to the owner of the only indelible pencil stub left in the camp. While the few remaining Germans and the Russians had no interest in writing letters, a number of us from the Baltic countries did. We found some clean birch bark in the forest, smoothed it out, borrowed the pencil for a half ration of bread, and wrote home. We had to write in Russian, which we didn't really know, and could only manage a few sentences to let the receiver know we were alive. We used

---

[196] First line of "Song of the Motherland," a popular Soviet song composed in 1936 by Isaac Dunaevsky.

no return address, since *Lagpunkt* or *Peresilk* would be unhelpful guides to our location. There were hundreds of these camps in the Gulag.

Since no one was at home for me anymore, I wrote to Sapuļi.[197] We folded the strip of birch bark into a triangle, wrote the address on the outside, and, parting from another half ration of bread, gave the letters to the minihorse driver to drop in the mailbox at *Peresilk II*. Maybe he actually did mail them, but as it turned out, no news from our *Lagpunkt* ever reached Latvia. The Russians in our camp were smarter; they ate their bread themselves and did not entertain any hopes of contacting relatives or friends. In my time in the camps, I never received any mail, although I had sent out four birch bark letters. But I did not allow myself to become disillusioned. Life had taught me to live with disappointment.

A serious cold spell set in during February (1946). After three men froze to death one day in the forest, the camp commandant decided to keep the prisoners in the barracks on minimum rations. Only a few of us had padded coats (*fufaikas*), and many of us would have perished in our frayed German army clothes. An assortment of old but clean clothes was brought over from the main camp and divided among the prisoners, giving precedence to the stronger forest workers. None of the *fufaikas* fit me, but I did gain a winter cap with earflaps and some good foot wrappings, which helped keep my exposed toes from freezing. We idled in camp for three days, until the cold eased. Since the need for logs in the Vorkuta coal mines was constant, we returned to the struggle according to the food-for-work formulas, though our ranks had been thinned.

Because of the drier air, it's easier to stand minus 40 degrees in the Russian north than back in Latvia, which draws moisture from the Baltic Sea. Another climate difference is that in the north, from October to May, it remains winter, with no thaws or slush confusing the issue. The snow gets slightly denser in May but does not melt till the end of the month when the temperature rises, and winter is gone within a few weeks. At the beginning of June, there are still snow islands in the forest, but the trees are quickly putting out buds, the grass is growing, and the frozen world revives as though responding to a wizard's wand. Tiny multicolored flowers bloom everywhere, birds sing, and we are

---

[197] Formerly (before collectivization) a farm owned by the author's maternal aunt Marija.

amazed to realize that not only wolves and bears can survive here. The brief vegetation period burgeons, making use of a meager sun to fulfill the commands of nature.

In June, our emaciated bodies began to recover. The death rate went down. Though the sun did not heat the air, it filled the forest with light. The days were very long now; the nights shrunk almost to minutes. The sun sank behind the horizon only at 11:30 p.m. and was up again at 1:00 a.m. Around *Jāņi* (June 24), we noticed the sun slowly sinking toward the horizon and then quickly rising again, leaving the night bright as day. These were the real white nights, much brighter than the ones they talked about in St. Petersburg.[198] It would have been hard to sleep in this light if we hadn't been so tired after the long hours of work. Freed from the cold, we shed some of our clothes and let the sun caress our bare skin. It was summer.

Our delights were short-lived. After *Jāņi*, the gnats and tiny flies descended on us, finding the low marshy area around our camp an ideal breeding ground. A few hours after beginning work, we were bitten everywhere and swollen like measles sufferers. Wrapping rags around exposed skin still left faces and hands vulnerable. The bites were painful and itchy. The tiny flies crawled into our eyes, ears, and noses. The only relief was to crouch within the campfire smoke, but this was unacceptable to the work team aiming for larger rations. We tried smearing ourselves with mud, but the little flies kept attacking our eyes, crawling under the eyelids till the eyes swelled shut.

As usual in a Russian operation, countermeasures were sought only after the production plan was threatened. A supply of gauze sacks was brought over from the main camp. We pulled these sacks over our heads, protecting the eyes, but leaving noses and other parts of the face that touched the gauze open to continuing attack from the tiny tormentors. Our vision and breathing were also affected, and soon we pulled the sacks off. We staggered around with swollen faces and hands until the camp commanders hit on the solution of switching the workday to night.

Starting in July, we went to work at nine in the evening and came "home" at seven in the morning. The change had several advantages: it was cooler at night, and we sweated less and attracted fewer gnats as

---

[198]   St. Petersburg is at 59.6 north latitude, about the same as Oslo. *Lagpunkt No. 2* was above the Arctic Circle, which is at 66.3 north latitude.

a result (who might also have been sleeping). On the other hand, it was harder to sleep during the day, not so much because we were unused to the time frame but because the bedbugs had multiplied so much they were able to suck up all the blood the gnats had left in us in the forest. The army of bedbugs had grown so vast you only had to draw a hand across your chest to fill your palm with them. We lost sleep and spent most of the days fighting the bedbugs, and it was easier in some ways to spend the nights working in the forest. A cycle of torments was now complete: lice in the prison cell, gnats and flies in the forest, and bedbugs in the barracks.

There was to be a different trial for me as well. Trimming the branches from a felled tree, I swung my axe into the toe of my work boot. The blow had been strong enough to remove most of the boot's toe. After a moment, I felt a pain in my foot, and the boot filled with blood. As I took the boot off, something rolled out into the grass. It was the fourth toe of my right foot. I had sliced it off like a wedge of potato. My workmates gave me advice on how to save it: put the toe back on, tie it tightly, and it will grow back on. I tore a strip of my shirt off, tied the severed toe back on, and went on chopping branches. Yet I couldn't move on the foot and didn't last long as a worker. Our Russian work team leader cursed me out thoroughly but did allow me to sit down and prop my foot against a tree stump. A few hours later, I hobbled back to camp with the others.

The medical orderly changed my dirty foot rag with a clean bandage. "Maybe it will grow back on, maybe not," he said resignedly and sent me back to the barracks. *At least I can use my other boots with the gouged out toes now*, I thought and lay down to sleep as the sun was rising already. Then the signal to wake up sounded. I was still unable to move around, though our work group leader let me know he would not put up with this: *"Sabotažnik, simuļant! Ja ķebjā nauču, svoloč, fašistskaja gaģina!"*[199] I limped outside but didn't get to the gate before a guard headed me off, cursing with equal ferocity. There's only one response to saboteurs and fakers, he said—the isolation chamber in the bunker.

The bunker was a half-basement log structure with a small door and a miniature window. Only half the building showed above ground. To enter the bunker, you had to descend a set of sod-covered stairs leading to the basement part. The guard unlocked the door and motioned

---

[199] "Saboteur, faker! I'll teach you, you bastard, you Fascist scum!"

me inside. Impatient with my slow progress, he pushed me down the stairs and kicked me inside. I lay on the cold floor in the dark with my throbbing foot. Gradually, my eyes adjusted to the half light from the little window. I listened to the work groups being counted and recounted and the usual yells and curses. I felt almost satisfied that I had chopped off a toe but not the whole foot and that I didn't have to go to work and had been left here alone. It was good to get some rest. The space was about three by four meters, with a crude pallet in the corner, where I lay down and raised my foot higher to ease the pain. I didn't know how long I would have to stay here, but I had eaten breakfast and felt content for now. On my chest, I had a small bag of sugar that I was saving for tough times.

The bag was a relic from my service in the German army and had originally held an oval identification tag to be used in case of death on the battlefield. The tag had disappeared after our capture. (I don't recall whether I threw it away or lost it during interrogation.) The bag survived, and when our work group twice outperformed the norm in a good section of the forest, we were awarded a few spoons of sugar. I knew where to put them. I crawled under my blanket to hide from predatory eyes and poured the treasure into my bag to keep for a rainy day. I had always been frugal, even miserly, wanting to keep something in reserve.

But the saver's reserves can also be the predator's prey. Having arrived alone in the bunker, I thought about consuming my sweet treasure then but decided to delay the moment again. I had just eaten and thought I would save the sugar for a time of real hunger in case there was no food coming to me in the bunker. I slept all night peacefully. Next morning, after the work groups had been fed, a guard brought me an American tin can with water. (*How far for the Americans to reach*, I thought.) I knew that would be all for the first twenty-four hours, yet when I heard the prisoners hurrying with their mess kits to get soup, I felt a tingle in the pit of my stomach. My body was reminding me of the established routine.

The camp went to sleep. I sank into a state of half sleep, half unconsciousness. Conscious awareness had fled to somewhere outside of myself. I heard the bunker door open and felt someone next to me, who pushed me deeper into the corner and lay down murmuring something. Everything seemed all the same to me, and I slept on. Perhaps they brought water again, but I didn't get up. I didn't want anything. I had seen how the old Germans died—silently, submissively, as though transfigured. I had seen so much death in the past two years that it no longer frightened me. At one point, I felt someone fumbling around my clothes, trying to pull them off, but I didn't have the strength or the inclination to resist. I slept again—for a long time.

Then a guard was shaking me, pointing to a cup of soup. How long I had been sleeping without eating I couldn't say even today. Friends later told me it was three days and nights, but to me, it seemed much longer. I forced myself to drink the soup and felt the blood begin coursing again. Then I touched the front of my jacket. It was open at the chest, and the sugar was gone. Enraged, I gathered my strength enough to grab my neighbor by the shirt and yell, demanding my property back. There was a blow to my head, and consciousness left me again. When I came to, I heard through the low background noise in my head my neighbor calling out, "*Uberi mertveca. Ja bojus!*"[200]

Later, my Latvian friends carried me back to the barracks. The medical orderly came by, patted my cheeks, and promised me *usilennij*[201] starting tomorrow. Strange that they had starved me for three days but after that let me stay in my bunk for three days and even brought me my food. "The Lord works in mysterious ways," and that can be said about the labor camp regime as well. My severed toe grew back, though not quite in the right place, because the dressing had shifted during my stay in the bunker. I grew used to it, and it didn't interfere with walking afterward. After my three days of rest, the return to hauling logs required special effort, but I managed. And I stayed alive this time too.

In late July, an NKVD officer with documents arrived at *Lagpunkt No. 2*. We had just crawled into our bunks after working the night shift. They drove us outside, lined us up, and, calling out last names from the list, divided us into two groups. We noticed that the Russians remained in one group and all the other nationalities in the other. Our group was ordered to gather our belongings and line up by the gate. We would be going to another camp. The sick and the incapable were further separated into another group, and the rest of us were called out one by one. Once we were outside, under guard, we were told to wait. An hour later, we walked away to the south down the same road, by which we had arrived on New Year's Day in the middle of the forest

---

[200] "Take the dead guy away. I'm afraid!"

[201] The extra rations granted to the sick.

to build a camp. A lot had changed since then; all the trees had been leveled for a kilometer around the camp, and a road built from logs fastened together now led from our gate to the main camp. The logs were a precaution against heavy loads sinking into the marshy ground, which stretched away from us in all directions.

IN THE MAIN CAMP: PERESILK II

The blare of the *Peresilk II* loudspeaker greeted us a good distance from this main camp, which we had heard so much about since our arrival in the north. After the usual round of searches, we were inside again. This was a major city compared to our little *lagpunkt*. Thousands of prisoners, hundreds of guards. We were shown to a very old and very dirty barracks. All the windows were closed, the air was stale, and the barracks was a magnet for various unsavory types, probably criminals hoping to plunder something from the arrivals. They were in for quick disappointment, since we no longer had anything worth taking.

The camp had a disinfection chamber, a barber, and a sauna. To enter the sauna was an indescribable joy, despite being driven through it in such haste that we didn't quite manage to cleanse ourselves of a year's accumulation of dirt. Still, it was a welcome treat. We met Latvians from other camps, who had been sent here a few days before us. A rumor said we would be released from the camp but without permission to leave the Vorkuta region. Another rumor held we would be sent home. We had heard all the rumors before and didn't believe them anymore. But this was a camp also used for sorting and distributing prisoners, and so we were not sent outside to work but stayed in camp and lived off minimal rations, which were subject to further reduction at the hands of the numerous thieves. The fact that there was not a single stalk or blade of anything green inside the camp signaled that hunger was even greater here than at our previous camp.[202] Before every barracks sat emaciated men whose only remaining joy was to warm

---

[202] A sign that the prisoners had been plucking grass and vegetation to supplement their rations.

themselves in the sun. They were no longer fit to work, but they were kept alive by the minimal rations.

The interrogations resumed at night, with the same NKVD officer as at Toruń, comparing current and earlier testimony and checking home addresses. He was polite in his way and did not threaten anyone with a pistol. A medical exam was next. All of us received the classification "malnourished." What else could be said about men who were just bones and skin? The men with swollen hands and faces from the gnat attacks were no longer in evidence, either from recovery in the sun or from an early death.

A few weeks later, we were moved again to a camp similar to our *Lagpunkt No. 2*, this one a bit smaller and distinguished with the number 5. It was early August, and the northern summer was nearing its end. This camp was also built at the edge of a forest and linked to other camps by a road built from connected logs topped by wooden tracks. We saw our first truck traversing this road with a pile of lumber intended for construction work. We also determined that only prisoners from the Baltic states had been brought here and wondered why and what the distinction would lead to.

The workload was a light one at first—preparing winter food for the horses. We cut birch branches, tied them together into bunches, stacked them on drying racks, and built a roof of fir branches over them. The daily goal for a ten-man work group was a birch-branch stack ten meters long and two meters high. This was not a difficult task since the area was covered with the wiry little birchlets of the northern forests. The Chekists must have finally decided that we were no longer capable of the heavy work we had done the last seven months, which had sapped our strength to the limit.

On the morning of August 12, we were assembled in front of the camp gates, and our names were called out. The camp commander read an announcement, which said that, thanks to the undying generosity of Josef Vissarionovich,[203] we would become free citizens from that day, and the guards would be removed. We would, however, continue to live in the camp and to work as before and were required to stand inspections every evening. Violators of these rules would be sent back to a closed camp with guards and put on trial. Here in our open camp, we would be able to buy boots and *fufaikas* (padded jackets) from the

---

[203] Stalin, referred to by his first name and patronymic.

warehouse but only once we had earned the required sums of money. We would also have to pay for our food. So on this day, having reached the age of twenty-three, I became "free as a bird." Like the serfs who gained their freedom but couldn't make use of it,[204] so we had no place to go in this northern tundra without documents or money. Removal of the guards had a symbolic meaning at best, but we rejoiced anyway to see that the guard towers were empty and the camp gates wide open.

Bundling birch branches would not earn us enough to live on, so we volunteered for logging duties again, though we knew well how difficult this work was. We took our field kettles along to the forest and brewed our own mid-day meals. We traded the berries we picked during free moments for fish and brewed a good soup from fish heads blended with wood sorrel, which grew everywhere. The logs we cut were shipped out by truck once we moved them to the side of the road and rolled them on to the open platform of the vehicle. How dangerous this was we learned already on the second day. A log rolled back and smashed the head of a worker, who was dead on the spot. For the first time, we buried the dead man, a Lithuanian, in a halfway decent fashion. He had been our group's best worker. His newfound "freedom" had lasted a week.

August and September are autumn months here in the north. Winter arrives in October along with snow and cold. Remembering the hunger pangs of the previous winter, we sought to take advantage of the gifts of autumn and searched for vitamins. The intensive vegetation period of the short summer months generated berry clusters and whole berry regions such as we had never seen in Latvia or elsewhere. Blueberries and cowberries, in particular, were spread like a carpet over the undergrowth. On Sundays, if we didn't have to put in extra work to fulfill the "plan," we simply walked a hundred paces beyond the gates, sat down in the berry clusters, and grabbed handfuls of blueberries and cowberries. Then we moved a meter forward, sat down, and grabbed for more. Kettles were quickly filled, followed by hats and tin cans. When all available receptacles had been filled, we filled and refilled our mouths. It was quite a sight—"freed" prisoners hauling their bony frames through berry bushes, smearing their bug-bitten faces and

---

[204] In 1861, Tsar Alexander II freed the serfs to the extent that they could buy the land they were farming, but the limited acreage they were allowed, along with the high taxes they had to pay, made their emancipation a continuing struggle.

hands with the juice of blueberries. No one there found it strange, of course.

In the evening, we traded berries for bread and herring. The camp veterans and the elite prisoners did not bother with berry picking and gladly traded for ours. The berries enriched our diet and theirs and helped combat the bleeding gums and loosened teeth (though once the teeth had fallen out, they were gone for good). We felt that things were slowly moving in a better direction, and our chances of survival were improving. At the end of August, the peak berry season was over, the weather grew cooler, and the gnats stopped biting. We thought now and then of our advantages over the mine workers in the Vorkuta camp, which stood out in the open, with no forests or berries within reach. We convinced ourselves that every misfortune has its share of fortune.

Our berry-picking delights soon ended. On September 6, all the "free" prisoners were ordered to report back to the main camp. We left the veterans behind in a nearly empty camp and hoofed back to *Peresilk II*. Having arrived here half alive some forty-five days ago, we walked steadily and firmly this time, relishing the absence of guards. We remembered the phrases from the past: "A step to the right, a step to the left . . . I'll shoot without warning!" No one drove us this time; we knew the way ourselves.

As "free" prisoners, we were not admitted to the main camp and were glad to forego its pleasures at last. A sizable crowd had already collected before the camp gates, including many Baltic prisoners from the surrounding *lagpunkts*. Our smallish contingent swelled the totals. We were about fifty men, all that were left from the several hundred who had been interned in the area. The attrition rate had been high.

An air of expectation stirred the crowd on the strength of a rumor that we would be sent back to the Baltic states. We believed it and didn't believe it. It was good in itself that the guards were gone. Now there were new arrivals, and our numbers grew by another few hundred. We heard Latvian, Lithuanian, and Estonian spoken. The now-familiar NKVD officer arrived with his document packet. He called out last names. Those called had to respond with their first name, father's name, and year of birth. If the data matched, the prisoner was sent to a designated area away from the crowd . . . where he received a shock.

A number of guards with firearms were standing around this area. It looked like another deception, like the usual lies. My heart nearly stopped. The bastards! We had long ago given up the thought of fleeing since only the wolves would welcome us here. It was hopeless. When everyone had been checked, we were formed into a column with the officer and several guards at the head and the remaining guards bringing up the rear. We did not have far to go to the station, which consisted of a guard shack and a sidetrack of three hundred meters, with two track switches. On these rails stood the red cattle cars with the barred windows that we knew so well. They looked like the same wagons we had tumbled from on New Year's Eve to "build a new world ruled by justice and work."[205]

---

[205] One of the Soviet slogans of the Stalin era.

HEADED WEST AT LAST

At the station, our Baltics contingent was ordered to line up in formation. Then the NKVD officer stepped forward and announced that we would be going home. We would travel through Leningrad to Estonia, where the Estonians would disembark, the rest continuing to Riga, where the Latvians would stay put, and the final destination would be Vilnius, for the Lithuanians. There should have been cheers, hats thrown in the air, but a curious silence was our only response. We heard only veiled threats to our newly acquired half freedom behind every word. We had been deceived before.

But things unfolded as promised for now. Thirty men were assigned to each railcar, which contained two-level plank beds and a toilet trough but no stove. The return trip in September promised to be more comfortable than our winter arrival. We counted twenty-six cars and from that reckoned about 700 plus travelers. Settled in the wagons, we received food meant to last the whole trip; each man got a loaf of bread, 300 grams of sugar, and four dried carp. The officer warned us that no more food would be distributed along the way.

We wondered why we hadn't been divided by nationality among the wagons. What could be simpler? Uncouple six cars in Tallinn, thirteen in Riga, and pull the remaining five to Vilnius; and that would distribute us properly, in our actual proportions. But we didn't puzzle over it long, having learned that whatever would be would have to be. Each wagon also received a pail, which, once underway, we were to use to provide water for ourselves. That seemed a promising prospect; we would be able to get out of the car along the way and do some raiding in the countryside.

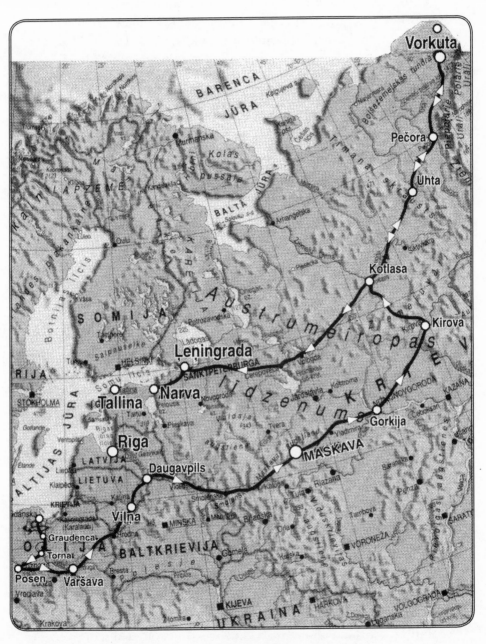

Author's route to the Gulag and back

For now, they gave us a ration of water and closed the wagon doors to keep out any unauthorized Gulag inmates who didn't have permission to return to Europe. On the first evening, there was food in profusion, and everything suddenly took on a rosy cast. We had not held so much food in our hands for so long that we didn't hold back and treated ourselves to a substantial meal. Estimates were confidently made that the trip to Riga would take three or four days. That meant we could divide the loaf of bread into four parts and eat one part along with one fish each day. The sugar would best be consumed right away (as I could attest from my own experience with saving sugar for later). The most delicious treat was the berries we had gathered just yesterday, now sprinkled with sugar—absolute heaven.

Next morning, the train began to roll, and on the following day, they let us open the doors and keep them open. It was the first time we could stand by opened doors after twenty months of imprisonment, and the feeling was wonderful, most fully felt by those who had been looking only through bars for too long a time. Clacking and creaking, the train rolled through the unending forests. Here and there, we caught glimpses of labor camps with their fences, guard towers, and barracks, all so familiar to us. The fact that we were riding by and not *to* these camps was so exhilarating, so beautiful that I wanted to cry.

We crossed the Kozhima River, passed Pechora and Ukhta. I remembered this stretch of railroad from last Christmas, when in my fevered state I licked frost from the wagon door mountings, and the frost was more delicious than ice cream. I remembered this stretch also for the prisoners who had starved to death and whose bodies littered the embankment till they were kicked into a ditch. I remembered the agony of the old Germans muttering about dishes they had made ("*Ein bisschen Salz, ein bisschen Pfeffer . . .*"). Compared to that grim journey, this was a wedding excursion. But were we really going home? We still found this promise hard to believe.

The train rolled briskly along at first, with only brief stops at the stations. As soon as the wheels stopped rolling, we all jumped out to stretch and move around and find some water but always with an eye on our wagon. We knew if we got left behind in our current condition—without documents and wearing the remnants of our German uniforms—we would quickly find ourselves back in the Vorkuta lager system. But the farther southwest we went, the slower our progress. When the train was shunted onto a sidetrack, we knew

enough not to expect a quick resumption of the journey. Our trip to
the north last winter had lasted eighty-three days. I remembered Vilis
Lācis's portrayal in *Vecā Jūrnieku Ligzda* of the Zītars family returning
to Latvia after World War I. In those days, the refugees had been able
to speed up the progress of their trains by chipping in to bribe station
officials. We didn't have that capability.

Our food rations had been consumed by the third day already, but
we had covered barely a fifth of our journey. The route took us through
regions where we saw few inhabitants and no animals, and we doubted
our chances of finding something to eat. We rode through thick
forests, but the train did not stop, leaving the berries and mushrooms
ungathered and the small animals unpreyed upon. For several days, we
drank only water. We realized we would not make it to our destination
this way. We had to change the situation, and we did. Beyond Kotlas,[206]
we began to see buildings, poorly cultivated fields. Near the stations, we
could see the potato furrows of the railroad workers and the cabbage
heads dotting their garden plots.

Beyond Vologda and near Cherepovets,[207] the train stopped in the
middle of a *sovkhoz*.[208] Perhaps the guard commander had arranged with
the train engineer for this unplanned stop. Perhaps he hadn't wished to
deliver a trainload of skeletons to the higher-ups in Leningrad. Maybe it
was just a coincidence, but suddenly we were looking, on both sides of
the tracks, at a carrot plantation, the first and only such enterprise we
saw in Russia. We had been weakened by hunger but retained enough
strength to climb down from the wagons and pull up bunches of
carrots with all their tops. These carrots differed from Latvian carrots
in their shape, color, and size, but a carrot is a carrot . . . is a rare treat. I
can't explain how our loosened teeth managed to chew them up or how
our stomachs digested them so we didn't get some stomach ailment.
We just brushed them free of dirt on our trousers and chewed away,
praising the *sovkhoz* agronomer.

Our train stopped in the outskirts of Leningrad on September 20.
We were not allowed into the city but were routed around to the Baltics
train line, where we stood for two days more. The city was visible in the

---

[206] Town about 1,100 kilometers (670 miles) southwest of Vorkuta.

[207] Vologda is 1,500 kilometers (930 miles) and Cherepovets 1,580 kilometers (980
miles) southwest of Vorkuta.

[208] A state farm, a variant of the kolkhoz.

distance. Our undiminished hunger wasn't enough, it seems, and we were mobbed by lice again. The train stood near a ditch filled with dirty water, but we had no soap and were too feeble to wash off properly. Only the thought that we were near Latvia prompted us to pull off our shirts and do manual battle with the lice. We masked our shock at one another's appearance in casual gibes: "How bony you are, with all those ribs showing. Your girlfriend won't recognize you."

After ten days without any warm food, we were served from steaming kettles of soup, and everyone received a loaf of bread along with a warning to make sure it lasted till Riga. But it wasn't in our power to make the bread last longer than a day, and it melted in our mouths like something that had never been. Next day, they brought the soup again, which, compared to the watery stuff in Vorkuta, could really be called soup.

On the twenty-third of September, we rolled a while and then stopped again. Here, there was no soup or bread, and everything we had received had been gobbled up. Our raids on the railroad workers' gardens resumed. We spurned nothing that was edible, stole anything we could reach, and quickly devoured it. Several more days of rolling along and stopping passed, and our hunger grew. I was overtaken by a feeling of weakness again and stayed in a corner of the railcar to save energy. It's a good thing that September was warm and sunny. Our return trip had taken twenty days. We were half starved, dirty, lice ridden but by some miracle remained free of illness.

In the early morning darkness of September 26, the train stopped. We slept on. But then we heard the yelling of the guards outside. We had forgotten about them, and they about us, for twenty days. They lived in their own car, where they ate, drank, played cards, and lived it up. We had nothing to offer in trade and never went near them. In the evenings, we usually closed the wagon doors ourselves from the inside. Now one of our guys tried to open the doors to get outside but found them locked. "Boys, we're in trouble again!" someone yelled. We tried to see where we were through the barred railcar window. In the morning's half light, we could make out the silhouette of a Russian church and only ruins beyond that. That meant we were still in Russia. We couldn't see the terminal building. Why had the doors been barred? It couldn't be a good sign.

As the sun rose, the guards finally opened the doors and ordered us to disembark with all our belongings but to stay near the train. We saw that the locomotive had stopped at the station, and our car was a hundred meters from the end of the platform. The sunlight played over a ruined city. Untouched by the devastation, the red brick cathedral with its massive central cupola, bright green roof, and four small towers reminded me of the Russian Orthodox church in Riga. We heard only Russian spoken by the railroad staff and civilians. A guard, waving his weapon, ordered us into groups. Riders were combined from each set of three wagons, then the next three, and so on, till the whole train had been emptied.

I was so weak from hunger I found it difficult to crawl out of the wagon. Friends spotted some sticks with forked branches at one end (perhaps from some hay-drying operation) and threw me a pair of these. I braced them under my arms as crutches and joined the others. I had nothing to carry by then. The tattered remains of my blanket stayed in the railcar. My field kettle was hanging around my neck, my spoon in my pocket.

I am not the only weakling, I see, as several boys slide down to the ground, too weak to stand, not responding to the guards' orders. "Our" NKVD officer appears with his documents, attended by a group of Chekists in blue trousers and red hats. These types we would rather see going than coming. We are not interrogated, however. The officer calls out last names, to which we must reply with our first name, father's name, and date of birth. Those born in 1922 and later are ordered to the right, those who are older to the left. The hour-long process forms us into two approximately equal groups. I'm in the younger group, which is flanked by a reinforced guard unit. What now?

When all the wagons have been checked, prisoners counted, and misplacements resolved, the officer gathers our "younger" group around himself and explains dirty, lice-ridden men such as we can't be sent home for now. Therefore, we will be fed first, then taken to the sauna, disinfected, and given clean underwear and clothes. Meanwhile, the railcars will be disinfected and washed as well. It sounds logical. It cheers us up. We like best the promise of being fed. Why we have been divided into two age groups, they don't clarify. The "older" group is also told something that we can't hear. They are led around to the other side of the terminal building, and we can't see whether they have guards there or not.

The kitchen kettles are across the tracks in the ruins, away from the station. We walk around the train until we find ourselves on a cobblestone street beyond the grade crossing. The distance is not long, but it's hard going with my crutches. We sit down in front of the ruins, but the guards remain standing. We wait. We hear the pushing and pulling of the railcars in the station, the whistle of the locomotive, the switchmen barking commands. We wait for the food . . . and then we are each holding a piece of bread, and there's a tasty soup in our field kettles. The days of hunger are behind us, we hope.

We are led to the sauna in the basement of the ruins. The space is dingy, but there's cold water flowing from an actual tap and warm water in a wooden tub, and a dab of green soap squirted into our hands. Then there's the shaving of heads and the rest of the disinfection procedure we have learned from our various camps. We are told to throw our tattered German uniforms, which have completely lost their color and shape, into a pile in front of the sauna for burning.

The modest space of the sauna admits 20-25 men at a time, and the purification process takes a while. We sit on the rubble in front of the sauna and wait for our turn. The purified men are released through another door on the other side of the ruins, and we dirty men can't see them. Then it's our turn. When I exit through the door of the purified, I see a hundred naked, skeletal men hopping around to get warm. There are no cloths to dry off with, and even on a sunny day in September, it's cold when you're naked and wet. We chuckle at each other; the disinfectant solution hasn't been rinsed well from our underarms and from between our legs, and our newly shaved heads look like veined, gray-tinged, irregular volleyballs. Our legs and arms are so thin we resemble spiders more than men. But let that be. We have eaten, and we are clean. At the moment, our thoughts reach no further.

With half of the prisoners yet to wash, an army truck with a canvas-covered frame pulls up, and Russian soldiers throw underclothes, shirts, and trousers out the back. The clothes are used but have been laundered. They have a Red army stamp on them. Every man gets a set, which fits some but not others. Trading begins. My pants reach to my knees, the shirt to my navel and elbows. But there's a cheerful atmosphere among us as we dance the *lambetvok*[209] in our underwear and laugh at each other. To be clean again and to put on clean clothes

---

[209] The Lambeth Walk, a walking-hopping dance of cockney origin popular in the 1930s in Europe.

seems as exotic as a tale out of the *Thousand and One Nights*. Is there a better feeling than the feeling of being clean?

We converse with the Estonians and Lithuanians in German, which somehow seems appropriate, but the Russians don't like to hear such talk. To them, the German language and everything associated with the Germans are like a red cape in front of a bull. We can understand that. The Germans have really cursed themselves for a hundred years.

Several more trucks pull up filled with Red army uniforms—pants, blouses, hats, socks, and *kirza* (oilcloth) boots. For us? It seems so, but why Russian uniforms? Patience, you'll find out. A few more hours pass while all 360 of us freed prisoners are washed and clothed in the new uniforms (but without insignia or belts) and while we trade for clothes and boots that fit. I manage to pull on my new clothing and boots but find it difficult to walk. The boots feel like wooden shoes. I have to learn to walk again, it seems, but I and the others have an edge over the recent past now; once our bones are covered, we look almost stately in our new army clothes.

A Red army or, as recently ordered by decree, a *Soviet* army major pulls up in a Willys jeep. He doesn't climb out but stands and addresses us in a loud voice:

"You have fought on the enemy's side against your own people, which is a serious crime. But Soviet power is not vindictive. Josef Vissarionovich (Stalin) has pronounced that those who were conscripted into the German army and have not committed crimes against humanity can be released from imprisonment and put to work rebuilding the cities. Over the past year, all of you went through a screening process,[210] which told us that, among you, there were no volunteers for the Wehrmacht and that you haven't murdered civilians. Therefore and on certain conditions, you are to be entrusted with the honored name of true Soviet citizens. From now on, you will be allowed to use the term 'comrade.' Since young men your age are all in the Soviet Army, you are, as of this day, being enlisted in that army. Of course, you will not be receiving weapons, since trust must be earned through hard work. You are being inducted into a construction battalion, and for now, you will be working to rebuild this ruined city. Your future will depend on your willingness to work and on your good

---

[210] Screening involved repeated interrogations to check for inconsistencies, as well as follow-up at the indicated school or work sites, as well as testimony of relatives and neighbors.

behavior. You will renew what you yourselves destroyed.[211] We'll decide later what to do with you then. Is that clear? Don't forget you are all subject to army discipline. There's no joking around with a court-martial. Failure to obey commands will send you back to where you just came from. And now I will introduce you to the commander of the 4th Work Battalion, who will take you to your barracks. Tomorrow you will begin your service in the ranks of the Soviet Army. With your good work, you will redeem your guilt."

On the morning of September 26, I had been a "freed" prisoner without the confirming documents. Above all, I had been a "Fascist." In the evening of the same day, I am a soldier of the victorious Soviet Army and for an indeterminate term will be serving in a construction battalion to work off my sins. I had been freed from the blue-gray uniform in a moment and just as quickly put on the green. My transformation and rebirth had been conducted with the aid of a smelly disinfectant, a glob of green soap, and a splash of warm water.

Today I open a new page in the colorful story of my life. But I doubt I am really the page turner. I'm really a pawn, pushed by the will of others. Was it the will of Hitler and now Stalin's will? More likely, it has been a game played by a higher power.

---

[211] Narva, a city in northeastern Estonia, was largely destroyed by Soviet air bombardment in March 1944.

RECOVERING IN NARVA

When they led us toward the barracks on the city side of the railroad tracks, we read the sign on the terminal building's façade: NARVA. And so we finally learned that we were to stay in this nearly destroyed Estonian border city. Our train had departed, along with all the red railroad cars and all the Baltic soldiers older than us. Were they taken away in the same train? Did the train take them home? We knew only that half of our group was gone and couldn't learn anything more at the time. But we did understand then why they had given us no documents up north and why we were met and guarded by Chekists in Narva. A new life had begun, and the old one was no longer worth remembering. Maybe someone from our age group managed to escape and later found his way home. This is something we would find out only years later.[212]

The city is almost completely destroyed. The Estonian Legionnaires had defended the city and its environs desperately and for a long time, but the Russian force advantage had been too great. When the Germans, "straightening the front," retreated, the city's ruins finally fell into Russian hands. With the loss of Narva, the Germans had rapidly retreated westward, leaving the road to Tallinn[213] open. All of Estonia had been quickly occupied. We learned this from the Estonian prisoners, with whom we now shared a common fate. The pre-war religious sentiments of the Russians had not been completely lost,

---

[212] Among the author's schoolmates who actually did escape and returned to Latvia years later were the poet Ziedonis Purvs, the actor Harijs Liepiņš, and several others.

[213] Tallinn, the capital of Estonia, is 196 kilometers (122 miles) west of Narva, on the Gulf of Finland.

however, and while bent on destroying everything else, they had spared their Orthodox church. All the other churches, of various confessions, had been destroyed, but the Russians had not fired at their own place of worship. And so the cathedral was the only building left in the city with its walls and roof intact, although it had lost all its window glass. The cathedral was now being used as a warehouse, and its little side rooms housed some of the bombed-out residents of the city.

Ivangorod fortress ruins on the right bank of the Narva River, fall 1947

Before the war, Narva was a unique medieval city with historical stonework buildings, ancient fortifications on the left bank of the Narva River, and two notable forts—the ruins of the Swedish fort on the left bank (city side) and the ruins of the Russian fort on the right bank,[214]—both rich in historical value. Now all the streets were filled with rubble and impassable. Our newly formed work battalion crawled single file along the trodden paths between the chunks of rubble. The streets were narrow and winding, like those in the Old Towns of Riga and Tallinn. Not one roof, or window, or door was left; everything combustible had burned and collapsed. There were city sections like

---

[214]   The right, or eastern, bank is the site of the Russian city of Ivangorod.

these in Germany after the Anglo-American air raids, but there, people could still inhabit the edges. Narva was a city swept free of its civil inhabitants, or so it seemed to us in the beginning.

And yet here in the middle of the ruins stands a building with a new roof. Before the war, it had been a club or a cinema, a sizable hall with a stage at one end and with several smaller rooms behind it. The hall is to be our barracks sleeping area, the other rooms our kitchen and storage spaces. Some windows have been glazed again, others covered with cardboard. The hall is filled with bunk beds as yet without any bedding. Someone has been thinking of us, it seems, and has provided the essentials. For now, we are not interested in comforts, only in food and sleep. This has been a strange first day "home." Since we are now members of the Soviet Army, we receive army rations in the evening. These are less than we would like but much more than we have been getting the past two years. On the first night, we drop where we are and sleep before our legs even have a chance to stretch out.

Next day, they divide us by companies and squads, designate sleeping places, and orient us to the barracks and the battalion regulations. The building next door has a suitable space for a dispensary, where the "doctor" will be a second-year Latvian medical student with similar experience already gained in the north. In *Lagpunkt No. 2*, the medical orderly had only some gauze dressings and a tincture of iodine. It looks as though the 4th battalion dispensary will be better outfitted, at least according to our commander. A pair of shiny new kettles has been set up in the kitchen, drawing our interest and feeding our expectations.

Then all 100 of us are lined up in formation in the courtyard. The others have been sent a kilometer or two outside the city, where they are to occupy the horse stables of an undamaged estate. There are no other suitable buildings with roofs in Narva for now. The battalion commander, a Jewish major, elicits a guarded kind of trust from us, no more. The three company commanders are Russians. For their platoon and squad leaders, these lieutenants select some of us former "Fascists" who understand Russian. We are pleased that our own boys have been picked. The major and the lieutenants strictly forbid us to use the German language, on pain of confinement in the stockade. We Latvians are in the majority and get by in our own tongue while using Russian with the Lithuanians and Estonians (as well as German when all the Russians are absent). After six months or so, the German language begins to die a natural death, as everyone has learned Russian.

Swedish fortress ruins on the left bank of the Narva River, fall 1947

Every unit is sent to a different location, but in the beginning, everyone's work is the same—clearing the streets of ruins, renovating buildings, laying water mains, pulling electric cables, and similar reconstruction tasks. For the first few days, I and ten other "slackers" are left in the barracks. The commanders can see that nothing is to be gained in construction work from weakened inductees like us. We are employed glazing windows, repairing pallet beds in the sauna, helping in the kitchen, and patching the fence around the barracks. After issuing their orders, the commanders leave us alone. We complete our assignments, rest up, and decide to go out on food raids again. The stealing of food has seeped into our blood by now, our weakened organisms crying out for extra rations. As much as our shaky legs allow, we toddle among the ruins looking for something to eat, finding nothing there. We need to get outside the city to the fields.

Indeed, there are vegetable gardens around the half-restored buildings in the outskirts of the city. But we have no departing train to climb into after our raids in order to escape punishment for our mischief. At first, we try to sneak into the potato furrows unseen, but after being caught and threatened with a variety of thrashings, we realize our tactics need to be changed. We decide to switch from

stealing to begging, with due attention to psychological nuances. Yet
our Russian Army uniforms harden the hearts of the Estonians, and
we are abruptly turned away. But the same uniforms make us one of
"theirs" in the Russian homes, where we gain access to a few boiled
potatoes or an onion. For the Russians, a new life in the ruins of the
war has yielded little as yet, but there's much kind-heartedness, as well
as little interest in work, among the Russian people. The inhabitants of
the nearest undestroyed houses are almost as poor as we are. So while
this first time we eat enough to fill our stomachs, the begging seems
humiliating to us. We are no longer prisoners, after all, but soldiers
of the victorious superpower. This is the last time we go begging, we
promise ourselves.

Since work has always been the basis of human advancement,
Kārlis Trejs and I decide to advance human development by forming
a crew of two and offering to saw and split firewood for the local
inhabitants. Our year's experience in the north gives us the necessary
qualifications. And the project is successful. The men here have been
killed in the war or not yet freed from service. The women and children
try to fill in for the men, but they're glad to get help. Kārlis and I bring
no exceptional powers to the task, but no one hurries us either, and we
don't have to strive according to the old food-for-work formulas: 1–2,
2–2, 2–3, and more. We saw some firewood, rest up, split some wood,
and rest again. After a while, the desired quantity of firewood is neatly
piled in place.

After completion of the task, a Russian hostess invites us to sit
down at her table to partake of the steaming boiled potatoes and the
pile of unrefined salt poured right on the table, along with some tea and
a discussion of life. The Estonian women take a different approach;
when the job is done, the lady of the house brings out a bag of raw
potatoes for us to boil "at home" ourselves. With the Russians, we
speak Russian, but our accents and skimpy vocabulary give us away, and
we have to admit we are *Latishi*. This takes us down a peg, but since
we are not Germans and almost "theirs," we part on friendly terms.
We speak German with the Estonians, who reply only in Estonian,
but this is enough to gain us some goodwill. If we also explain we
are from *Latvia* and are *Letten*, our Russian uniforms no longer seem
so objectionable. The Russians see our fate as similar to theirs, but
the Estonians see in us the good old pre-war days. The war and the

post-war years uncover each person's bright and dark recesses. It's a fertile field of observation for the psychologists.

That first month in Narva, we strive to raise our status from "malnourished" to "adequately nourished." The construction battalion kitchen is not a bad operation, but it gives us too little. We spend every moment outside of work on supplementing our rations. Campfires are burning in the courtyard every evening. Stoves have been devised from scrap materials, kettles and pails scrounged up. Potatoes boil in pails over the fire; potatoes bake in the coals and ashes. Two of us can empty a pailful of boiled potatoes with nothing added, in one sitting. This may sound like a fisherman's tale, but the proof is in my first post-war photograph.

After we have spent a few months recovering from the starvation regimen of the north, we take turns sitting before a white sheet to be photographed for the identity cards that will prove we are not bandits dressed in Russian uniforms but certified members of our work battalion. The photos show us all with rounded cheeks and cheerful "horse faces" that bear no relation to the Buchenwald inmate look-alikes of the previous fall. Such extremes—from the edge of starvation to near plumpness in two months' time—can only be achieved by youthful organisms interacting fervently with pails of mashed potatoes.

The bad years are behind us now; even their memory is unwelcome. Having spent all of 1946 thinking about and wrestling with the problem of finding food, we find other interests in ascendancy in the spring of 1947 and begin to change back from animals to people. There's a postal service in Narva, and you can buy paper, ink, envelopes, and stamps. All the "newly inducted" boys hasten to send news of themselves home. In the post-war period, hundreds of thousands weep for the fallen, search for the missing, and hope. A few weeks after our arrival in Narva, the first letters appear in our barracks, followed by parcels and then by mothers and fathers carrying full coffers and packages. Some of the pre-war prosperity still holds in the Baltics, and country people do not lack for butter, bacon, and honey. Parents bring all their bounty to their half-starved sons in Narva. These fortunate fellows gladly share their windfall with those who have not yet received packages or those who have no hopes of ever receiving such things. We have not yet lost the sense of duty and fellow feeling that bound us together in the war, and many are given a helping hand.

Where is my family now, I wonder, *if they haven't been lost in the air raids?*
In the fall of 1946, I don't know the answer to this question. I only
know that I no longer have a home. I write to Sapuļi, Brīvzeme, and
Vārpas[215] with the same questions: What do they know of my family,
and what is happening now in Latvia? I write to Arnolds too, though
I know nothing about his fate since our parting in Kudevera in 1944.
Mother's sister, Marija, replies briefly and to the point: she and her
family are fine and living in their home, but she knows nothing about
my family. Mērija, head of the Brīvzeme household, relates that, in
October 1944, the Germans had asked all the residents in her area
to retreat from the Soviets to the west. Brīvzeme would be part of a
line of defense for Riga. But the Wehrmacht unit stationed there had
received a sudden command to pull back to Riga, and my parents had
accepted the offer to leave in a truck along with the troops. Mērija has
been living at Brīvzeme and is watching over our family's possessions
there.[216] She invites me to come stay with her, and she will rent me my
former room.

A great idea. Get on a train, and ride home to reclaim your piano
and your "Latvian painting" portfolios. Live with Mērija like an aimless
idler. Father's former colleague from Vārpas writes that his son Gunārs
had been called into the Red Army but has now been freed. The whole
family is living in Vārpas, and he asks me to join them there. "Come
join us," he writes, "You'll have a roof over your head and a job in the
school here. You'll finish your teacher certification by correspondence."
There's little I can say in response to these impractical offers.

Arnolds also writes. He has recently been released from a prison
camp in Riga (after internment in a lager near Moscow) and is working
as a production specialist in a furniture factory. He's been able to get
in touch with several of our classmates. And so some of the loose ends
have been pulled back together. I begin an intensive correspondence
with Arnolds, Sergejs, and Ziedonis, my classmates from the Teachers
Institute. The process serves as a spiritual renewal for me. I wait for
their letters impatiently and write long replies myself.

Shortly before Christmas, on a Sunday morning when we're
assembled for "prayers"—that is, for the obligatory political

---

215 Relatives' and acquaintances' homesteads near the author's own.

216 The author's family had been staying at Brīvzeme and left most of their
possession there when they fled.

indoctrination—Viesturs Ozoliņš and I are summoned to the receiving area. We see several women with bags standing beyond the gate. Viesturs goes out first and falls into his mother's embraces. I see Aunt Marija, and our delight at meeting again after three years is consumed in a barrage of questions and answers about ourselves and family. There's a basement area nearby set up by our boys for receiving guests, since the barracks would be too crowded and noisy. We all head for the basement, having received leave from the barracks till Sunday evening—in exchange for some Latvian bacon for the commanding officer.

Marija and Viesturs's mother have become acquainted on the train. They have both lived through a night of unpleasantries and alarms. In the post-war period, the trains are afflicted by thieves and robber gangs, and many parents coming to see their sons arrive empty-handed and even without money or passports. Our brave travelers have been fortunate to get through with only anxious moments, while at the other end of their car several people have been robbed, their clothes torn. Anna has sent me a warm jacket, Edvards a pair of boots, grandmother some mittens;[217] they're all intent on helping me through the expected cold winter. A full bag of victuals also testifies to the efforts of the Sapuļi cows and bees. Viesturs, in addition to clothes and food, also receives books. We're both excited.

We show our visitors parts of the ruined Narva and the new city rising from the rubble through our efforts. In the evening, we accompany them to the station. They have an unpleasant night journey ahead of them with a long wait in the Tapa station and a transfer to the Tallinn–Riga train. The railcars are not lighted as yet, the stations half dark. This encourages the gangs wielding knives and razor blades to invade the bags and wallets of travelers. Viesturs's mother does not let that scare her away and comes to see her son twice a year, bringing books each time, which we both read with great enjoyment. The second year, she brings him a camera as well, which he puts to good use, and many in our battalion gain a unique perspective on our Narva years. I'm grateful that fate brought Viesturs and me together; he has proven to be an extremely generous person and a good friend.

From the first, the morning lineup in the barracks has included a call for service specialists—a cook, a medical orderly, a clerk, a mailman, a

---

[217] Anna was another aunt of the author's, Edvards her husband.

shoemaker; these are to be the "headquarters company," the elite. Over the following days, selection focuses on various construction specialties. I've spent several weeks in the barracks doing odd jobs, spending my free time in the city outskirts with Kārlis chopping firewood, and I'm an expert in mashed-potato preparation. Through this specialty, I've managed to recover and even put on weight. As a result, I'm soon a roofer working on the damaged buildings of the former city high school complex. The work is not difficult, though up on the roof, the winter's cold and wind feel like claws tearing my soul out, even through Anna's wool jacket. But compared to our forced labor in the northern forest, this kind of work is nothing. We are working according to a plan and don't have to kill ourselves just to get something to eat. We're all fed alike. That's the construction program as we experience it for the first month.

One morning as we're getting into formation, I notice another major standing next to our commander. He's looking for a geodesist (a surveyor). My hour has struck, it seems. The major asks if I'm familiar with the theodolite and the nivellier,[218] and I tell him I certainly am. "You'll work for me," the major says. "We're forming a surveying unit." I'm thankful to my surveying masters, Baumanis and Mazpolis, for teaching this craft to me during the summers of 1939–42 as I was earning money for school. Now I'd be able to apply my knowledge and add to it as well. From this moment on, I no longer had to do construction work, carrying cement and bricks, lumber, and metal; clearing ruins; digging and filling in pits—everything that was done by the rest of our construction battalion soldiers for four years.

Major Kozel and I took a liking to each other. Kozel was the only intelligent Soviet Army man in Narva in those days. He had graduated from a technical college in Leningrad before the war, led a construction crew during the war, and ended up near Berlin at the end. Now Kozel was heading a construction organization in Narva, and our 4th battalion was attached to this organization as a labor force. Having learned of my Teachers Institute background and four summers of surveying practice, the major checked me out on the geodesic instruments and on calculation of coordinates and was satisfied. He handed all the instruments over to me and told me to select an assistant. I chose Kārlis

---

[218] Both are measuring instruments used in surveying.

as the bearer of the surveying rods and later after getting to know Viesturs brought him along as an assistant on the theodolite.

As the workload increased over the next year, we formed a collegial, friendly group—Vilnis, Kārlis, Viesturs, Sirelis, Jānis, the Estonians Pastak and Vīress, and the Lithuanian Česlav. We served not only all the construction projects in Narva and the new buildings in the suburbs but we drove also to the village of Sillamäe[219] to fix the boundaries of the factory and the residential sectors there, along with all the above- and below-ground communication lines. We also worked in the towns lying between these two: Lagna and Ustnarva. It would be fair to say that in 1947–48, all the new buildings in the Narva region were raised with the assistance of our geodesic unit.

The Narva-based construction administration was a large organization, headed, of course, by the Russian military, but its workforce consisted primarily of Baltic construction battalions (former Legionnaires) and prisoners in closed camps who hadn't yet served their time (both men and women, about 1000 each in Narva and Sillamäe). Because the prisoners needed to be guarded, most of the new construction took place behind fences and inside closed camps. Our construction battalion was almost entirely dedicated to this kind of work—building fences, guard towers, and gates for enclosing new construction projects—so that the prisoners inside the fences could work on the projects in proper confinement. There were about ten such projects in the city alone, lit up day and night by searchlights. It could be said that Narva was rebuilt from rubble by the efforts of former Legionnaires and current prisoners, in partial fulfillment of the Soviet major's September 26, 1946, command[220] (or, less harshly, his wishes).

Moving from one building project to another, we frequently met Latvian boys we knew from the campaigns in Prussia, or from prison, or the camps up north. We shared recollections of our ordeals, remembered friends we had lost. The current working conditions bore no resemblance to the regimens of the past. Baltic soldiers were well regarded because they worked productively and won bonuses for their Russian superiors. The iron discipline of the German army was no longer in fashion, yet compared to the Russian Army units in Narva,

---

[219]   Twenty-five kilometers (fifteen miles) from Narva, on the Gulf of Finland.

[220]   To rebuild what "we" had destroyed.

our construction battalions always stood out, both in the barracks and the workplace. The Russians could learn a few things from us.

But our commanding lieutenants were interested only in booze and girls. As models of discipline, they were hopeless. On occasion, a drunk company commander had to be carried home by his soldiers so that both he and they could avoid further difficulties. In contrast to the officers, at least half of the soldiers had a high school education, and they read books. (About books, the lieutenant was dismissive. The stiff paper wasn't suitable either for rolling a cigarette or for hanging on a nail in the toilet; the newspaper *Pravda*, now, was a different matter altogether.) Our company commander was not a bad man, just prone to quick anger, violent cursing, and prompt forgetting of the cause. He could also be easily bribed and mollified. An even more colorful personality was our company *starshina* or *Spiess* in German (the First Sergeant). He was a Lithuanian but with pronounced Soviet mannerisms. "Not everybody could be the *starshina*," he intimated, "You had to have balls." But we found his weak spot and used it to gain more freedom within the battalion as will become clear in time.

Our first company renovated the classically styled main building of the former city high school, added a second story and a roof. Our battalion was later transferred to these comfortable, well-heated rooms. The second company worked on projects in the city (the uranium ore processing center,[221] the lumber yard, the power station, and others) and had dealings with the prisoner workforce, which was a highly varied group, ranging from a university professor to a three-time murderer serving 25 years. The third company built prefabricated Finnish homes outside the city on a stretch of level ground toward Soldino.[222] The Finns were sending lots of materials for building comfortable one- and two-family wooden homes of a kind the Russians had never lived in. The homes had to be assembled, erected, and hooked up to utilities. All the sites and projects were in the purview of our survey group. The surveying was pleasant work in good weather, not so pleasant in the snow and slush but even then preferable to the heavy construction duties of our compatriots.

By now the hunger pangs of the first months had been satisfied, and food was no longer the primary concern. The battalion kitchen

---

[221] There was a uranium mine in Sillamäe during 1946–48.

[222] Town 7 kilometers (4 miles) west of Narva.

offered limited variety but adequate nourishment. Since postal service to our homelands had been restored, many of the soldiers had heartier fare under their pillows. The focus shifted to appearance and dress. The Russian uniforms were improved by tightening and shortening the blouse. The boys found a shoemaker in the city who was willing to sew leather boots in exchange for Latvian bacon and cigarettes. It was an entirely different feeling during our Sunday afternoon free hours to walk around in leather boots in place of our floppy, stretched-out *kirza* boots. Belts and hats also improved, and there were even sightings of white collars in the German style. It was quite an evolution over the six months since we discarded our rags from the north. Both our standards and capabilities had shifted by 180 degrees.

Special-interest groups began to form and operate on Sunday evenings. The musicians put together an ensemble featuring a band (accordion, guitar, drums), singers, a mime, and a master of ceremonies. The battalion commander supported the group, since its shows increased the battalion's prestige when it visited other construction units and appeared at state festivities with an appropriate program. The performers were multitalented and the programs varied and colorful. Ivars Krastiņš began his career on the fourth battalion's stage with a Radames aria from Verdi's *Aida*. Jānis Pirvics entertained us with his mime performances. A virtuoso accordion player was the Lithuanian Balčunas. "Black" Andrejs played all the instruments in turn and sang pop songs in Latvian and Russian, like a natural stage animal. He was also an outstanding master of ceremonies, a skilled raconteur, and the tireless leader of the ensemble for the whole period of our service.

The program included Latvian, Lithuanian, Estonian, Russian, and even German pop songs, performed mostly in Latvian or Russian. These were enthusiastically received by the soldiers. And where there's music, dancing is sure to follow. Like flies drawn to honey, girls of various ages appeared at the camp gates early on Sunday evenings. Women were not to be seen during the work week, except for some of the women prisoners clad in their padded jackets, performing men's heavy work. On Sunday evenings, these women were back in their camp behind barbed wire. But it turned out that actual civilians lived here and there amid the ruins. Some of the girls lived in the outskirts, some on the other side of the railroad tracks, in the region of the textile factory Krenholm Manufacture. They were all Russians.

The few remaining Estonian families steered clear of the Red soldiers. Gradually, the Estonians left Narva, and the city was populated by Russians from the war-damaged areas of Pskov.[223] The Russians lived frugally in temporary shelters amid the ruins, worked in the Krenholm factory or in construction, and waited for a promised apartment in the new buildings. Within two years, Narva turned into a completely Russian city, where no other language could be heard.[224] Reminders of the old days were still present in the Old Town, but this sector was not rebuilt. Remnants of Narva's rich history were also accessible in the fortresses on both sides of the river. On free Sunday afternoons, we liked to climb over these ruins and immerse ourselves in the times of four and five hundred years before.

Our surveying unit had pulled in men of similar interests. We gladly attended the first part of the 4th battalion events (the concerts) but usually did not stay for the second part (the dances). Shyness or lack of self-assurance held us back from trying to approach the girls, who seemed rather earthy or even coarse to us. Then too, each of us had a girl back in his homeland or somewhere else in the world—a dream image that had to suffice for now.

A major event in the city of Narva was the setting up of regular movie showings. The films were presented in three showings on Sundays only. We were able to attend the first showings, since the evening inspection in the barracks was at nine. Given our lack of cultural opportunities for the past several years, we eagerly attended the showings each Sunday without regard for the quality of films or the poor viewing conditions— the unheated barnlike hall, the imperfectly covered windows, and the temperamental projector. Some showings took twice as long as planned, when the film broke repeatedly and had to be mended. But this was all part of our Sunday diversions, and we accepted the downside with good humor. Most of the viewers were soldiers from the construction battalions, who did not spare their commentary on the heroes of the films, as well as the film projectionists. For us, the movies were the most entertaining of events, particularly for those of us who did not go to the dances. Among many forgettable films, I still remember a few notable productions starring Zarah Leander, Beniamino Gigli, Marika

---

[223] Russian city southeast of Narva.

[224] 82% of Narva's population today is ethnic Russian; Estonians are 4%. Russian is spoken by 94% of the population.

Roekk, and others.[225] After these shows, I hummed the film melodies all the way back to the barracks. These Western productions brought a little light into the grayness of our barracks.

When they transferred us to the second battalion, I still worked as a surveyor; but in the evenings, I became the battalion "artist." After work, I was engaged in lettering posters, subtitles, slogans, charts, etc. The battalion leaders felt that the more of this kind of "art," or visual propaganda, there was in the barracks, the better. Fastened on every barracks wall were my political products praising the invincibility of the Soviet Army and the growth and development of the superstate. On one occasion, I was given a book listing the yearly production numbers for coal, iron ore, and crude oil from 1917 to 1940, with no data included beyond that.

"What should I do to bring the numbers up to date?" I asked.

"Put down that production in 1947 is twice that of 1941. I can guarantee you won't be in error."

I prepared the information in approximately this spirit: all the lines, all the arrows, all the bars in the charts only rose higher and went further. I understood that the truth did not interest anyone here and drew up what was expected.

Luckily, I was not asked to enlarge portraits of Lenin and Stalin. A recent order from Moscow restricted the drawing and painting of these leaders' images to artists with special qualifications, awarded only after special examination. I would certainly have ended up in solitary confinement, since my portraits were not realistic and did not always resemble their subjects, which in this case had to be treated as holy images. Reproductions of the approved portraits were shipped in large quantities from Leningrad; these had to be framed and hung in the barracks, around the courtyard, and above the gates.

My status as "artist" provided various privileges. I no longer had to doze through the political indoctrinations, which were obligatory for other battalion members, no longer had to join the cleanup campaigns. Instead, I was able to make use of pencils, paper, paints, and canvas— for my personal needs, as well as the official ones. It meant a lot to me that, after a four-year interruption, I was once again able to draw and paint in my free moments. The bunks in the barracks were jammed so

---

[225] Zarah Leander—Swedish actress of the 1930s; Beniamino Gigli—Italian opera tenor and actor (in 20 films, 1935–53); Marika Roekk—Hungarian dancer, singer, and actress in German films, 1930s to 1944.

closely together they had to be entered, at both levels, from the ends. At night, the air quality in a space with so many sleepers, as well as foot wrappings hung up to dry, was not good. So I spent most of my time till the evening roll call in our workshop, which was shared by the carpenters, shoemakers, and other craftsmen and where I had staked out a corner also for my table, frames, and paints.

Compared to the north, we were now living very well. But you always want to live better, live freer. The barracks routine was unappealing to us. After the day's work, we had to spend another hour marching, turning right, turning left, all the elementary moves that we had absorbed and exceeded in the German army ad nauseum. We saw no weapons and had no tactical training. We were still considered politically unreliable and, as former "Fascists," needed to be watched. An unexpected incident helped me partly free myself from this barracks regimen.

After the day's work, our surveying instruments were stored in the attic of the construction administration building. One morning, one of the theodolites was not in its usual place. Interrogation and a search did not turn up the missing instrument. To guard against the continued risk of theft, Major Kozel decided to leverage his plan to build a light-copying workshop in the attic for copying technical drawings. At the same time, the new workshop was to serve as a locked storage room for our surveying instruments. He didn't want to rely on a lock only, so he made me the night watchman. This arrangement was much to my liking, except that I didn't want to serve by myself. One person couldn't stay awake all night if he also had to work next day. I convinced the major to let Viesturs stay with me. The major was receptive to the idea, discussed it with the battalion commander, and shortly, Viesturs and I received written permission to spend our nights in the administration building.

In the attic room of the Building Administration;
from left: Viesturs and Vilnis

It was a fine arrangement. After work, we walked a kilometer and
one-half to the barracks for supper. After the roll call at 9 p.m., we
walked back to our room in the attic. Then we bribed the company
starshina to let us leave the barracks right after supper. Our *starshina* was
a drinker. We bought some vodka with the money sent by Viesturs's
mother and took the bottles back to the barracks. The *starshina* also
ordered a "painting" from me; that is, I had to copy from a postcard
and enlarge on canvas a very sentimental scene with a pond and swans
and a pretty girl in the middle. For this work, I was able to live on the
loose for several weeks, without checking in at the barracks.

Our attic was in a building occupying the highest elevation in
the city. Before the war, the site held a Catholic church and, next to
it, a two-story brick residence for the priest. This building was now
occupied by administration staff, while Viesturs and I held sway in the
attic, which had a skylight in the roof, whose light I used in the light-
copying process.[226]

Our privileges in this arrangement were provided by Major Kozel,
and in that sense, we were under his protection. But nothing in this

---

[226] The process used coated paper that was sensitive to light to make copies of
technical drawings.

world comes for free. We also had to earn the major's goodwill. To that end, we took care of his residence in one of the newly built Finnish structures, where he lived with his wife and two kids. We rebuilt the firewood shed next to his house into a decent little cow barn. The cow needed hay, so we reaped hay in the nearby meadows. The house had a voracious stove, so the firewood was supplied by the same pair— Viesturs and Vilnis. Some of our friends opined that it would be better to live in the barracks than to slave for the major, but Viesturs and I were quite satisfied, since we valued personal freedom above all. While much of our free time was spent on the major's household, we were able to live undisturbed in the attic room where we didn't have to breathe the stale air of the barracks at night or stand mindlessly in formation waiting for the evening roll call.

I spent my free time, such as it was, drawing, while Viesturs copied technical drawings. When Viesturs brought in electricity to our attic room from the second floor, something didn't connect properly, and it was a good thing we noticed the resulting short in time. The damage was limited to a few charred floorboards, but this was enough to get us chased out of the attic. We wondered what we could do other than go back to the barracks.

To preserve our freedom, we decided to take advantage of the ruined Catholic church next door. Only the thick brick walls of this structure were left; its towers had been blown away, the roof burned down and collapsed. But a homeless Russian family had restored the roof of the priest's vestry, put in windows and doors, and so gained a cozy room for themselves. In the church itself, they stored firewood and hay, and their supplies covered only part of the available space. At the front of the church, under the towers on both sides of the entryway, there had been two small rooms, about three by three meters. When the towers collapsed, one of the rooms had been left filled with rubble, but the other was in better condition, its walls and window openings intact. It needed a roof and a floor; a door had to be installed, the window glazed, and the rubble moved to the basement. The family at the other end of the church provided a good example for us, and with Major Kozel's permission, we set to work. We found all the necessary materials right there in the area, except for the window glass, the hinges, and the nails, which our friends filched from their construction sites for us. Our new abode was ready in a week, guarded by a strong lock on the door. The major inspected our work and praised us for the initiative.

So we traded our attic room for a "holy seat" in a church. We would have agreed to renew the whole church to avoid returning to the barracks. Unfortunately, our *starshina* increased his demands for supplies of vodka, while our savings rapidly evaporated, until they had been completely depleted. The *starshina* was no longer mollified by the arts; he was now a devotee only of Bacchus. After an unsuccessful meeting between us, after the *starshina* had left without a bottle once again, we received an order from the battalion commander: all soldiers living outside the barracks must return to base. We were summarily driven back to the barracks, our hair was shaved to the skin, and we were shown to the least desirable bunks.

Viesturs and I schemed fruitlessly how to get outside the battalion again. Our patron Major Kozel was away on a vacation to his birthplace, and the battalion commander, a rival of our major, took this opportunity to put us in our place. We lost our privileges and for three weeks worked on construction sites and, like the others, marched in the courtyard in the evenings and dozed through the political lessons.

When the major returned, our plan of escape was ready. We offered to renovate his home in the evenings after work. As a first step toward restoring our freedom, the major got us excused from the evening inspection. Then I convinced him that it was unsafe to leave our instruments in the church overnight, given the recent theft of some cement and paints. We would guard the instruments ourselves. And so we got back to our quarters in the church. We were still subject to recalls to the barracks and, in the two years we spent in Narva, lived in the barracks more than in the refuge we had created. Nonetheless, the year 1948 in Narva remains in my memory as the best time I spent in those days after the ordeals of the north.

But all good things have an end. Major Kozel was elected a Party secretary[227] and transferred to another construction organization in Tallinn, where the workforce was also made up of army personnel and prisoners. Our own battalion commander immediately had us moved back to the barracks. However, a request from Tallinn quickly followed to transfer us both to Major Kozel as essential specialists. The

---

[227] In the Soviet system, nearly all organizations, including the military, had not only functional leaders but also political officers, who typically had the last word about decisions.

commander had to accede, in part since he couldn't refuse a request from a Party secretary. But he sent only Viesturs to Tallinn, and I was left by myself in the church, where at least I wasn't bothered by demands to return to the barracks.

I spent much of my free time drawing with charcoal and experimenting with watercolors. I had decided that, after demobilization, I would try to enroll in the Art Academy in Riga. If there was a competition, I would use the works I had created over that summer to attempt to gain entry. My ambition was supported by a classmate from the Teachers Institute, Laimdots Mūrnieks,[228] who was already at the Art Academy.

Major Kozel had not given up on his plans for me, however. He wanted me to join him and kept trying, until he succeeded in the fall. On the 25th of November, I was transferred to the construction battalion in Tallinn. I didn't really want to leave Narva, but I was not in a position to decide such things for myself.

---

[228] Later a successful artist in postwar Latvia.

TALLINN

It felt like an unfriendly reception at first—a strange city, setting the mood with rain, a sharp sea wind, and gloomy gray stone buildings. Perched on the edge of the city across from the Julemiste railroad station, the barracks were in the rounded Finnish style but with thin walls that allowed the wind to blow through and drain the last traces of warmth. They had been built for ten men, but installation of two-level bunk beds had increased the population to twenty. This construction battalion was also made up of Baltic soldiers led by Russian commanders. The messroom was a good distance away across a bare, muddy field. Discipline in the barracks was oppressive; every slight infraction earned a punishment, such as washing the kitchen floors, cleaning the toilets, and similar tasks. After the more tolerant atmosphere in Narva, I found this assignment unappealing.

My first winter in Tallinn was spent in these round barracks. We worked on construction projects nearby, together with prisoners again; our main task was to rebuild the *Dvigatel* factory destroyed in the war. Evenings were spent cleaning clothes (quickly soiled at a dirty worksite), eating supper, standing inspection, and then to bed. So it went day after day, in a gray, monotonous routine. Things improved toward spring. On Sunday afternoons, assuming no rule violations during the week, we received two- to four-hour passes to the city.

A completely different atmosphere held sway here. This was the capital of the republic, offering many cultural establishments and other attractions. Unlike the destruction visited on Narva, Tallinn had suffered from only a few air raids that had damaged only part of the city center. While Soviet soldiers and their family members were the majority in Narva, the army presence here was tolerably low, and

Tallinn Old Town rampart

the dominant group was civilian and Estonian. A trolley line from Julemiste to the center was available, and the center offered cinemas, theaters, a concert hall and opera, stores, taverns, and many other places and things I had only been able to dream about for four years. To slake my thirst for music, I needed money, and so I became the battalion artist once again. I sold my artworks to the better-off soldiers to pay for tickets to the concert hall and opera house.

I found ready companions for the cinema, but only my friend Alfreds, whom I met at the concert hall, was interested in going to the opera with me. He became a good friend during my time in Tallinn, and we shared interests in literature and poetry. I saw less of Viesturs now, since we no longer worked together. Until the concert season ended in June, I spent several hours nearly every Sunday afternoon at a concert, an opera, a play at the Russian Theater, or an exhibit at the art museum in Kadriorg.[229] These vital experiences in the world of art helped me overcome the empty vegetative existence in the barracks.

---

[229] The Kadriorg Palace built by Peter the Great in 1718, when Estonia was part of the Russian Empire.

Author sketching in Tallinn, summer 1949

Summer brought its own variety of joys. I wandered through
Tallinn's distinctive Old Town, admiring its medieval architecture. Better
paints and paper were also available, and I immersed myself in working
with watercolors. If the weather was conducive to painting, I found a
quiet corner somewhere in the narrow streets and forgot everything
else. This, and all I could see and learn here, helped me adjust to the
change from Narva and the loss of its life of relative freedom.

As Party secretary, Kozel decided to establish two libraries—one
for the prisoners in the closed camp, the other for the technical workers
in the newly built headquarters building near the fire station. The
major arranged for me to spend half the day on surveying tasks at the
construction sites but the other half working in the administration
building, assembling sets of project plans and copying technical
drawings for the builders. On one occasion, the major and I drove
to the city center to buy books for his new library. The major was an
intelligent man, well versed in construction engineering but with little
experience or knowledge of literature. His special interests had been
in the field of surveying but were now focused on political writings. I
couldn't really give him good advice on Russian literature, since I didn't

know it very well, especially the works written after the Revolution, and my command of Russian was still a work in progress. I counseled him to stick with the classics, but he largely ignored this advice.

In the bookstore, he walked along the shelves—in the Russian section, of course—and pointed to his selections with a show of confidence, hoping the choices would prove their worth. The salesgirl probably understood that we had plenty of money but not much discrimination or taste. The Party had decreed that a library must be established, and we spent the allocated funds to the best of our limited understanding. In my own self-interest, I convinced the major that we should include art books in our collection, and he let me choose these items as I thought best. Thus, the new library acquired reproduction albums of the works of Repin, Serov, and other Russian old masters, along with the illustrations of Kibrik.[230] Satisfied, we returned to the administration building and the room reserved for the new library.

Between us, we managed to acquire about three hundred books for each collection. "Enough for a start-up," pronounced the major. In time, I developed my skills, became more responsive to user demand, read the critiques in the literary bulletins, and became a librarian for two libraries. By the time I ended this career, each of the libraries held a collection of more than two thousand volumes. As the librarian, I was often asked for recommendations and judgments on particular books. Though my knowledge was limited, I dispensed my advice freely, thus likely also promoting the worthless and knocking down the worthwhile. I was determined to retain the librarian position in order to avoid returning to the barracks right after my surveying work. The major entrusted me not only with the library keys but with the acquisition function and the record keeping, such as it was for these small collections. I did my best to keep things in good working order.

Several times a week, I checked out books to the prisoners from their own library, which was an amenity in stark contrast to the no-books policy in the lagers of the north. This prison population was also diverse—from the criminals (who didn't read books) to science Ph.D.s, who carefully searched the shelves and sometimes even found an item suited to their interests. A Jewish dentist from Riga regularly checked out the latest novels and talked to me about Riga and Latvia,

---

[230] Ilya Repin (1844–1930), Russian painter and sculptor; Valentin Serov (1865–1911), Russian painter and portrait artist; Yevgeny Kibrik (1906–78), Russian book illustrator.

though we never discussed politics, remaining wary of each other as possible agents of betrayal.

The prison camp offered its own concerts with fairly proficient musicians and singers. But the camp also held cutthroats for whom murder was a minor offense that led to only minor punishments; it was a simple matter to kill a fellow prisoner and to be penalized with only five additional years to their twenty. (The death penalty was not in force at the time.) In all significant respects, life behind the barbed wire in Tallinn was a picnic compared to life in the Inta–Vorkuta region. To even dream about books up there was unimaginable, when prisoners gave up half their bread ration for a 5 × 5 cm square of newsprint for rolling a cigarette and when, on another occasion, one *zek* killed another in a quarrel over such a piece of paper. Here, the prisoners were fed just like the soldiers—three times a day. In the evenings, they organized concerts and read books, while we in the north, after ten hours of hard labor, were only able to crawl into our bunks, conceding the battle to our tormentors—the lice, the bedbugs, the gnat millions.

In March 1949, our work site was on one side of the Tallinn–Leningrad railroad line, while our barracks stood on the other, behind the Julemiste station. On the morning of March 25, our surveying group had to cross the tracks on the way to the work site. I carried the theodolite, Viesturs the nivellier, Ants—our Estonian surveying rod bearer—the rest of our instruments. The major led the way with the blueprints case. To cross the tracks, we had to go around a long line of cars standing on siderails near the station. Passing the cars, we saw the barred windows, the locked doors. A line of Cheka guards with automatics stood outside, not letting anyone near the wagons, which were filled with Estonian men, women, and children. We heard the crying of women and children from one side and the cursing of the men in other railcars on another track. People were trying to hand parcels to the prisoners, but the Chekists were chasing them away. It was just like the afternoon of June 14 eight years ago in Jelgava— another deportation. And we knew what lay ahead for the people locked in these railcars. We had returned half alive from that destination three years before.

We looked at one another and spoke without words. We assumed that Latvia was undergoing a similarly dark day.[231] The major noticed that we had become gloomy and uncommunicative. He turned toward us with a question, "You don't approve?" We stayed silent, though we wanted to scream. Then the major made his point: "It's the right thing to do. It'll be a better life without these enemies of the people." That said it all. We spoke not a word to Major Kozel for the rest of the day. The rift between us was too great. No discussions could close it.

On the whole, despite our political differences, the major treated us well. He knew our background as soldiers but never mentioned it. Once, he suggested to Viesturs that he should join the Komsomol[232] but did not insist on it when Viesturs declined. Perhaps knowing that my family was in Germany, he made no similar offer to me nor complained about Viesturs's decision. When Kozel left with his own family for a vacation in the south, he appointed me to guard his house, left all his keys, and even showed me where his money was hidden. I slept in his home for two weeks and relished my escape from the barracks. When the major was later transferred to Ukraine, I saw tears in his eyes at our parting.

Two weeks after our March 25 encounter with the deportation trains, I received a letter from Aunt Marija: "Things are going well for us now. We joined a kolkhoz, but the Krusas and Elza Bērziņš left on a visit." I understood that Marija's neighbors had been deported, but my aunt and her family were spared for now.

In June, Viesturs and I were visited by his mother and Aunt Marija. We were much more presentable now, no longer ragamuffins with distended, post-starvation faces but smartly dressed fellows with rosy cheeks. Our hair had grown back, clothes were pressed, boots shined. With passes in our pockets, we were not ashamed to be seen on the streets of Tallinn and to show our visitors the city's notable places. We listened soberly, however, as Marija recounted the events of March 25 in Latvia and her family's hasty decision to "voluntarily" join the kolkhoz.

---

[231] The March 1949 deportations from the Baltic states sent 95,000 people, 73 percent of them women or children, to remote areas of the Soviet Union. The operation was meant to accelerate the forced conversion to collective farms in the Baltic states and to eliminate a support base for the partisans fighting the Soviet occupation.

[232] The Communist Youth League for 14–26 year-olds.

I had also received a letter from Rendsburg:[233] "We would like to go to *Apvāršņi* next year," wrote my father.[234] "What do you think?" My reply was that "Studies in *Apvāršņi* are expensive. You might soon run out of money." My parents understood. And since they couldn't stay in Germany,[235] they chose another path—to the west. I have always regretted these few words to them. Maybe it wouldn't have been so bad if they had come back. Father was sympathetic to socialist ideas, though he had never mixed in politics. Who can say today what would have been the better course? Having only recently tasted the bitter cup, I didn't want my parents to experience the same. Who knows if my letter helped them decide their fate?

It's a wonder too that the correspondence with my parents, which definitely went through the censors, didn't get interrupted and that there were no penalties for me as a result of it. We did stay away from all politics in these letters and talked only of family matters. Even today, none of us has an inkling of what was collected in the archives of the Cheka over those years.

Sometime later, the battalion commander ordered me to prepare blank forms for passes. I copied a few dozen extras for personal use. Now Viesturs, Alfreds, and other friends were well supplied; we only had to write the desired dates and hours into the blanks. We still had to bribe the *starshina* to cover our absence from the evening inspections, but after Narva, we were skilled in bribery and had no trouble. The three of us neither drank nor smoked, and booze and cigarettes were the best currency in the Soviet Army, where they unlocked all doors.

Alfreds had come to know two Latvian widows in the city, and he took me along to visit them, with the inducement that they had Latvian books. He was trying to learn Estonian himself. The women were sisters. They had been refugees from Liepāja during the First World War, ended up in Estonia, married there, and lived in Tallinn in the years between the wars. Their husbands were dead now and their

---

[233] A city in Schleswig-Holstein, in the far north of Germany, where the author's family was staying in a refugee camp. They had learned of each other's whereabouts through Aunt Marija.

[234] *Apvāršņi* was the name of a summer cottage owned by the author's father, who is expressing in code his desire to return to Latvia. Replying in kind, the author warns his family that a return would not be advisable.

[235] The United Nations–sponsored refugee camps in Germany were being phased out at this time.

sons, who had served in the Estonian Legion, still away from home five years after the war. They lived in a small apartment in the city center, where we were warmly received. They wanted very much to talk in Latvian again, to discuss their sons, whose fate was similar to ours, which bound us together. I tried to console the sisters by suggesting their sons might have fled to the west, but I doubt they believed me. They had a seaside cottage in Pirita[236] and invited us to visit there on a free Sunday. We promised to come.

On a sunny August 14 afternoon at the cottage, five of us from the battalion—led by our guide to Estonian society, Ants—were received not only by the Latvian sisters but also by Ants's relative and her friends, Estonian girls. How to communicate with them? We had forgotten German, and Russian was unpalatable to the Estonians. The result was a mixed salad of German pop songs on the record player, a duet of Latvian songs by Valdis and Laimonis, songs and conversation in their own language by the Estonians, with Alfreds trying to hold the jumble of sounds together within bounds accessible to all. Youth does not require a precise linguistic understanding to establish communication, so we all felt cheerful and convivial.

One of the Estonian girls was placed next to me, with the encouraging comment that she was interested in drawing, so we should be able to find a common language even without sharing a language in common. Indeed. Since that day in Pirita, my drawing and painting time on Sunday afternoons diminished and was replaced by the duties of an escort. This did not serve the cause of art, but it did make life more interesting. The workday hours at construction sites and the evenings in the library passed quickly as I awaited the free hours of Sunday.

At the beginning of the year 1950, rumors grew of an impending demobilization. In February, they would release those born in 1922, in March those born in 1923, and so on, until all the "Fascists" had been released from service in the construction battalions and would be given a choice—to stay on as free workers or to go home. After seven years away from home, most of the fellows wanted to go back. But not everyone felt confident in taking this step. Some argued for demobilization right here in Estonia, acquiring a passport, working a while to earn some money, and going home only then. Others no

---

236   On the Baltic coast northeast of Tallinn proper.

longer had a place to return to (parents deported to the east or fled to the west). Some had established families with Russian girls in Narva or Estonian girls in Tallinn. For another, sins committed during the German occupation made it difficult to return. Still others argued that staying here offered a paid job, while back home they would have to work in a kolkhoz for kopeks a day.

I no longer had a home or family in Latvia and remained undecided. Aunt Marija wrote that I could find temporary lodgings at Sapuļi[237] until I got back on my own feet. I would need a home base if I wanted to study at the Art Academy. My friend Lorencs urged me to follow his example: obtain the necessary documents, and work here to earn money for the return to Latvia. His mother lived in Riga in a good apartment, and he had a girl there, but he was going to stay in Tallinn for now. My future was haunted by my past. My Teachers Institute diploma was decorated with the German eagle. Such a document would find a hostile reception at any university now. Even less promising would be my military discharge papers, noting my service in a construction battalion, whose staff were likely to inform potential employers or school directors of my past transgressions. And then the obligatory autobiography, which would have to include my service in the German army and the fact that my family had been lost in Germany (which would be understood as escape to the west). Turn whichever way I would, I saw nothing good for me in Riga. I would have to choose the path of Lorencs: stay in Tallinn, and find work here on the strength of my four years' experience.

But the decision remained in limbo, since demobilization remained only in the rumor stage. February was nearing its end, but no one had been set free yet. *Just another tease by the authorities*, we thought in resignation. How many more would they foist on us?

Soon enough, the question was answered for me by fate. On the 25th of February, construction work was being held up by a missing piece of metal meant for the end of a plumb line, which I needed to establish a starting point for a series of measurements with our surveying equipment. It was a rainy day, we were rushed, and under pressure to find a solution, I decided to mill an irregular piece of metal from the construction site into the rounded shape of a plumb bob. I

---

[237] The home of the author's aunt Anna.

was not wearing safety glasses as I applied the metal to the grinding surface on a lathe. A sliver of the metal flew into my eye.

Since it didn't hurt, I paid little attention to it. In the evening, I went to see the medical orderly, who told me to come back Monday to see the doctor. (There was only one doctor for several battalions, and on that Friday, she was receiving patients elsewhere in the city.) *No choice*, I thought, *I'll wait till Monday*. That evening, I even watched the film *The Fall of Berlin* before climbing into my bunk. Now I began to realize that my situation was not tenable. The eye was turning red, and my temperature was rising. Next morning, I could no longer see with the damaged eye.

I hurried to the outpatient clinic in the city, but they did not want to receive me. "The army has its own doctors," they said. Still, after several hours of waiting and after all the civilian patients had been seen, I was received and sent to the hospital. The same scenario unfolded there; the Estonian medics said they had nothing to do with army personnel. I left and found a military hospital, but they did not receive me either because my referral was to the city hospital. Bureaucracy to the third power.

Late in the evening, as the pain in my eye increased, I was back in the city hospital. There was a different doctor on duty now, who seemed willing to help but warned me that, since it was Saturday evening, the "professor" had gone home and was expected back only Monday. Meanwhile, treatment without a specialist's examination could not be started. I was determined to stay right there and sat in a corner and waited. A nurse came by, looked at my eye, and told the duty doctor that this Russian soldier needed to be put to bed immediately and the professor called. The doctor did not agree. We can't disturb the professor over every triviality (now if he was one of our boys . . . but this one in his Russian uniform . . . and anyway, who should decide these things—a nurse or a doctor?). A compromise was reached: they put me to bed, but treatment would have to be delayed two nights and one day.

On Monday, a strong course of penicillin arrested the blood poisoning in the eye, but the optic nerve could not be restored. "Treatment should have been started the first day," the famous professor told me later, "then the outcome would have been different." The blinded eye would now have to be removed to save vision in the other. After the operation, I remained in the hospital for ten more days. My daily visitor was Regina, the girl I had met six months ago in

Pirita. I was glad she was coming to see me, but I didn't want her to be tied to a crippled man. "I'm an invalid now," I told her. "You shouldn't come." But she came.

Regina in 1949

On the 10th of April, I was discharged from the hospital to a changed situation in the barracks. Someone else was in my bunk, and all the soldiers of my age group had been demobilized and had scattered to the four winds. My own demobilization orders were ready in one hour. Invalids were of little use in a construction battalion anyway. The accounting of wages and expenses for my four years of work showed that my earnings had been totally consumed in food, clothing, footwear, heat in the barracks, and other forms of consumption. I had nothing coming.

But I was free. I had already built a plywood suitcase and put my remaining drawings inside along with my treasures—a Ludolfs Liberts[238] monograph I had bought in a rare-books shop and a copy of Gogol's *Taras Bulba* illustrated by Yevgeny Kibrik. That was the extent of my possessions. Fortunately, Regina's mother advanced me the money for a train ticket, or I would have had to jump on a railcar and travel like a hobo, along with most of the other soldiers in those days. I knew I could not stay in Tallinn now. I was headed for Riga.

At our parting, Regina gave me a tiny blue flower and asked, "Do you know what this flower is called?" She answered her own question, "It's a forget-me-not."

---

[238] Latvian painter and set designer (1895–1959), who fled to the west in 1944 and emigrated to the United States in 1950.

HOME AGAIN

On April 25, 1950, the War Commissariat[239] in Riga officially demobilized me on the grounds of unsuitability for further military service. My discharge papers held a code that told any army personnel department that I had been in the German army, a prisoner in a filtration (screening) camp, a member of a construction battalion, and had gone without military training, not to speak of weapons training. The question now was whether I would be suitable for life generally after the seven-year journey I had just completed.

For the time being, I stayed with Arnolds. I needed a roof over my head but also the proper documents. The problem was that, unless I had a residence in Riga, I couldn't be registered there, and without registration, I couldn't get any other documents, including a passport,[240] without which I also couldn't get a job anywhere. Because his room was too small for more than one person, I couldn't be registered at Arnolds's address but found an available room in Jūrmala[241] with Sergejs. This gave me access to the passport. Now I could look for a job.

---

[239] The Soviet version of a draft organization for military-age men.

[240] The internal passport system in the Soviet Union was used to register people at their place of residence, which also provided local authorities with lists of residents and helped them monitor and control the movements of people.

[241] Resort area west of Riga.

Author's family: (from left) mother Emilija, brother Alnis, sister
Rita, father Andrejs–in refugee camp in Rendsburg, 1947

My first destination, however, was the Art Academy, where I
appeared with a portfolio of artworks under my arm, though the best
ones had been sold or given away in Estonia. I was well received in
the academy office, since soldiers demobilized from the Soviet Army
were now in favor. I was asked to write a brief autobiography and show
them samples of my works. One of the faculty members looked over the
drawings and indicated that these would be acceptable as meeting entry
criteria. Then he read my autobiography. He asked me to wait while he
went off for consultations. When he returned, he found it difficult to
resume the conversation.

"What happened to your eye?" he asked, staring at my bandage.
"One of my eyes is gone," I replied stupidly. Now my interlocutor
came alive and launched into a long explanation of why I couldn't
be admitted to the Art Academy. There was historical precedent for
artists without hands or feet or with other defects, he explained, but
two eyes were an essential prerequisite for becoming an artist, as well
as for enrolling in the academy. There were many appealing professions
related to the art field, he said, and I should be able to express myself
fully in any of these and study in the applicable schools, just not this
one. He spoke in a friendly and considerate manner and praised my
drawings after he realized they had been done before my eye injury. My
autobiography was not mentioned again, but it was clear that the loss of

my eye had allowed the professor to escape from a pointless discussion of politics. In the office, I asked them to return my application on the grounds that I had reconsidered my choice of schools and decided to enroll in the architecture department at the university.

A few days later, I unexpectedly ran into my surveying master Mazpolis, with whom I had trained during the summer months of my Teachers Institute career. He recognized me despite the Russian Army shirt I was wearing without the epaulets. "What are you doing these days?" he asked. "Nothing? Then come work for me. I need an assistant." I realized that I wouldn't have to worry about my future now. I was out of place in Riga anyway with my Russian Army uniform that repelled civilians, while my army documents were "dirty" in the eyes of potential employers throughout the city. Until I'm able to earn myself a change of clothes and acquire a prosthesis for my eye, it will be better to work out in the countryside away from the questioning looks of people. On the street, I always had the feeling that people were only looking at my bandage and nothing else. I knew this was stupid on my part, but I was captive to my lingering sense of inferiority. I wanted to get out, as soon as possible, from a city that had become alien to me.

"Good," I replied. "I'll go to the surveying department on Jēkaba street tomorrow and sign up for the position."

"No, no, you won't be accepted that way. Let me prepare the way first, and then I'll call you. Where do you live? Do you have a phone?"

"I don't really have a place of my own," I replied. "As for a telephone, I haven't even dreamed about something like that. Let me come to your place."

"Good," he replied, and thanks to his recommendation, I was accepted for the position. The very next morning after my acceptance, with a warm May sun shining, I traveled on assignment to Trikāta in northern Vidzeme to measure land boundaries. Because of the combining and dividing of acreage for collective farms in 1950, the total amount of land and forests now controlled by the state had to be measured. Much to my liking, the workload was heavy. Living was also cheap in the countryside, and I was able to set aside half my salary for the planned purchase of a new wardrobe. Most importantly, I was almost always by myself except for the birds in the forest and the flowers in the fields. The local people were sincere and helpful; they offered shelter and sometimes even shared food from their own meager provisions.

Emilija visiting, 1964

I was able to work without restrictions, from early morning till late evening, unencumbered by schedules and regulations. It was wonderful to be able to organize my own working day. I was finally free from the army commands and the barbed-wire fences, working for myself under my own volition. I spent all summer walking over the roads, the fields, the forests, and the wetlands of my beloved Latvia. I liked the work and did it well. I overfulfilled the quota by 50 percent, and for this, I received praise and was awarded a bonus.

In the fall, with a wad of money in my pocket and accompanied by Arnolds, I headed for the best department store in Riga to buy the material for a suit. Arnolds knew a good tailor, who did his work well and converted me from a former soldier into a solid citizen—Mr. Surveyor. Later, he tailored my army greatcoat into a civilian overcoat. And so I changed my appearance and identity again. Who could now say that this young dandy had once walked in rags, wrapping his feet tightly to keep his toes, which protruded from a Russian tankist's boots, from freezing in forty-below weather?

* * *

Has the war ended for me now? The formal end came in April 1950. The reality is that those ten years of war and postwar life have not really ended for me or my comrades. Our feeling is that the war will end for us only with the end of this life. A similar conclusion was reached after the First World War by people like Remarque and Hemingway[242] and others. After the Second World War, the feeling and belief are the same for any of us who served in the front lines. The memories and occasional nightmares still haunt us in our comfortable civilian existence. The younger generations might accuse us of excessive digging around in the past and of a tendency to complain. And they will be right—until the cannons start roaring again. Only then will the current generation understand and justify us, on the basis of their own experience.

---

[242] Erich Maria Remarque (1898–1970) served in the First World War on the German side, was wounded, and published *All Quiet on the Western Front* in 1927. Ernest Hemingway (1899–1961) served in the war on the Allied side, was wounded, and published *In Our Time* in 1925 and *A Farewell to Arms* in 1929. For both authors, the listed works reflect most directly the disillusionment and alienation of the Lost Generation.

ADDENDUMS

In January 2003, Vilnis Bankovičs received a letter from the Commission for Evaluation of Crimes of Totalitarian Regimes, which had been established in the years following the renewal of Latvia's independence. The letter read as follows:

To Vilnis Bankovičs:

Having reviewed your submission of a certificate of compulsory military service No. 0661028 (19.10.1963), the Commission for Evaluation of Crimes of Totalitarian Regimes finds that you spent the period from September 26, 1946, to April 25, 1950, as a **politically repressed** person employed within the construction administration (No. 907) of the USSR Interior Ministry's Primary Industrial Enterprises in Estonia.

Dainis Vanags

Commission Chairman

The commission did its work by reviewing documents and records that had been compiled by the occupying regimes during the war and afterward. Like the Germans, the Soviets were scrupulous documenters of decisions reached within their vast bureaucracies. In the decisions that related to former Latvian Legion draftees, such as Vilnis Bankovičs, the operative documents were the April 13, 1946, Order No. 843-342 of the Council of Ministers of the USSR and a September 8, 1947, letter

(No. 888-s) from Vilis Lācis, Chairman of the Council of Ministers of the Latvian Soviet Socialist Republic, to Lavrenti Beria, Deputy Chairman of the USSR Council of Ministers.

From a review of these documents, the Commission concluded: "It is clear that the construction battalions were repressive formations, within which persons born in the years 1922–24 and sent from Latvia or from filtration camps [such as Lagpunkt No. 2 and Peresilk No. 2] were not being set free, but according to a top secret order, were conscripted without their agreement and as prisoners of war systematically assigned to construction work. Although these persons were formally classified as members of war reconstruction battalions, they were not members of the military. They were not given terms of service, they did not go through military training, did not give an oath, but were used only for heavy physical labor."[243]

* * *

The findings of this commission have altered not only Vilnis Bankovičs's legal status in an independent Latvia but also the import of his memoir. In the legal sense, he and many of his fellows have finally been recognized as victims of a foreign regime, one to which they were subject for 45 more years beyond the end of World War II. Though Vilnis in time was able to find suitable work and lodgings for himself and his family, for all the years of this regime's existence, he remained a guilty person and a politically unreliable member of society. This status limited and constrained his choices in education and work, as well as the professional level and salary he was able to achieve. Along with many other politically repressed Latvians, he spent the postwar years as a second-class citizen in his own country.

The Commission's findings and declaration have unmasked this injustice, and an unjust status has been removed from people who were not guilty but were rather abused by a totalitarian power. Although this recognition comes after too many years, it is nonetheless meaningful and morally satisfying—to those who are still alive at least and to their loved ones.

---

[243] From the June 26, 2000, letter from J. Osis of the Office of the Attorney General of the Republic of Latvia to Dainis Vanags, chairman of the Commission for Evaluation of Crimes of Totalitarian Regimes.

But why hasn't the politically repressed status been awarded to those who, also without choice, were conscripted into the German army? The author himself says that the question should be posed to the government of the Latvian state but that his own understanding is that the signatures of such Latvian leaders as Dankers and Bangerskis[244] on the documents establishing the "voluntary" Latvian Legion precluded a similar definition of this service. But in the author's view as well, service in the German army must be distinguished from that in the Soviet: "I did not go to war voluntarily, but once I was called in, I hoped I could help Latvia regain its independence. I felt it would be dishonorable to evade this duty. I still think so today."

And how does the commission's declaration alter the meaning of the author's memoir? As readers, we realize that this declaration changes the way we receive the Red Army major's address in Narva about the mercies of Stalin to his audience of recent Gulag inmates. In the same way, we look differently on the four years the author and his fellows spent in Narva and Tallinn, when, as it turns out, they were not draftees into the Red Army but still prisoners of war, with the same kind of "freedom" as they were granted in the main camp in the Gulag.

The author's own outlook on the war has not changed, he says, not even a little. Nor has his view of either power changed. His outlook in this regard is clearly understandable to every reader of the book, but in reply to my questions, he states the following:

> It was my "fortune" to experience the power, brutality, deceit, and lies of two totalitarian regimes from 1940 to 1950. My youth, its most beautiful years, was spent as an army conscript, a prison camp inmate, and later as a second-class citizen during the occupation years. I wanted to be a patriot of my country. I did not die in the war, and I was lucky to survive the Gulag after the war had ended. In the final reckoning, I count myself lucky: I established a wonderful family, I have wonderful children, Latvia has finally regained its independence and will in time regain its economic strength and cultural richness.

---

[244] Oskars Dankers (1883–1965) was head of the "self-government" organization set up by the Germans, and Rudolfs Bangerskis (1878–1958), a prewar general in the Latvian army, was designated Inspector-General of the Latvian Legion.

These are the views of Vilnis Bankovičs, who endured all that was forced on him and who demonstrates his personal victory over repression by remaining in his final years the same optimistic, contented, generous person who in 1943 began his fight for Latvia's freedom.

Maris Roze

Epilogue

Rita Drone

It was early January 1948, in the Fockbek refugee camp in Germany, when we received the first postwar letter from my brother, Vilnis. I can still recall the image of Mother falling on her knees to thank God for His mercy. The rest of us surrounded her, standing in various stages of shock, before breaking into broad celebratory smiles. That was one of the few times I saw my self-controlled mother so strongly display her feelings. A few years before that moment, Father had received a letter from one of Vilnis's acquaintances with the probable news that Vilnis had fallen in battle. A fellow soldier had reported that Vilnis had been wounded and then not seen again in their unit. All the official information we were able to get stated that he was "missing in action." In my own mind, however, I could never accept that he had really been killed.

After we received Vilnis's letter, an intensive correspondence began, within the allowable bounds of the time. The letters had to be carefully structured if they were to get through the censors at the Cheka, the secret police. Because many letters simply did not arrive, we numbered them and used pseudonyms and code words.

Some three years before, our family had arrived in the Schleswig-Holstein district in northern Germany. On May 8, 1945, along with the rest of war-weary Europe, we celebrated the end of World War II, although the occasion was not an unadulterated joy to us, as well as to other Baltic refugees. Our hopes for a restored and independent Latvia were not to be realized. At the moment, all the major powers

From left: Andris, Lija, Emilija, Vilnis in 1964

seemed to accept the *de facto* incorporation of the Baltic states into the Soviet Union, although later Great Britain, the United States, and other nations refused to accept the incorporation *de jure*. This fact had a great influence on our family's later life.

The early postwar years were a difficult time in Europe, especially so in Germany, a country defeated in war, bombed out, plundered, flooded with thousands upon thousands of refugees from the east— both German and those of other nationalities, all fearing to end up under a Soviet regime. After a few years in the refugee camps, it was clear that we had no future in Germany and had to seek shelter elsewhere. Emigration was the remaining option. At the end of the 1940s, a number of countries were ready to open their doors to the stateless masses. The most promising of these seemed to be the United States. Our family was fortunate to obtain sponsorship from a farmer in Michigan, and in April 1950, we arrived in New York harbor.

The decision to emigrate to the United States rather than return to Latvia was not an easy one for our parents. They both understood that, with this step, they would begin a completely new life, one for which they were not prepared. Without a command of the English language, they would be unable to make use of their education and

would have to work in unskilled jobs. But this was not the main issue
for my father. He was deeply patriotic and found it very difficult to
leave his country for whose independence he had fought in World War
I. Then too, his political sympathies were closest to the socialist ideals.
Being a rather naive idealist, he was never able to accept the premise
that the Communist regime was really as monstrous as the experience
of the Soviet occupation in 1940–41 had shown. His mind embraced
these realities, but his heart could not. Using various cover names, he
had written to Vilnis and to several friends in Latvia, asking whether
he should return. Most of the replies had been negative. With a heavy
heart, he decided to choose emigration, primarily for the sake of his
children's futures.

We spent our first summer in the United States on the farm in
Michigan, but by early fall, it was already clear that this work could
not support our family. Our sponsor released us from the agreement,
and we parted on friendly terms. We moved to the nearby city, where
my brother quickly began working in construction, Mother found a job
in a hospital, and Father and I went to work in factories. In time, my
brother and I also managed to complete our delayed education, Alnis
earning a master's in engineering and I a master's in education and
library sciences. Though our father never fully settled into our new
circumstances, Mother readily learned English and found work in a
hospital as a nurse's assistant.

In time, our correspondence with Vilnis grew to include visits. In
1964, Mother was one of the first émigré visitors to Soviet Latvia, when
she literally shocked Vilnis; his wife, Regina; and their kids by showing
up unannounced in their communal apartment in Riga. (Her letter
announcing the visit had never arrived.) Visitors then were required
to stay at an Intourist-designated hotel, participate in organized tourist
activities, and were forbidden to travel outside Riga. Later, Mother
described her impressions of this first return visit to Latvia: "Though
I had lived under this regime, over the years, I had forgotten what
that really meant. I was so relieved and thankful to God to escape this
oppressive atmosphere when we finally reached Stockholm."

Still, it was an opportunity to meet loved ones and talk things
over—carefully, of course. Our parents, both singly and together,
traveled to Latvia five times each. In 1974, I too went back, to let
my eleven-year-old daughter meet her relatives and see her parents'
homeland. We met with Vilnis at agreed-upon places in the Esplanade

park or by the National Opera house. In the hotel, we were careful in our conversations, knowing that there were listening devices in the rooms. We were happy to visit Vilnis at his little home, which was detached and away from the city center. We were playing by the local rules, but these could not overcome our joy at seeing one another again.

And how did Vilnis's life unfold after his return to Latvia? As recounted in the last chapter of his book, he was taken on as a surveyor by his old master Mr. Mazpolis. Working for the surveying department of the Ministry of Agriculture, Vilnis spent the first five years after his return measuring farmland. Though he enjoyed the rural environment, he found that he had developed an allergy, which made it impossible to continue this work. Again, with the help of friends, he found a position as a technical draftsman/designer at the design institute of the cellulose and paper industry in Riga. In time, the institute gave Vilnis an opportunity to round out his technical education through correspondence courses. These helped him finish his career in 1989 as a project group leader and a certified engineer-designer.

His personal life also provided fulfillment and satisfaction. As he was leaving Tallinn, Regina had mentioned that she would love to see him in Riga sometime, and Vilnis had invited her to visit. In the fall of 1950, she made the visit, and they spent a lovely Sunday together. A correspondence and additional visits followed, until they decided to get married in 1952. The wedding was in Tallinn, with Regina's parents as witnesses.

In Riga, a severe apartment shortage had been created by the waves of migrants from the east. With the assistance of a friend, Vilnis was able to get access to a single room, in which the newlyweds began their married life. Regina learned Latvian with admirable speed and skill, as we noted from reading her letters in America. In May 1953, their daughter, Lija, was born. Four years later, the family welcomed their son, Andris. Regina chose to deliver both children in her native Tallinn. She also raised them to speak both languages.

Having lost their one-room "apartment," the Bankovičs family moved into a communal-living arrangement, which included sharing the kitchen and bathroom with four other families. This strained situation was fortunately relieved when Vilnis's recently widowed godmother invited him to come live with her. She and her late husband had begun to build a house in central Riga but had to interrupt the process because of the war. Vilnis now had a chance to complete the construction project and also gain a much better living arrangement for his family.

Summer 1967; from left: Emilija's brother-in-law Eduards Kalniņš;
Andrejs; Emilija; Emilija's sisters, Marija Sapule and Anna Kalniņa; Vilnis

And what happened to Velta and her family, whose trials Vilnis
describes in his first chapter? Only Velta and her older brother were able
to escape the June 14, 1941, deportations and the likely consequence
of an early death that visited most of her family. Only Velta's mother
returned from her exile in Siberia but died soon thereafter. Velta's
father died in the concentration camp at Vjatlag; her younger brother
and older sister died and were buried in the Krasnojarsk district, her
brother-in-law in the camp at Solimkamsk.

After Vilnis was called into the Legion, Velta corresponded with
our mother, and thus we learned about her dramatic escape with her
brother, Robert, from encirclement by the Red Army in Pomerania,
when—shortly before the German capitulation, together with a group
of Latvian soldiers—they had set out across the Baltic Sea in an
improvised boat to Sweden. A few years later, Mother had received
Velta's last letter from Sweden, informing us that she had met her future
husband and was getting married.

We had no news of Velta for a long time, until 2003, after the
publication of the first edition of *Los, Los! Davai, Davai!* when she
was visiting Riga and rang up Vilnis. They met several summers in a
row, when Velta traveled to Riga to deal with issues related to family

property. In these visits, Vilnis learned more about her life in Sweden and afterward. After the tragic incident of Sweden's acquiescence to Soviet demands for repatriation of former Latvian legionnaires in 1948, Velta and her family were among those who undertook an unauthorized departure from Sweden to seek asylum as political refugees in the United States. Their request was granted. Velta and her husband raised three sons and a daughter in America.

Velta's husband died in 1998, Regina in 2006, and Velta followed them in 2010. Vilnis received this last news from Velta's daughter, Gundega, who surprised him in Riga in a visit during the Song Festival of 2013, shortly before his 90th birthday. They look forward to continuing their acquaintance.

Genesis of a Book

Though I had heard a number of Vilnis's accounts of his experiences directly from him, as well as from our parents, I was never as moved by them as in 1989, when Vilnis was finally able to get an exit visa and come visit us and our 95-year-old mother. He spent three months with us in Minneapolis and took the opportunity to recount his experiences freely, without any apprehensions of being spied upon. Hearing his story from beginning to end, I decided that it was something that should be heard not only by his family but also by the general public, which, in Soviet Latvia, had been prevented from hearing or reading about the fate of prisoners of war on the Eastern front.

Vilnis's account was not exclusive, since many Latvian men had experienced similar circumstances. But in 1989, among the many legionnaire memoirs, there were almost none that included the experience of falling into enemy hands on the Eastern front. I thought that such an account could fill a gap in our country's history. I encouraged my brother to write down his recollections, and eventually, he agreed that they were worth preserving for the benefit of a new generation of readers.

Since the publication in 2003 of the first edition of Vilnis's book, a number of other memoirs of the times have appeared. Still, very little else has been written about the themes so well reflected in Vilnis's recollections about the strong similarities between the opposing sides in Eastern Europe—their warmaking and warcraft, their indifference to the everyday person and the rank-and-file soldier, their determination to reach their goals at any cost. Such testimonials were especially notably absent in the foreign language histories of the times.

To help correct the imbalance of views, I resolved to seek an English language translation of Vilnis's work and was very happy when my friend Maris Roze, having read the work in Latvian and deeply felt its power, volunteered to take on a translation.

Printed in the United States
By Bookmasters